Alan Brown
71 Elm Bank Gardens
Barnes
London S.W.13
(PRO: 1816)

D0613828

# MONUMENTAL BRASSES

# MONUMENTAL BRASSES

*Together with a Selected Bibliography and County Lists of Brasses Remaining in the Churches of The United Kingdom*

BY THE REV

## HERBERT W. MACKLIN

D.D.

*Former President of the Monumental Brass Society*

WITH A NEW PREFACE AND REVISION, BY

CHARLES OMAN

*Victoria and Albert Museum*

*London*

GEORGE ALLEN & UNWIN LTD

RUSKIN HOUSE MUSEUM STREET

SIXTH EDITION 1913
SEVENTH REVISED EDITION 1953
REPRINTED 1960, 1963, 1965 AND 1966

*This book is copyright under the Berne Convention. Apart from any fair dealing for the purposes of private study, research, criticism or review, as permitted under the Copyright Act 1956, no portion may be reproduced by any process without written permission. Enquiry should be made to the publisher.*

PRINTED IN GREAT BRITAIN BY
NEILL AND CO. LTD., EDINBURGH

# PREFACE

IF the Rev. Herbert Macklin had not died at the early age of forty-nine, in January 1917, this book would not have had to wait so long for a fresh edition. Though thirty-nine years have elapsed since the appearance of the sixth edition no better introduction to the subject has been issued, so that the publishers were entirely justified in their decision to reprint this book which had enjoyed such a deserved popularity early in the century.

It should be emphasised that the text remains entirely that of the Rev. Herbert Macklin and that the only alterations consist in provision of a bibliography revised so as to include recent works and a list of brasses which have been war casualties. Though the study of monumental brasses has been carried on intensively in this country for over a hundred years, there is still no danger of the subject becoming exhausted. As evidence in support of this, we may point to the fact that, although the Monumental Brass Society has been operating since 1886 (with the exception of one interval of twenty years), the quality of the contributions to its *Transactions* shows no sign of deterioration but seems on the contrary to improve. Though interesting discoveries have been made in recent years, the general outline of the subject had been settled long before Macklin's death, so that there is no risk of the novice being led seriously astray by reading his extremely well-arranged and informative book. The corrections which have to be made are mainly of a minor character. Perhaps the most serious are those which have to be made on pp. 16–17 when he quotes Haines's theories with regard to the origin of brasses. The idea that monumental brasses were evolved from the champlevé enamels of Limoges is now entirely obsolete. Memorial plaques of Limoges champlevé enamelled copper would appear to have been always rare, and it is unlikely that any found their way up into Belgium where the monumental brass appears to have originated, as that region was already notable for a very vigorous local school of champlevé enamellers, at least as old as the French one. The earliest monumental brasses of which we have record are all northern. The earliest examples of which we have mention in Belgium are those of two successive bishops of Liège, Hugues de Pierrepont (1200–29) and Jean D'Aps (1229–38), and so these would appear to be roughly

5

contemporary with the extant brass of Bishop Ysowilke (1231) at Verden, near Hanover.   The idea of the monumental brass was already well established in England by the middle of the thirteenth century, when the cathedrals of Salisbury and Wells, and Westminster Abbey, all possessed examples.   A small one which was once at St. Paul's, Bedford, probably belonged to the first quarter of the century but it would be rash to assume that England had any priority in the manufacture of these memorials. There is, in fact, no reason to doubt that the monumental brass was evolved in the Low Countries, where skilled engravers on metal abounded, in competition with the incised stone memorials. Similarly, modern Continental writers are also unanimous that the centre for the manufacture of the brass plates, which formed the raw material of the monuments, was in the Low Countries and not at Cologne, despite some rare references in English records to "Cullen plates."

The instructions for copying brasses still hold good, but fewer readers are likely to benefit from them than at the time that they were first printed sixty years ago.   Modern housing conditions do not favour the accumulation of bulky collections of rubbings, so that the collections, all nearly complete, at the British Museum, Victoria and Albert Museum and the Society of Antiquaries, are becoming increasingly useful for reference.   Though the rubbing of monumental brasses has ceased to be a fashionable hobby; their study still remains indispensable for anyone seriously interested in English social history of the later Middle Ages and of the Renaissance.   Similarly, every writer on costume or arms and armour in this country has found in monumental brasses a rich source of illustrations such as is available to no writer dealing with the same subjects in any foreign land.

In one respect the decline in brass-rubbing has not been a loss. For the student of costume or of arms and armour a rubbing is good enough, but only by the examination of the brass itself is it possible to appreciate its beauty fully.   Rubbings may do sufficient justice to the more mediocre late mediæval brasses, but no one with any sort of appreciation for mediæval art will regret a pilgrimage to such churches as Stoke D'Abernon, Westley Waterless, St Margaret's Lynn, Cowfold, Hunstanton, etc. Perhaps, as a result, the artistic qualities of brasses are appreciated better nowadays.   There is no doubt that this is the case of the late sixteenth- and seventeenth-century examples, which have been studied much more seriously by writers who have not been oppressed by comparisons with those of the best mediæval periods.

Chapters III and IV call for no special comments. When we reach Chapter V it will be found that Macklin was inclined to attribute some of the most celebrated brasses of admittedly foreign origin to Lübeck. Though the resemblances between the brasses in St Margaret's Lynn, with some of those in North Germany is undeniable, the tendency amongst Continental writers at present is to attribute both the brasses in England and those in the old Hanseatic area, to Flanders and to Bruges in particular.

Turning to individual brasses in this section, a protest must be uttered against Macklin's use of the long obsolete name South Kensington Museum when referring to the Victoria and Albert Museum. The most important of the brasses so misdescribed is that of Ludowic Cortwille, which it is now known came from the church at Wattoo, near Furnes and close to the Belgian coast, not from the chapel of a castle near Liège. It should be noticed also that another fine Flemish brass, that of Thomas Pownder, is now to be found in Christ Church Mansion Museum, Ipswich, to which it has been moved from the derelict but not yet ruinous church of St Mary Quay. The variations in the successive editions seem to indicate that Macklin could never quite make up his mind about the origin of some of the brasses which he latterly described cautiously as showing foreign influence. It is necessary to realise that, before the French Revolution, many of the mediæval churches of Paris and of Artois and Picardy were rich in monumental brasses. We have nowadays to take into account the probability that there was a school of brass-engravers in northern France, whose work has almost entirely perished. Of the brasses in this country, those which are most generally attributed to France are those to Sir John Northwode and lady at Minster-in-Sheppey, and John de Grovehurst, priest, at Horsemonden, Kent.

The editor accepts full responsibility for the overhauling of the Select Bibliography. He did not feel it necessary to retain the headings of Costume and Heraldry. The subject index in any good library will direct the enquirer to the standard works. Some works dealing directly with monumental brasses have been omitted as having become obsolete. On the other hand, it has been necessary to include a number of important books and articles which have appeared since the 1914 edition. The most important of these is, of course, Mill Stephenson's *List of Brasses in the British Isles*, 1926, and its appendix issued in 1939.

The mention of Mill Stephenson's work leads on naturally to a discussion of the County Lists contained in Chapter VII. The introductory remarks might lead the reader to suppose that within the self-imposed limits—inscriptions not accompanying effigies were nearly always excluded—the lists were virtually complete. Mill Stephenson included inscriptions and used a somewhat less condensed form of description, yet his book runs to six hundred pages of lists as compared to Macklin's forty-six. Granted that Macklin's lists with a few exceptions, such as that of his home county Bedfordshire, are rarely complete, it would be wrong to assume that their value was much diminished. The sometime president of the Monumental Brass Society kept himself well informed about recent discoveries, and by the time that he published the sixth edition of his book practically all the brasses of real artistic interest had been noted. Those which have turned up since are not such as demand inclusion in a book which only aims at providing a good introduction to its subject. It is always possible to start a discussion about the date or the individual commemorated when a brass has lost its inscription. Macklin's attributions seldom call for serious modification.

Whilst leaving Macklin's County Lists as they were, the editor has done his best to save the reader from a sense of frustration resulting from a visit to a church (or the site of one) where a brass is no longer to be found. He has not attempted to list brasses temporarily displaced, *e.g.* one which has worked loose from its stone and has been taken for safety to the rectory until its reinstatement is possible. It was not to be expected that in the late war, when so many ancient churches were damaged or destroyed, monumental brasses should have escaped unscathed. The ability of a brass to stand up to rough treatment had been demonstrated on many previous occasions, and it is on the whole satisfactory that the total losses were not more severe. It is believed that the list at the end of this book is the first attempt to record the losses and the alteration of locations resulting from the war. It is probable that it is not complete, and it must not be assumed that the condition of all the other brasses belonging to blitzed churches is entirely satisfactory. The editor knows of one brass which is still *in situ* in a church which lost its roof ten years ago. It is hoped that appeals will result in a faculty being granted for its removal to a place of greater safety as it is still undecided whether the church will ever be rebuilt.

Danger to monumental brasses does not result only from enemy action but is commonly due to the failure of the attachment of the brass to the stone after centuries of wear and tear. Generally the authorities of the church take action before the risk of loss or of damage becomes serious, but for many years the Central Council for the Care of Churches and also the Monumental Brass Society have interested themselves in the safeguarding of neglected brasses. The secretary of the latter society has had many years experience of dealing with this problem and is generally in a position of being able to call upon a member in the neighbourhood for fuller information and an expert report. It is worth reminding readers that when a brass works loose there are two problems created: 1. To get it replaced securely in its stone without damage; 2. Before this is done to look to see whether it is a palimpsest. All the interesting palimpsest discoveries have been made in this way.

Lastly, the editor would like to record his thanks to the curators of provincial museums who kindly supplied him with information on the condition of brasses in the blitzed ancient cities. The same is also due to Mr Geoffrey Thompson who dealt with the same matter in York.

CHARLES OMAN.

### PREFACE TO THE NEW EDITION

The preparation of the present edition provides an opportunity for drawing attention to the principal developments since 1953.

Readers who experience difficulty in procuring heel-ball for their rubbings are advised to get in touch with the Monumental Brass Society which has made arrangements for the continuance of supplies. The address of the secretary is— The Hon. Secretary,
The Monumental Brass Society,
c/o The Society of Antiquities,
Burlington House,
Piccadilly, London, W. 1.

The Central Council for the Care of Churches has issued a pamphlet (price 6d) "The Care of Monuments, Brasses and Ledger Slabs in Churches" which is very suitable for presentation to incumbents who are discovered neglecting or maltreating brasses.

The additions to the Bibliography are grouped together on page 141.

CHARLES OMAN

# TABLE OF CONTENTS

# LIST OF ILLUSTRATIONS

# INTRODUCTION

OUR ancient churches are full of abounding interest. Their architecture, with all its details and subdivisions, opens out a wide and extensive field of enjoyment and research. Their furniture and fittings are in like manner the subjects of various branches of study, and touch upon a large proportion of the arts and crafts of the Middle Ages and of the Renaissance. Thus we may turn our attention to fonts or other objects of sculptured stonework, such as piscinas, holy-water stoups or sedilia; to screens, stalls, bench-ends and wood-carving of all kinds; to coloured glass, wall-paintings, floor-tiles or ironwork; to bells, both ancient and modern; and to a multitude of beautiful examples of altar plate or of embroidered vestments.

Besides these things we have Monuments of all kinds. First, sculptured effigies and carved tombs, memorial slabs and heraldic ledger stones, and finally the subject of this handbook, *Monumental Brasses*, which form a class by themselves.

They are to be found in all parts of the country, and consist of flat metal plates cut to shape and let into the surface of a tomb, of which they are a part, and from which they ought never to be separated. They take the form of engraved figures of the persons commemorated, accurately portrayed in the armour, vestments or other costume which they wore in life, canopies and devices of various kinds, shields of arms and inscriptions.

These brasses of mediæval and renascent England are of the greatest possible interest, and form a valuable series of illustrations and a commentary on the history and manners and customs of our ancestors. Commencing, as they do, in the reign of Edward I., and from the time of the last Crusade, they continue in use, without a break, through the troubled periods of the French wars, the Peasants' Revolt, the struggle of the rival Roses, the Revival of Learning, and the Reformation, to the Great Rebellion, the establishment of the Commonwealth, and the Restoration, and thus form one of the many links of the chain which binds us to the past. All classes of the community are commemorated by them. The carved figure upon its lofty marble tomb and beneath its vaulted canopy was suitable only for persons of the highest rank: the noble, the knight, the lord of the manor, the bishop of the diocese, the abbot of the monastery. The brass might be used, and was used, by all ranks alike; and moreover, being usually let into the pavement of the church, occupied no valuable space. In brasses, as in monuments of stone, we have our nobles and knights and bishops, but we can add to them the franklin, the yeoman, the merchant, the mechanic, the servant, the parish priest, the monk, the student, the schoolboy. The scope of the brass-engraver was a wide one, and his work applicable to the humblest purse as well as to the richest. In St Alban's Abbey, once the wealthiest and most important religious foundation in England, lies the magnificent memorial of one of its abbots. His life-size figure is engraved upon plates of brass of exquisite workmanship and surrounded by canopy and diaper work, by saints and angels. Close by are the humbler memorials of some of the Benedictine monks of his monastery, simple figures or half-figures, of small size and no great value, save to the student of the past.

But it is as memorials of middle-class and commonplace life that brasses gain their greatest importance. The vast majority of persons pictured and commemorated by them are the possessors of names absolutely unknown to history, of whom without their brasses we should have known nothing. A new light, for instance, is thrown upon the Wars of the Roses when we find that in spite of troublous times brasses became more and more common, from which, as from other indications, we can infer that the struggles of the rival factions could have had little influence upon the peaceful middle classes, who were all the time steadily increasing in wealth and importance.

And in particular, brasses give a complete pictorial history of the use and development of armour, dress and ecclesiastical vestments from the thirteenth to the end of the seventeenth century—a long array of Crusaders, conquerors of Wales and Scotland, fugitives from Bannockburn, opponents or supporters of Gaveston and the Spencers, heroes of Creçy and Poitiers, of Shrewsbury and Chevy Chase, of Agincourt and Orleans, of St Alban's and Barnet and Bosworth; knights of the Garter, and rivals in the joust and in the tournament; stately ecclesiastics, archbishops, bishops, canons, parish priests, abbots, priors, monks, abbesses, nuns, and the professors, lecturers and divines of the Reformation. Among civilians, the wealthy burghers of the fourteenth century, contemporaries of Chaucer and of Wiclif, of Wat Tyler and Jack Cade, wool-staplers, brewers, glovers, salters, and so forth; men who saw the monasteries suppressed, the Bible first printed, the Marian martyrs burnt, who prepared to receive the Spanish Armada, contemporaries of Shakespeare, mayors, aldermen, notaries, jurats and many more. All these we see, not in fancy sketches, but in actual contemporaneous portraits.

To the herald also brasses are of no small importance. Nearly all the better examples are, or have been, furnished with shields of arms, either in or about the canopies, or at the corners of the stone slabs in which the plates are set. In the fifteenth and sixteenth centuries, ladies of good birth often wear their own and their husbands' coats-of-arms embroidered upon their kirtles and mantles, while their husbands wear a short coat or tabard-of-arms over their body armour.

The inscriptions which usually accompany the engraved effigies are of peculiar value to the student of archæology. They form the key to the chronology of art, and give invaluable aid in fixing the date of any works of painting, sculpture, enamelling or metal-working. Brasses, in fact, are almost the only dated mediæval works of art. In themselves, too, these inscriptions are of value to the palæographer and to the philologist as well as to the collector of epitaphs. Stone inscriptions speedily wear away, but not so those on brass.

# MONUMENTAL BRASSES

## I.—Origin and History of the Manufacture of Brasses

### MATERIAL AND DEVELOPMENT

THE material with which brasses were made was an alloy of copper and zinc, called latten. Until the middle of the sixteenth century it was manufactured chiefly at Cologne, where it was beaten into rectangular sheets, and thence imported into England and other countries. From the place where they were produced these sheets commonly went by the name of Cullen plates. The Flemish brass of Ludowic Cortewille and his lady, 1504, now in the South Kensington Museum, was formerly assayed for the Jermyn Street Museum of Practical Geology and Mineralogy, and found to contain the following proportions :—copper, 64 per cent. ; zinc, 29½ ; lead, 3½ ; and tin, 3. A fragment of an earlier brass, of the fourteenth century, perhaps from Westminster Abbey, was also assayed in 1866 for Mr T. J. Gawthorp, and contained no lead, but more than 66½ per cent. of copper, nearly 33½ zinc, and only the faintest traces of iron and tin. Lead and tin, however, are usually present in small quantities. The result is a remarkably hard metal, which resists all attempts at disfigurement, and after the lapse of hundreds of years, brasses are found to be in almost as perfect a state as when they were fresh from the engraver's hand.

Stone effigies of equal antiquity are frequently mutilated almost beyond recognition. The hands, the feet, the noses, the very heads are broken and lost, and the bodies are hacked and disfigured with names and initials.

The brass alone defies the hand of time and the penknife of the desecrator. In the Chapel of St Edmund, in the Abbey Church of Westminster, lie side by side the brazen effigies of

Alianora de Bohun, Duchess of Gloucester, daughter and wife of two great Constables of England, *dramatis persona* of Shakespeare's *Richard II.*, and Robert de Waldeby, Archbishop of York, the tutor of Edward the Black Prince. Elsewhere lie the brasses of John Estney, Abbot of Westminster, of Dr Bill, the first Dean, of Sir Thomas Vaughan, beheaded by order of Richard III., of Sir Humphrey Stanley, knighted upon the battlefield of Bosworth, and others. Of these, some are slightly worn, and some slightly broken, but on no single one of them have wandering sightseers succeeded in scratching so much as an initial. The material of which brasses are made is of such strength and durability as to withstand the misfortunes to which effigies of stone would quickly succumb. The action of fire is an instance. Churches have been burnt to the ground, and their monuments for the most part reduced to dust; but the brasses have escaped with little or no damage. The Surrey Archæological Society has in its possession a beautiful little brass, originally in Netley Abbey, which was discovered some years ago in a cottage, doing duty as the back of a fireplace. It is quite uninjured.

## ORIGIN OF BRASSES

According to Haines, brasses were more particularly derived from two allied but older forms of memorial,—

(1) Stone incised slabs.
(2) Limoges enamels.

*Incised slabs* are precisely the same kind of memorials as brasses themselves, differing only in the material used. Figures, canopies, coats-of-arms, crosses and the like, are cut in the Purbeck marble, slate or alabaster, which are commonly used for these purposes, by means of incised lines. But the difference of material is by no means unimportant. As has been already pointed out, the durability of brass is beyond comparison greater than that of the hardest stone, and consequently the number of incised slabs which have remained to this day are inconsiderable. Even those which we have are worn down to such an extent that the design is almost obliterated, and in all cases alike an ordinary heelball rubbing is practically an impossibility. One method alone may be employed with any likelihood of success, and was so employed by Mr Creeny, of Norwich, the Continental brass-rubber. A very light heelball rubbing must first be taken, so as to indicate the position of the component parts of the design, and then the details may, as far as possible, be painted in with printers' ink from careful notes and measurements or a rough sketch.

Crosses were at an early date incised upon stone slabs, and more especially on coffin-lids, and were followed during the twelfth century, both in England and on the Continent, by effigies. In the fourteenth century brasses began almost entirely to supersede them in England, though in Germany, France and Flanders the incised slabs still held their ground. Even in England they lingered on, and occasional examples may be found of each of the principal classes of effigies—ecclesiastics, men in armour, ladies and civilians—throughout the fourteenth, fifteenth and sixteenth centuries.

Among the earlier examples of the thirteenth century the most notable are as follows:—

A knight (cross legged), c. 1260, Avenbury, Herefordshire.
Bishop William de Byttone, 1274, Wells Cathedral.
Sir John de Botiler, c. 1285, St Bride's Glamorgan.
Archbishop de Freney, c. 1290, Rhuddlan, Flint.

These were preceded by effigies carved in low relief, almost invariably on coffin-lids, and by effigies partly in relief and partly incised. Good examples may be seen in Salisbury Cathedral, to Bishops Roger and Jocelin, 1139 and 1184, and at Bitton, Gloucestershire, near Bristol, to Sir Walter de Bitton, 1227.

*Limoges enamels* came into use in France and Western Europe generally about the twelfth century, and therefore shortly before the era of brasses. The art of enamelling metals had originally been introduced from Byzantium, though not at first as a form of memorial for the dead. This application was reserved for the artists of Limoges. Rectangular sheets of copper were overlaid with costly and many-coloured enamels, the colours being divided one from the other by narrow ridges of metal. The whole composition would present somewhat of a resemblance to a beautiful mosaic. For monumental purposes an effigy would usually occupy the centre, and be surrounded by canopy, diapered

B

background and inscription. Such memorials were always of small size, on account of their costliness, which must have been considerable, and are very rare. Their general design is reproduced in the rectangular brasses of Flanders and Germany.

It is perhaps due to the existence of enamels that colouring matter was frequently used in connection with brasses, especially with their armorial details, and in isolated shields of arms, as they are commonly found at the corners of a brass-containing slab; the field is almost invariably cut away in order that the plate may receive its heraldic tinctures. But plaster, resin, wax or some other substitute was generally used instead of enamel, and has almost invariably perished in the lapse of time. Examples of actual enamel, nevertheless, do sometimes occur, as in the shield borne by Sir John Daubernoun, 1277, whose brass, the earliest still existing in England, lies in the chancel of Stoke D'Abernon Church, in Surrey. It is figured on page 59.

The brasses which have survived the Reformation, the Civil War and the carelessness and havoc of later times are but a remnant, a tithe of those that were once laid down. Vast numbers were produced during the fourteenth, fifteenth and sixteenth centuries, and must have given employment to many engravers. The latter were in all probability divided into guilds, established in London and some of the more important provincial towns, such as York, Norwich, Ipswich and Bristol. Peculiarities of style and design may often be traced to these provincial guilds. But the men of the London guild were probably by far the most important, and their works were conveyed to all parts of the country. They had an extensive factory at Isleworth, in Middlesex, though little is known of either it or them. Their work was that of skilled artists, working, however, from certain well-defined types supplied by the leading draughtsmen of their day. Thus, although no two brasses are exactly alike, yet there may be very close assimilation, and a great number of brasses of the same decade or half-century may so nearly resemble one another as to be indistinguishable until they are placed side by side.

Before reaching its destination, the engraved brass passed into the hands of the mason, who inlaid it in its stone or marble slab. For this purpose Purbeck marble of several varieties was very commonly used, of a grey colour, marked with shells, and susceptible of a high polish, but unfortunately brittle, and the surface liable to perish.

Separate casements or matrices were cut for the various parts, and they were fixed in position by small rivets of the same material as the brass itself, sunk into little holes filled with lead. The under surfaces were also smeared with pitch, in order to secure a better hold. Where brasses have been torn away and lost, the matrices often remain, and exhibit the exact outlines of all the plates of which they were composed. It is thus possible to ascertain the approximate date of a tomb and the nature of its adornments. Such matrices deserve to be carefully preserved, and should always be recorded.

## PROGRESS AND DECLINE OF THE ART

It is a noteworthy fact that the earliest brasses are the finest and the best, alike in boldness of design, in accuracy of workmanship and in excellence of material. The engraved plates are of great weight and thickness, so that it is not only not uncommon, but even usual, for the oldest examples to be now in a far better state of preservation than those which were laid down hundreds of years later. The results of daily and weekly wear and tear will be found to be in directly inverse ratio to the date of execution. The history of brass-engraving after the close of the fourteenth century is one of deterioration and decline. Strange as this may at first seem, it will bear a different aspect if brasses are considered in relation to the fabrics which they assisted to adorn.

*Gothic architecture* reached its middle and best period in the decorated style of the fourteenth century. Monumental brasses arrived at their highest point of excellence at the same time, and, declining with it, lost their beauty when Gothic architecture fell from its high estate, and art was turned into new and as yet unexplored channels. The old objects of art, and among them brass-engraving and glass-painting and the illumination of manuscripts, were flung aside that men might plunge without let or hindrance into the luxuriance of the Renaissance.

Each age is found to have its special characteristics and distinguishing features, and these will now be indicated in a series of seven periods.

## (1) Edward I. and Edward II. 1272-1327

The figures are usually life-size, and cut from very thick plates of metal. The drawing is bold and unconventional; there is an entire absence of shading, and the lines are deeply incised.

Brasses are representations, on a flat surface, of sculptural effigies, and keep many of their distinctive features. The persons commemorated are therefore represented as in a recumbent position, with the head resting upon a helmet or cushion, and the feet against (not upon) a lion, hound, or, in the case of ladies, one or more lap-dogs, while the hands are joined in the attitude of prayer upon the breast. Examples are few in number, and the knights are commonly cross-legged, at least during the earlier reign, and shown with shields upon their left arms.

The inscription is set round the border of the slab, and its Lombardic-Uncial letters are made from separate pieces of metal, each set in its own matrix.

Under Edward II. canopies are first introduced. They are of simple design, and when used the figures are generally rather less than life-size.

## (2) Edward III. and Richard II. 1327-1399

Brasses now attain their greatest magnificence and variety, and all orders of the realm have their representatives. The figures are usually about four feet in height, but examples can be found of all sizes, from a foot or so upwards. The drawing is a little more conventional than before, but nevertheless of great beauty.

Knights are represented without their shields, but still with an animal at the feet, and often with crest and helmet at the head. The border inscription is retained, but on continuous strips or fillets of brass, and a second inscription placed immediately below the figure or figures. The language employed is often Norman-French. Floriated crosses of great beauty now appear, and enclose within their heads figures or half-effigies.

Bracket-brasses appear at the same time, in which figures are represented upon a canopied bracket, or sometimes kneeling at its foot, and supplicating certain saints above.

This period extends itself also into the first few years of the next century.

### (3) *House of Lancaster.* 1400-1453

Figures become smaller, but are still carefully and accurately drawn, and there are a great number of really fine brasses.

Children are sometimes given, boys and girls being placed on separate plates below their parents.

The border fillet is sometimes omitted, but never the foot inscription.

Floriated crosses give place to crosses fleury without figures, and finally, together with bracket-brasses, disappear.

### (4) *House of York.* 1453-1485

The average size of brasses continues to decrease, and the engraving, though still excellent, is not so good as formerly.

Figures are attired in exaggerated forms of dress, and often present the face in profile. This was necessitated in order to exhibit the butterfly head-dress fashionable among ladies, and the husbands were obliged to follow suit.

Knights are found bare-headed, with hair at first short, but afterwards long. The recumbent position was sometimes, indeed commonly, abandoned, and a ground of grass and flowers shown at the feet. Shading, in the form of cross hatching, began to be used.

Shroud and skeleton brasses came into general use, especially in the eastern counties.

### (5) *The Tudor Period.* 1485-1558

Brasses are more numerous than at any other period.

Figures are clumsily drawn, and are often out of proportion.

Single figures are usually given in profile.

Children have separate brasses, and chrysoms (*i.e.* swaddled infants) are found.

Mural brasses come into fashion. They are small, and usually set in moulded tablets, with a certain amount of canopy work and other architectural ornament. Or they are placed in the recess of high canopied tombs. The principal figures kneel at desks or faldstools, with their children marshalled behind them.

English becomes the common language of all inscriptions, except those to ecclesiastics, which still retain the Latin.

The use of shading increases, and there is less boldness of design. Local artists are often employed, and the engraving is sometimes very poor.

### (6) *Elizabeth and James I.* 1558-1625

Art very much debased.

Thin plates of cheap metal are used, to the ruin of the memorials. The lines are spoilt by an excess of shading.

The figures stand in constrained attitudes upon a pavement or pedestals, and portraits of the deceased are evidently intended.

Small and pictorial rectangular mural brasses become common.

### (7) *Final Period*

Brasses become very rare, and the few that are to be found show a remarkable deterioration even from those of James I.'s reign.

At the year 1642 brasses come almost to an end, and only about forty more are recorded. The latest example, commemorating Benjamin Greenwood, 1773, at St Mary Cray, Kent, is of a most degraded type, and might have been merely scratched upon the metal.

### HISTORIC TREATMENT OF BRASSES

1. Before the Reformation.
2. At the Reformation : Henry VIII., Edward VI., Elizabeth.
3. The Great Rebellion.
4. The Eighteenth Century.
5. Modern Treatment.

Of the first period there is little enough to say. Brasses and monuments in general received the treatment they deserved, and in times of civil war the combatants fought only against one another, and not against the dead. No disrespect was shown by either Lancastrians or Yorkists to each other's tombs.

In the year 1536, by order of King Henry VIII., came the dissolution of the lesser monasteries, and in 1539 that of the greater. This was the beginning of evil and sacrilegious times. Priory chapels and conventual churches were sacked and destroyed in all parts of the country, and with them of course went all the monuments they contained. Great numbers of brasses must have perished among the rest; but while the majority doubtless found their way to the tinker and his melting-pot, a considerable number returned to the hands of the monumental brass-engraver, to reappear in a new form on other men's graves. Thus we find that the brasses which were laid down in the latter part of the sixteenth century were often cut from earlier plates, and newly engraved upon the reverse side.

But the reign of Edward VI. was even more destructive, when regularly appointed commissioners were sent round to the various cathedrals and parish churches, with orders to destroy or carry away everything that was popish. And it may be noted that the more intrinsic value anything possessed, the more papistical it seemed to be in the eyes of these worldly commissioners. Had Edward VI.'s reign continued but a few years longer, we might have been obliged to count our brasses only by hundreds instead of by thousands.

A good account of these times is found in Weever's "Ancient Funeral Monuments," published in 1631, and therefore but a few years before the outbreak of the Great Rebellion. He tells us that—" Toward the latter end of the raigne of Henry the eight, and throughout the whole raigne of Edward the sixth, and in the beginning of Queene Elizabeth, certaine persons of every County were put in authority to pull down and cast out of all Churches, Roodes, graven Images, Shrines with their reliques, to which the ignorant people came flocking for adoration. Or anything else which tended to idolatrie and superstition. . . . But the foulest and most inhumane action of those times was the violation of Funerall Monuments. Marbles which covered the dead were digged up, and put to other uses, Tombes hackt and hewne apeeces; Images or representations of the defunct, broken, erazed, cut, or dismembred, Inscriptions or Epitaphs, especially if they began with an *orate pro anima*, or concluded with *cuius animae propitietur Deus*. For greedinesse of the brasse, or for that they were thought to bee Antichristian, pulled out from the sepulchres, and purloined. . . . This barbarous rage against the dead (by the Commissioners, and others animated by their ill example) continued untill the second yeare of the raigne of Queene *Elizabeth*, who, to restrain such a savage cruelty, caused a Proclamation to bee published throughout all her dominions."

This was " A Proclamation against breaking or defacing of Monuments of Antiquitie, being set up in churches, or other public places, for memory, and not for superstition." Twelve years later a second proclamation was published by Elizabeth to the same purpose.

*The Great Rebellion.*—Again Weever, though now by anticipation, strikes the keynote of the treatment of brasses by the Puritan party,—

" These proclamations (of Elizabeth) took small effect, for much what about this time, there sprung up a contagious broode of Scismatickes; who, if they might have had their wills, would not onely have robbed our Churches of all their ornaments and riches, but also have laid them levell with the ground; choosing rather to exercise their devotions, and publish their erronious doctrines, in some emptie barne, in the woods, or common fields, than in these Churches, which they held to be polluted with the abhominations of the whore of Babylon."

When the " contagious broode of Scismatickes " at last did have their wills, churches naturally suffered, and especially cathedrals. Cromwell and his army of " godly men " left their mark wherever they went. Once more commissioners were appointed in every county to " reform " the churches, and so thoroughly was their work performed, that scarcely a brass is now to be found in any of the cathedrals, and many parish churches also were stripped entirely of their memorials. The empty slabs with which they often abound are a melancholy sight. Brasses were made of valuable metal, and were sometimes found useful in the casting of cannon. Numerous instances occur in which brasses were torn up wholesale, and sold by weight for ridiculously small sums, sometimes at as low a rate as three-pence or fourpence per pound. Nor must this ill treatment be laid wholly at the door of the Parliamentarians. Charles and his cavaliers were equally unscrupulous in all matters where money was concerned, and it is only reasonable to suppose that when college and family plate was sacrificed to the king's use, the safety of brasses which happened to be under the care of royalist parsons would be greatly endangered.

*The Eighteenth Century.*—During this period little care was taken of any kind of antiquities, and great numbers of brasses were lost, mutilated or destroyed. A few instances may be given. A correspondent says in *The Gentleman's Magazine* of 1794 : " The venerable church of St Alkmond, in Shrewsbury, being to be taken down and rebuilt, I went to transcribe some old monumental inscriptions, for fear they should be destroyed by the workmen ; but to my surprise, there were several inscriptions on brass plates gone. This led me to make enquiry, and I found they were sold, by order of the churchwardens, to a brazier ; on which I went and desired to see the plates, and carefully copied the inscriptions. That is, all I could find ; but there were more taken from the church, which I fear are lost." His concluding remarks are also worth quoting : " I am sorry, Mr Urban, we have such Goths and Vandals at this time, who would not scruple to destroy any *memento* for the paltry sum of four or five shillings. Such people must certainly be void of humanity, of honour, and, I believe I may safely add, of honesty."

For that same paltry sum, and at about the same time, a magnificent foreign brass was sold at King's Lynn, similar to the two that remain in that town, and therefore one of the finest engravings in Europe.

Instances of such usage might be multiplied indefinitely, and in every county.

*Modern Treatment.*—At the beginning of the nineteenth century, and in the early years of the Gothic revival, brasses were treated almost as badly as before. So-called "restorations" have passed in a great wave over all our parish churches, and have in many cases inflicted irreparable damage. Monuments have been displaced, and brasses torn from their slabs. Here again hundreds of instances might be adduced, of which the following is only too typical. In 1841 the Church of St Giles, Camberwell, was almost wholly destroyed by fire, and an entirely new edifice was built on its site by the late Sir Gilbert Scott. The brasses were left to the tender mercies of the contractor and his men. Out of half-a-score of brasses, one figure, two inscriptions, and two shields escaped, and were roughly cemented to the wall of the new vestry. The rest were scattered broadcast through the parish. Most of them have fortunately been since recovered and replaced.

But the record of the last few years is not in the main one of destruction and loss, but rather of recovery and restoration. Brasses, formerly in private possession, are being restored to the churches from whence they were abstracted, as at Hereford Cathedral. The interest of brass-students is gradually arousing a corresponding interest in brass-guardians. Often missing portions of mutilated brasses have been restored, and well restored too, as at Cobham, in Kent, and Lingfield, in Surrey.

It is unfortunate that in some cases it has been thought necessary to refix brasses against the wall, instead of upon the pavement to which they belong. In such a position they usually look unnatural and out of place, and also suffer from corrosion. They should never on any account be separated from their original slabs, if these exist.

## II.—Making a Collection

### METHODS OF COPYING

By means of a collection of rubbings, it is possible to bring together and compare the brasses of each era and of each distinctive style. The process of making a rubbing is a purely mechanical one, and can be performed by persons altogether unskilled in drawing. As in other things, however, a little practical experience is needed before the collector can expect his rubbings to be quite up to the mark. Practice makes perfect.

The method usually adopted is as follows :—Purchase at a paper-hanger's shop a roll of white lining or ceiling paper, of medium thickness and quality. If the paper is too thin, it will tear easily, and if too thick it will not press sufficiently into the incised lines of the brass, and so will give only a bleared rubbing. If the quality is poor, the paper will turn a dirty yellow colour, especially after being exposed to the light. It is sold in pieces of twelve yards each, and in two widths—viz. 22 in. and 30 in. Wider paper is rarely met with, and is exceedingly inconvenient to carry about. When a brass is more than thirty inches wide, it must be rubbed in separate pieces, which may afterwards be pasted together. Some few collectors prefer to use tinted paper, but it is not so satisfactory as white.

The rubbing is performed with heelball, a composition of beeswax, tallow and lamp-black, which is sold by leather-cutters (not saddlers) in small cakes about as large as a penny. It is used by cobblers, and can sometimes be bought at their shops. The best make is by Ullathorne, and can be procured everywhere. He also sells larger cakes, of about three inches in diameter, which will often be found useful. Heelball is either hard, medium or soft, according to the amount of tallow it contains. The quality can always be

ascertained by application of the thumb-nail.  It is as well
to be provided with all three kinds, as some brasses require
rather different treatment to others.  The softest heelball
cannot be used in hot weather, since it has a tendency to
melt.

With a not too hard nail-brush and a duster in his pocket,
the collector is now equipped for work, and may attempt his
first brass.  A preliminary and very necessary operation is to
carefully brush and dust away every speck of dirt from the
surface of the brass.  If this is not done, or any grits are
left, the paper is sure to tear before the rubbing is half
completed.  We will first suppose the brass to be upon the
pavement of the church, or upon the flat surface of an altar-
tomb.  The roll of paper must be laid upon it, and its upper
edge firmly secured by weights, books or hassocks; the rest
of the paper can be unrolled as it is needed.  The heelball
must be rubbed evenly over the whole brass, when a perfect
impression will be obtained, the incised lines appearing white.
Greater clearness will often be gained by first pressing the
paper into the lines.  This can be done by the hand, or better
by taking off the boots and walking up and down upon the
brass.

If the brass is small and finely engraved, covered with
diaper work or hatching, it will be well to use the hardest
heelball.  Longer time and more trouble will be needed to get
a black rubbing, but the lines will be sharper, and the whole
capable of receiving a beautiful polish by being simply rubbed
over with a handkerchief.  A heelball rubbing is quite fixed,
and will not smear.  If the brass has much plain surface, a
uniform blackness can be far more easily obtained with softer
heelball.  Care should be taken not to rub beyond the brass
over the stone slab, and so spoil the outline.  Some, however,
prefer to ignore the outline, and afterwards to cut out and
mount the rubbing.  Should the brass be fixed upon the wall,
it will be necessary to fasten up the paper in some way.
Drawing-pins are not available against a stone wall, and
other means must therefore be found.  Most collectors use
wafers.  This is the cleanest and most convenient way, and
of course care must be taken not to damage or mark the
wall.  For carrying the materials, it is as well to have some
sort of case, made of waterproof, to sling over the back.

A needlecase and an umbrella cover will suggest two of the forms which it may take.

The heelball method has been thus fully described, because it is the one most usually adopted, and is also the simplest. It was not, however, discovered until some years after brasses began to be copied, and collections of their impressions to be made. In about the year 1780, Craven Ord, Sir John Cullum and the Rev. Thomas Cole commenced the first known collection, and their method of procedure was as follows :—Printers' ink was poured upon the brass, and wiped into all its lines ; damped paper was then laid upon it and pressed well in, producing a printed facsimile, though of course the position of the brass was reversed. This was a great disadvantage, especially as it rendered illegible all the inscriptions. The process has not been made use of at all in late years, and it is doubtful whether many incumbents could be found who would permit the pavements of their churches to be made in the mess which it would necessarily entail.

At the death of Craven Ord, in 1830, his collection was purchased by the late Francis Douce for £43, and by him bequeathed to the British Museum, where it was deposited in 1834.

While Ord and his friends were printing, other collectors began to make use of blacklead in the same manner in which heelball is now used. The result was very bad, for the rubbings would soon become so smudgy and faint as to be almost worthless.

The Messrs Waller next introduced a new method. Their plan was to prepare rubbers of wash-leather, stiffened with paper, of a triangular shape, and primed with a thin paste formed of very fine powdered blacklead mixed with the best linseed oil. The rubbings were taken on stout tissue paper. This method is still in use, and has certain advantages. An accurate rubbing can be made in a few minutes, which would perhaps take an hour or more if done with heelball. It is, however, very faint, and is absolutely useless for exhibition.

Another method is mentioned by Albert Way in the *Archæological Journal* of September 1844. He says that some collectors prefer the use of rubbers of soft black leather, the waste pieces which remain in the shoemaker's workshop, especially those parts which are most strongly imbued with the " dubbing," or black unctuous compound, with which the skins are dressed by the curriers. The plan has not found general favour with brass-rubbers, though it stands high in the favour of campanologists, being admirably suited for taking rubbings of the inscriptions and devices upon church bells.

In 1844 there appeared Richardson's Metallic Rubber, a bronze-coloured composition, intended to give to the rubbing the appearance of the brass itself. It was intended to be used upon a dark paper, so that the lines might be black and the surface the colour of the original. It was used in the same way as heelball. In giving an almost perfect facsimile of the brass, one of the greatest advantages of a heelball rubbing was at once lost. A rubbing in black and white is a great deal clearer than the brass from which it is rubbed, and this clearness is of course lost by the use of a bronze rubber.

A more elaborate method of the same general character was attempted in 1900, by the use of a material called the Delamere Brass-rubber, sold by Messrs Parker & Co. of Oxford, and perhaps still obtainable. A yellow rubbing on special white paper was treated with liquid black, intended to darken the incised lines. Its use entailed a good deal of labour and difficulty, and did not become popular.

Brass-rubbings are greatly improved by being mounted, but the process of mounting occupies a good deal of time and trouble. It is essential to mark each brass with its name, date and origin.

## ARRANGEMENT

A collection of brass-rubbings is bulky, and to some extent inconvenient. At the British Museum rubbings were pasted into half-leather albums of enormous size, some of them ten feet or more in height. But such a method is usually prohibitive on account of cost, and a majority of rubbings must be stored away in rolls. In order to make individual rubbings accessible it will be necessary to keep an index-catalogue, and carefully to number and label every roll, and

Sir William Harper and Wife, 1573.
St Paul's, Bedford.

every brass within the roll. The following particulars should be recorded :—

(a) Place of origin, and county.
(b) Person or persons commemorated.
(c) Date, or approximate date.
(d) Date of rubbing.

It is also useful to keep a larger catalogue, modelled upon a plan long ago adopted by Haines for the Oxford Architectural Society's Manual, published in 1848. Here a description and full particulars should be given, with measurements, exact position, coats-of-arms, etc. An example will best explain the method.

### No. 355

### A.D. 1573. Sir William Harper and Wife

*St Paul's, Bedford*

*Position.*—Relaid on floor of south chapel of choir.

*Component Parts.*—Two figures, each about 20 in. in length, a black letter inscription of five lines, and a coat-of-arms.

*Description.*—The knight in Elizabethan armour, with mail-skirt protected by tassets, etc. Sword and dagger to left and right. Over all, a cloak, fastened at the neck by three buttons over the right shoulder. Head bare, but resting on helmet. Small ruff.
  Lady in quilted petticoat and open dress with small waist sash. Sleeves with large diagonal slashes. Queen Mary head-dress and small ruff.

*Coat-of-Arms.*—Harper, now borne by Bedford Grammar School. [Unless well known, it is necessary to describe the coat.]

*Inscription.*—"Obiit 27° die Februarii, 1573. Año aetatis suae 77° |
Here under lieth buried the body of Sir William Harper knight Alderman and | late Lorde Maior of the Citie of London withe dame Margarett his last wife wch | Sir William was borne in this towne of Bedford, and here foūded & gave lands | for the mayntenance of a Grāmer Schoole.

  [The | indicates the end of a line.]

Great accuracy is necessary, especially in copying inscriptions. Every capital letter or the want of it should be reproduced, as well as the various forms of contraction. It is really remarkable to note how few printed inscriptions can be relied upon as being absolutely correct.

A great deal of useful work can be carried out by means

c

of notes, and valuable collections of such notes can be formed. The brasses of a particular church or district, for instance, can be verified, and illustrated in every possible way, by drawings, photographs and measurements. In recent years it has been found possible to take direct photographs of many brasses, even when they are upon the floor of a church, by a special arrangement of the camera and its stand. Such photographs are most useful, especially in combination with rubbings.

It should always be noticed whether a brass retains its original position, and remains in its original slab; and the outlines of all lost parts should be indicated, and a rubbing or sketch made of the entire composition. In the case of a sketch, every measurement, as well as of the whole slab, should be accurately given.

Heraldry is another point in which the notebook or album can often provide additional information, for the same armorial bearings as those upon a brass may perhaps be found in stained glass in a window, with the proper tinctures, or carved or painted upon a marble tomb. In any church it is well to exhaust the whole field of inquiry, and to search for slabs and tombs which have lost their brasses as well as those which still retain them. All notes should be dated.

A collector may of course specialise in any direction he pleases. Suppose that his interest lies chiefly in the history and evolution of costume, armour or ecclesiastical vestments. His collections may then consist chiefly of drawings and tracings of various details with which he is concerned. With tracing-paper and ink he can quickly copy from rubbings, and the effect will be excellent. Thus it is easy to make a series of sword-hilts, bawdrics, separate pieces of armour, ladies' head-dresses, girdles, pendants, etc. ; or of amices, the apparels of albs, morses, the orphreys of copes, bishops' mitres, croziers and other insignia, and so on ; and all these may be preserved in albums or portfolios which will in time become of the utmost interest and value. But let it never be forgotten to mark every example clearly with its date and origin. Another will perhaps be attracted by the early Norman-French inscriptions. Let him range them together, and add the few which can be gathered from stone and marble originals. To another the heraldry will assume special importance, and the armorials to be gathered from brasses, especially in the earlier examples, will be found of the greatest value. Yet another will group together the representations of saints and angels, who often appear in canopies, side-shafts, ornamentation or in isolated figures. And thus in many and various ways the pursuit of brass rubbing will lead to the accumulation of a great many differing points of interest and knowledge.

# III.—Classes of Effigies

## BRASSES OF ECCLESIASTICS

PERHAPS the most interesting classes of effigies are those which represent respectively Sir Priest and Sir Knight. Of these it is more convenient to take Sir Priest first, because his vestments are an inheritance from a far earlier age, identical in name and use, thought not in shape and material, with those worn centuries before, and because they underwent no changes, except in form, during the period of Brasses down to the Reformation. Moreover, the earliest brass in existence—viz. A.D. 1231—represents one of the clerical order, the German bishop Ysowilpe, still lying in the Church of St Andrew, at Verden. The clergy were divided into two great classes :—

### 1. The Minor Orders.

Doorkeeper ; symbol, a key.
Exorcist ; symbol, a holy-water pot.
Lector ; symbol, a book.
Acolyte ; symbol, a candle.

All orders received the tonsure, and all wore the same dress—viz. the long white *alb*, with the single exception, and that only in parish churches, of the sexton, who ranked as a doorkeeper.

### 2. The Major Orders.

Subdivided into two divisions.

(a) *The Sub-deacon*, whose symbol was an ewer and basin, and who was sometimes also called the *Epistoler* and the *Patener* (*i.e.* he who held up the empty paten).
*The Deacon*, or *Gospeller*.
*The Priest*.

(b) *The Lords Spiritual*, bishops and archbishops, with priors and abbots.

Hic iacet Magister Galfridus Byschop,
quondam huius Ecclesie Vicarius, qui obiit
secundo die Non' Nou' A' d'ni M CCCC lxx vii.
Cuius anime propicietur Dominus. AMEN.

Geoff. Byschop, Vicar of Fulbourn, Cambs, 1477.
Priest in Eucharistic Vestments.

| | |
|---|---|
| *a.* The Amice. | *e.* Ends of the Stole. |
| *b.* Sleeve Apparels of the Alb. | *f.* The Alb. |
| *c.* The Chasuble. | *g.* Foot Apparel of the Alb. |
| *d.* The Maniple. | |

The mediæval vestments of the Western Church received their full development before the ninth century. From the beginning of the Christian era there had been three great tendencies always exerting themselves on the dress of the clergy :—

(a) For a real article of dress to become little more than a useless, though symbolic, ornament.

(b) For a plain white linen vestment to become gorgeous in colour and material.

(c) For the lower orders of the clergy gradually to assume the vestments properly belonging to the higher ranks.

We are not, however, concerned with the various stages through which the different vestments passed, but must take them as we find them in the fourteenth century.

The usual vestments which appear in the brasses of parish priests are those worn at the celebration of the Holy Eucharist, or Sacrifice of the Mass. They consisted of the amice, alb, girdle, stole, maniple, and, most important of all, the chasuble.

(1) *The Amice* was originally a hood, but soon became a mere neckerchief, or square of linen, with a cross embroidered upon it, and with a border sewn along the edge

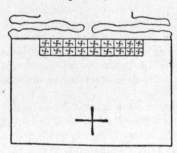

The Amice.

to which its strings were fastened. This border was called an *apparel*, a name given to any piece of embroidery sewn upon a vestment, and it was often ornamented with gold, silver, and jewels. The name orphrey is frequently used interchangeably with apparel for the same kind of work, but more often it implies a narrower strip of stuff, such as will be found down the centre and round the edge of the chasuble. The apparel of the amice is never called an orphrey, and in brasses always appears like a broad collar.

(2) *The Alb* was a linen vestment reaching to the feet, with close sleeves, and ornamented with six orphreys, or apparels, a square being sewn to the lower hem both in front and behind, while the other four adorned the back, breast and cuffs. Those on the cuffs sometimes, in the earlier examples, entirely encircle the sleeve, as at Horsmonden, Kent, c. 1330, and Wensley, Yorks, c. 1360, but usually only cover the upper part. The alb was confined at the waist by a girdle or belt, and was not open in front. In a cathedral church all orders wore it, and most the amice also. Angels are almost invariably represented in this attire.

(3) *The Stole*, almost entirely confined to the higher orders, was a long and richly embroidered band passed round the back of the neck and hanging down in front. It was crossed over the breast, and was kept in position by the girdle. Bishops usually wore the stole straight, and by deacons it was only worn over the left shoulder. Its fringed ends, appearing from beneath the chasuble, are alone seen in brasses, with a few exceptions, as at Horsham, Sussex, and Sudborough, Northants.

(4) *The Maniple*, once a napkin, and intended for use as such, at about the time of the Norman Conquest dwindled down to a silk and gold strip, very similar to one of the ends of the stole. It was looped or buttoned to the sleeve of the left arm.

(5) *The Chasuble* was the distinctive mark of a priest. It was a large oval vestment, sometimes slightly pointed, with an aperture in the middle for the head. It was put on over all the other vestments, and was originally of a soft and pliable material. It was usually ornamented in front and behind with a Y-shaped orphrey, which in later times became a straight-armed cross.

These were the vestments which were worn by the priest at the altar, and in which he was commonly buried. He is frequently represented in brasses as holding a chalice and wafer, and the chalice was often buried with him, being laid upon his breast. In most instances the chalice is held in the hands, but there are exceptions, as at Wensley, in Yorkshire. Brasses of chasubled priests are common everywhere, and are usually of small size, with an average height of perhaps twenty inches.

Tranllus ihu faluis oipur quod tryc iitr ,
pontifics gii truclau cup tumulatuu
Iudugia qua cmus du bua buos henuer,
dhus carms huus fub hunu leui fub ffur.

Annus bus huus pir alut Aliup' cpinus,
Sont faitus liugnus bns pontiatus,
Spur aput ho att yalms muotan
Quj tic pins muuls fib yfis Anikan

Thos. Cranley, Archbishop of Dublin.
New College, Oxford, 1417.

An archbishop in full pontificals.

NOTABLE EXAMPLES :—
    Lawrence de St Maur, Higham Ferrers, Northants, 1337. **Large.**
    John de Grovehurst, Horsmonden, Kent, *c.* 1340. **Large.**
    Thomas de Horton, North Mimms, Herts, *c.* 1360.
    Simon de Wensley (name uncertain), Wensley, Yorks, *c.* 1360. **Large.**
    Priest (unknown), Shottesbroke, Berks, *c.* 1370. **Large.**
    Priest (unknown), Fulbourn, Cambs, *c.* 1370.

## Episcopal Vestments

The higher orders, bishops, abbots and archbishops, were entitled to wear all that could be worn by their subordinates, together with certain additional and distinctive vestments. Bishops and mitred abbots were of equal rank, and cannot be distinguished by their dress. It was once supposed that, contrary to the usage of a bishop, an abbot held his pastoral staff with the crook turned inwards, to signify that he had no jurisdiction outside his monastery. This, however, has no support from existing effigies, in which the staff is held indifferently either way.

In addition to the eucharistic vestments already enumerated, bishops wore both—

1. *The Tunicle* of the sub-deacon, and
2. *The Dalmatic* of the deacon.

These reached to the knee, and were alike in shape and material. They were fringed, and the latter often richly embroidered. Both were slit up for a short distance at the sides. The tunicle is represented as rather the longer of the two, in order that both may be seen. They were worn under the chasuble, while the stole was sometimes below them, as at Westminster Abbey, Burwell, Cambs, and New College, Oxford; and sometimes below only the dalmatic, but above the tunicle, as at Ely Cathedral. Other episcopal insignia are the mitre, sandals, gloves, ring and pastoral staff or crozier.

3. *The Mitre* began as a plain white linen or fur skull-cap, with long strings. It attained the form by which we know it during the twelfth or thirteenth century, and its further developments were slight. In the earlier examples it is low in height and without crockets, which were first added at the end of the fifteenth century. Two *infulæ* or *lappets*, richly embroidered strips of silk, were attached to the lower edge of the mitre, and hung down one behind each ear. They may

be seen in the brasses of Archbishop Grenfeld, at York, 1315, and of Bishop Boothe, at East Horsley, Surrey, 1478.

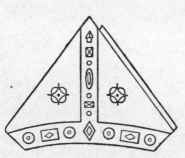

Mitre, 14th Century.

Crocketed Mitre, 16th Century.

4. *The Sandals* were pointed slippers ornamented by three strips of embroidery, forming a sort of orphrey.

5. *The Gloves* were of white netted silk, with a jewelled ornament upon the back. The middle finger of the right hand was cut away, in order to show the episcopal *ring*, which was worn below a guard upon that finger.

6. *The Crozier* terminates in a heavy crook, ornamented with jewels, and frequently containing the symbol of the lamb and banner. To it is often attached a scarf, known as the *vexillum*, and supposed to be derived from the Labarum, or Standard, of the first Christian emperor, Constantine the Great. The end of the staff is furnished with a small spike.

Archbishops used the same vestments as bishops, with two additions :—

1. *The Pall*, a circle of white lambswool, adorned with crosses, and with pendent and weighted ends in front and behind, was thrown over the shoulders above the chasuble. Its history is interesting, since it was first conferred as a mark of distinction by the early Byzantine emperors upon the patriarchs of Constantinople. Being adopted in the West, it became the special prerogative of the pope to confer this vestment, and the various metropolitans always received it straight from the chair of St Peter.

2. *The Cross-staff*, in practice usually substituted for the crozier, though an archbishop might use both. The head

Thos. Wilkynson, Prebendary of Kipon and Rector
of Orpington.  Orpington, Kent, 1511.

**Priest in Cassock, Surplice, Almuce and Cope.**

46

is a plain cross, or sometimes a crucifix, as at New College, Oxford.

EXAMPLES :—

*Archbishops.*

Grenfeld, of York, York Minster, 1315.
Waldeby, of York, Westminster Abbey, 1397.
Cranley, of Dublin, New College, Oxford, 1417.
Unknown, Edenham, Lincs, *c.* 1500.

*Bishops.*

Trilleck, of Hereford, Hereford Cathedral, *c.* 1360.
Wyvill, of Salisbury, Salisbury Cathedral, 1375.
Waltham, of Salisbury, Westminster Abbey, 1395.
Boothe, of Exeter, East Horsley, Surrey, 1478.
Bell, of Carlisle, Carlisle Cathedral, 1496.
Stanley, of Ely, Manchester Cathedral, 1515.
Young, of Callipolis, New College, Oxford, 1526.
Goodrick, of Ely, Ely Cathedral, 1554.

*Abbots.*

Delamere, St Alban's Abbey, *c.* 1360.
Estney, Westminster Abbey, 1498.

## Processional Vestments

Ecclesiastics are often represented as wearing other vestments than those already described.

1. *The Cope* is the chief among these, and is worn over a cassock and surplice. It is a cloak-like outer vestment, with a broad ornamental orphrey along the edge, and is semi-circular in shape, fastened at the neck by a large clasp, called a *morse*. The whole of the cope is sometimes richly diapered, as at Winchester and Balsham.

2. *The Almuce*, a fur hood, with long ends pendent in front, is worn with the cope. To represent the fur conveniently, the surface of the brass is commonly lowered, and the depression filled up with lead or some similar substance.

Examples of coped priests are exceedingly common, and often very fine, thus affording a marked contrast to the memorials of their brethren in Eucharistic vestments.

NOTABLE EXAMPLES :—

Canon Campeden, St Cross, Winchester, 1382.
Canon Fulburne, Fulbourn, Cambs, 1391.
Canon Sleford, Balsham, Cambs, 1401.
Prior Prestwyk, Warbleton, Sussex, 1436.

Dean Blodwell, Balsham, Cambs, 1462.
Professor Sever, Merton College, Oxford, 1471.
Bishop White, Winchester College, Hants, c. 1548.
Archbishop Harsnett, of York, Chigwell, Essex, 1631.

Canons of Windsor were entitled to wear, instead of the
cope, the mantle of the Order of the Garter, of which they
were members.  It was purple in colour, and bore upon the
left shoulder a circular white badge with a red cross.

EXAMPLES :—
Canon Lupton, provost, Eton College, 1540.
Canon Cole, S.T.B., Magdalen College, Oxford, 1558.

The almuce is frequently worn without the cope, and then
its full dimensions become apparent.  It is brought well
together over the breast, and slopes down over the arms.
Its edge is fringed by a row of small tufts of fur or tails.

EXAMPLES :—
Archdeacon, Goberd, Magdalen College, Oxford, 1515.
Prebendary Adams, East Malling, Kent, 1522.
Provost Hacombleyn, King's College, Cambridge, 1528.
Canon Coorthopp, Christ Church Cathedral, Oxford, 1557.
Provost Brassie, King's College, Cambridge, 1558.

### Academicals

At the two universities, and more particularly at Oxford,
there are to be found a number of brasses of priests in
academical habits, though they are rare elsewhere.

Among them there is considerable diversity, and it is
exceedingly difficult to discriminate between these diverg-
ences, and explain their meaning.

All wear the cassock.  They may be roughly divided into
several classes, according to the dress.

1. *The Doctor's Dress*, probably (*vide* illus., p. 49).
    (a) *Sleeveless Gown*, reaching to the feet, and having a
        single slit in front, through which both the arms
        were thrust.
    (b) *The Tippet*, a large cape, distinguished from the
        almuce by having a straight edge and no pendants.
    (c) *The Academical Hood*, either added to or substituted
        for the tippet.  It is best seen in profile, as in the
        kneeling figures of Dr Billingford, at St Benet's,
        Cambridge, and of Archdeacon Polton, at All
        Souls' College, Oxford.

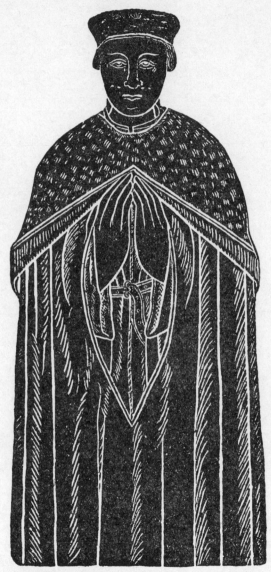

A Doctor, *c.* 1480.   Little St Mary's, Cambridge.

(*d*) *The Cap*, stiff and round, and rising slightly to a point in the middle. Dr Billingford and Dr Hautryve, of New College, wear skull caps instead. Neither kind bears any resemblance to the modern college-cap.

EXAMPLES :—

William Hautryve, LL.D., New College, Oxford, 1441.
Richard Billingford, D.D., St Benet's Church, Cambridge, 1432.
John Argentein, D.D. and M.D., King's College, Cambridge, 1507.
Unknown, Little St Mary's, Cambridge, *c.* 1480.
William Towne, D.D., King's College, Cambridge, 1496.
Unknown, Great St Helen's, Bishopsgate, London, *c.* 1500.

2. *Bachelors of Divinity*, perhaps.

(*a*) *Gown with two slits*, instead of one.
(*b*) *Tippet*, half-furred.
(*c*) *Academical Hood*, sometimes omitted.

This class is a doubtful one, and two of the examples below, from Queens' College and Trinity Hall, are, to say the least, peculiar.

EXAMPLES :—

John Bloxham, S.T.B. (*Sanctæ Theologiæ Baccalaureus*), Merton College, Oxford, *c.* 1420.
John Darley, Herne, Kent, *c.* 1450.
William Blakwey, Little Wilbraham, Cambs, 1521.
Unknown, Trinity Hall, Cambs, *c.* 1530.
Unknown, Queens' College, Cambridge, *c.* 1535.

3. *Masters and Bachelors in other faculties.*

(*a*) *Rochet*, worn over the cassock, or an academical tabard.
(*b*) *Tippet*.
(*c*) *Hood*.

In this class are included the great mass of academical brasses. The different degrees are probably distinguished only by the colour of the hood, which does not appear. The linen rochet has short sleeves. So has the cloth tabard.

EXAMPLES :—

John Mottesfont, LL.B., Lydd, Kent, 1420.
Walter Wake, S.T.S., New College, Oxford, 1451.
David Lloyde, LL.B., All Souls' College, Oxford, 1510.
Nicholas Goldwell, M.A. (no tonsure), Magdalen College, Oxford, 1523.
Abbot Lawrence, of Ramsey, Burwell, Cambs, 1542.

Sometimes the surplice is apparently omitted, but whether this has any special significance or not it is impossible to tell.

EXAMPLES :—

Ralph Vaudrey, M.A., Magdalen College, Oxford, 1478.
Nicholas Wotton, LL.D., Great St Helen's, Bishopsgate, London, 1482.
Richard Spekynton, LL.B., All Souls' College, Oxford, 1490.

4. *Undergraduates*, or more properly, students. It is possible that in the brass of Thos. Baker, student of civil law, 1510, in All Souls' Chapel, we have the attire of the mediæval undergraduate. He is dressed in a belted tunic, a fur-sleeved gown, and a mantle, to which is attached a small hood, gathered up upon the left shoulder. He has no tonsure.

### The Monastic Orders

Monastic brasses are comparatively rare, in consequence doubtless of the spoliation and destruction of the monasteries under Henry VIII.

*Abbots*, in episcopal vestments, are to be found at St Alban's, Westminster, and a few other places.

The only one in distinctly monastic attire is at Dorchester, Oxon, representing Richard Bewfforeste, *c.* 1510. His hooded cloak is open in front, showing a surplice and almuce underneath. His pastoral staff rests on his right arm.

*Priors*. Of a prior there is a very fine example at Cowfold, in Sussex, the cloak and cowl alone being visible.

*Monks*, of the Benedictine order, in the same simple dress, are to be found at St Alban's and elsewhere.

*Abbesses*. Two only are known, at Elstow, in Bedfordshire, and Denham, in Buckinghamshire. Their dress is that of a widow in ordinary life—viz. a plain kirtle, mantle, veil head-dress, and barbe or wimple. The Elstow abbess has a pastoral staff.

*Nuns*. Some half-dozen nuns are similarly attired, but Margaret Dely, 1561, treasurer of the convent of Syon, in her diminutive brass at Isleworth, Middlesex, has no mantle.

### Post-Reformation Ecclesiastics

The divines of the Reformation are not very commonly commemorated by brasses; but when they occur, they are represented in the ordinary dress of citizens, which will be described under the head " Civilians."

NOTABLE EXAMPLES :—

Griffin Lloyd, rector, Chevening, Kent, 1596.
Dean Tyndall, Master of Queens' College, Cambridge, Ely Cathedral, 1614.
Dean Wythines, Vice-Chancellor of Oxford University, Battle, Sussex, 1615.

## BRASSES OF MEN IN ARMOUR

Mediæval armour is nowhere so well represented as on brasses. We have left to us specimens of every kind of armour, from the chain mail of the crusader to the latest development of the reign of Charles II., when gunpowder and shot caused it to be finally abandoned.

The student should, however, by no means neglect to visit the armouries in the Tower of London, where he may learn much that is not apparent upon an engraved brass—e.g. the methods of fastening together the various parts of a suit of armour, the way in which roundels are strapped and buckled to the breast-plate or épaulière, and similar details. The defences of the back are never shown in brasses. These can hardly be learnt but from collections of armour. The Tower is particularly rich in armour of the reign of Henry VII., and all later developments are represented. The Wallace Collection should also be visited.

Stone effigies deserve equal attention, chiefly for the light they throw on the earlier periods. Knights who fought under Plantagenet kings may be found in nearly all the great cathedral and conventual churches. Westminster Abbey must be specially mentioned under this head, and among lesser churches the Temple.

At St Paul's Church, Bedford, there is recorded to have been a brass of Sir John Beauchamp, 1208, and this, if it had survived to our day, would have been the oldest brass known. As it happens, little is known about it beyond the name of the knight whom it commemorated, and we can only regret its untimely loss. But probably it was a cross-brass, without effigy.

In knightly brasses we have brought before us the actual contemporaneous portraits of our forefathers as they fought in all the great battles and wars of English history, from the last Crusade to the close of the Stuart period. During this time the armour of the knights underwent almost as many changes as occurred in the passing fashions of their ladies. It may be divided into seven distinct classes, each a development of the one before it. But between each there is of course a short period of transition, just as between the different styles of Gothic architecture, with whose rise and fall the art of brass-engraving is intimately connected.

**I. The Surcoat Period.** During which entire suits of mail were worn, ending with the death of Edward I., 1307.

NOTABLE EXAMPLES :—

Sir John Daubernoun, Stoke d'Abernon, Surrey, 1277.
Sir Roger de Trumpington, Trumpington, Cambs, 1289.
Sir Robert de Bures, Acton, Suffolk, 1302.
Sir Robert de Setvans, Chartham, Kent, 1306.

(*a*) A period of transition, during which additional defences of plate began to be worn over the suit of mail, and with the surcoat. Extended through the greater part of the reign of Edward II.

NOTABLE EXAMPLES :—

Sir William Fitzralph, Pebmarsh, Essex, *c.* 1320.
Sir —— de Bacon, Gorleston, Suffolk, *c.* 1320.

**II. The Cyclas Period.** From the Despencer troubles at the close of the reign of Edward II., to the middle of that of Edward III., say to the founding of the Order of the Garter, 1350, between the battles of Creçy and Poitiers.

NOTABLE EXAMPLES :—

Sir John de Northwode, Minster, Isle of Sheppey, 1325.
Sir John de Creke, Westley Waterless, Cambridgeshire, 1325.
Sir John Daubernoun II., Stoke d'Abernon, Surrey, 1327.
Sir John Giffard, Bowers Gifford, Essex, 1348.

**III. The Camail Period.** From the founding of the Order of the Garter to the first few years of the reign of Henry IV.

NOTABLE EXAMPLES, exceedingly numerous, *e.g.* :—

Sir John de Cobham, and four others, Cobham, Kent, 1354-1407.
Sir Wm. Fienlez, Hurstmonceux, Sussex, 1402.
Sir Wm. Bagot, Baginton, Warwick, 1407.

Sir Robert de Bures, 1302.   Acton, Suffolk.
Knight in Chain Mail and Surcoat.

55

(*a*) Transitional, overlapping the two periods which it partially divides. A larger quantity of plate armour is worn in conjunction with the camail of mail.

NOTABLE EXAMPLES :—

Sir Thomas Braunstone, Wisbech, Cambridgeshire, 1401.
Sir John Hanley, Dartmouth, Devon, 1408.

**IV. The Complete Plate, or Lancastrian, Period.** From Henry IV. to the commencement of the Wars of the Roses in 1455, marked chiefly by Henry V.'s French wars and the battle of Agincourt.

NOTABLE EXAMPLES :—

Sir Simon de Felbrigge, Felbrigg, Norfolk, 1413.
Sir John Peryent, Digswell, Herts, 1415.
Sir Thomas Bromflete, Wymington, Bedfordshire, 1430.

**V. The Yorkist Period.** From the battle of St Alban's to the battle of Bosworth and death of Richard III. in 1485, covering the whole period of the Wars of the Roses. The defences of plate were made more numerous and exaggerated than before.

NOTABLE EXAMPLES :—

Sir Thos. Shernborne, Shernborne, Norfolk, 1458.
Sir Thos. Grene, Green's Norton, Northants, 1462.
Thos. Peyton, Esq., Isleham, Cambs, 1484.

**VI. The Mail Skirt, or Early Tudor, Period,** of the reigns of Henry VII., Henry VIII., Edward VI., and Mary.

Examples are so numerous that it is useless to mention any in particular, especially as none of them are of any very great merit.

**VII. The Tasset, or Elizabethan, Period.** Extending to the final abandonment of the use of armour. Armed men later than the reign of Elizabeth are of the same style. The series closes with the figures of Nicholas Toke, Esq., Great Chart, Kent, 1680, and Edm. West, Serjeant-at-law, Marsworth, Bucks, 1681.

### I. The Surcoat Period

The reign of Edward I. produces the earliest remaining knightly effigy—viz. that of Sir John Daubernoun, mentioned on p. 54, at Stoke d'Abernon, near Leatherhead, in Surrey. Here we have portrayed the full crusading panoply, though this particular knight never visited the Holy Land.

The armour is as follows :—

 1. A complete suit of chain mail, consisting of
     (a) *Hawberk*, covering the body and arms.
     (b) *Coif de mailles*, or hood.
     (c) *Chausses*, or stockings.
     (d) *Gloves*, continued from the sleeves of the hawberk,
and undivided for the fingers.

 2. *Genouillières*, or knee pieces, made either of steel or of a leather called *cuir-bouilli*, and strapped over the chain mail.

A *surcoat* of linen or cloth was worn over the armour. It was sleeveless, and reached to some distance below the knee, being slit up part of the way in front, confined at the waist by a narrow cord, and fringed at the bottom.

ACCESSORIES :—

  i. *Shield*, which was either small and *heater*-shaped, as worn by Sir John Daubernoun, or else rounded to the body, as Sir Robert de Bures has it. In both cases the coat-of-arms of the wearer was emblazoned upon it.
      It was worn on the left arm, and supported by a guige or strap, usually ornamented, passing over the right shoulder

 ii. *Spurs*. These were of the " prick " kind—*i.e.* they were cruelly long plain spikes, fastened by straps across the insteps.

iii. *Ailettes*. Curious square appendages, fastened in an upright position on the shoulders, fringed and emblazoned with the wearer's arms. They were not always used.

Sir John Daubernoun, 1277.
Stoke d'Abernon, Surrey.

The earliest existing Brass in England.

iv. *Tilting Helmet.* Only worn when in action. At other
times carried slung over the saddle. Made of heavy
steel, and padded inside. It is shown only in the
Trumpington brass, where the knight's head is
pillowed upon it. A chain connects it with the cord
which surrounds his waist in order to preserve it
from the danger of being lost.

WEAPONS :—

i. *Sword.* Large, and cross-hilted. Often very handsome, with a beautifully enriched scabbard. It is
hung in front, or a little to the left side, from a
broad belt adjusted over the hips.

ii. *Spear.* Only found in the brass of Sir John Daubernoun. It leans against his right arm, and is
adorned by a small emblazoned pennon.

In most cases the feet rest against a lion, though
occasionally a hound is substituted.

(*a*) **Transition Period.** The same weapons are used, and
the same armour worn, but with certain additional defences
of plate. These are as follows :—

i. *Demi-plates*, on the upper and forearms, called brassarts or rere-braces and vambraces.
ii. *Coutes*, protecting the elbows.
iii. *Roundels*, or palettes, spiked, buckled to the shoulders
and the bend of the arms.
iv. *Jambs*, or shin-plates.
v. *Sollerets*, or shoes of small steel plates jointed together
and protecting the feet.

The Gorleston knight is in banded instead of chain mail.

## II. The Cyclas Period

The close of the reign of Edward II. saw several important
changes in defensive armour. The suit of mail was still
worn, but was generally banded—*i.e.* instead of the little
rings being linked to one another, they were sewn in rows
upon a leather foundation. The sleeves of the hawberk
became shorter, and vambraces were worn beneath on the
forearm. The *coif de mailles* upon the head gave way to the

fluted steel *bascinet*, and the surcoat to the cyclas.   In other respects the armour remained the same as in the transitional period, except that prick spurs fell into disuse, and were replaced by the ordinary rowel type.   The cyclas differed from the surcoat in being slit up at the sides, and very much shorter in front than at the back ; even behind it did not reach below the knees.   Owing to its shortness in front, the garments worn beneath it can all be seen, one below the other.   Beginning from the outermost, the body-coverings were as follows :—

i. *Cyclas.*
ii. *Pourpoint.*  A fringed dress of rich materials, usually embroidered with some pattern.
iii. *Hawberk.*  Now usually with the lower edge pointed, but at Minster straight and slit up the front.
iv. *Hauketon.*  A padded garment, stitched in parallel downward lines, and intended to protect the body from the chafing of the heavy hawberk.

The Bowers Gifford knight, mentioned on p. 54 as a notable example, is really transitional, and also peculiar, since he wears a garment which can only be described as something between a surcoat and a jupon (speedily to be mentioned), and has no brassarts or jambs.

### III. The Camail Period

The armour worn during this period, which lasted half-a-century, was almost invariable, and moreover quite different to that which it displaced.

DEFENSIVE ARMOUR (*vide* illus., p. 65) :—

i. *Bascinet.*  A plain, acutely pointed steel cap.
ii. *Camail.*  A tippet of mail, chain or banded, laced to the bascinet, and covering the neck and shoulders.
iii. *Mail Shirt*, or sleeveless hawberk, visible only at its lower edge, and sometimes at the arm-pits.
iv. *Jupon.*  A tight-fitting short tunic without sleeves, generally of leather, and sometimes charged with armorial bearings.  Its lower edge was in most cases escalloped or fringed.

Sir John Daubernoun the Younger, 1327.
Stoke d'Abernon, Surrey.
Knight in Mixed Armour and Cyclas.

Sir John d'Argentine, 1382.
Horseheath, Cambridgeshire.

Knight in Bascinet, Camail and Jupon.

v. *Arm-defences*, now entirely of steel, and consisting of *épaulières* (epaulets), protecting the shoulders, usually of three plates one above the other; *brassarts, coutes,* and *vambraces.*

vi. *Gauntlets*, of steel or leather, or sometimes of leather faced with steel.

vii. *Cuisses*, or thigh armour. Steel plates, frequently covered by pourpointrie work—*i.e.* cloth or other material fixed with metal studs.

viii. *Genouillières*, small and plain.

ix. *Jambs*, in some instances showing a pair of mail stockings.

x. *Sollerets*, sharp-toed, and generally having the instep protected by what is called a gusset of mail.

xi. *Rowel Spurs.*

OFFENSIVE ARMOUR :—

i. *Sword*, cross-hilted, with a plain scabbard. It was fastened at the left side to a handsome *bawdric*, a broad straight belt adjusted upon the hips.

ii. *Misericorde*, a short dagger, without guard, fastened to the bawdric on the right.

An important change has not yet been mentioned. The shield is now no longer represented as an adjunct to the pictured knight. It disappears as completely as if it had fallen into disuse. The feet rest always against a lion or a hound.

(*a*) **Transition Period.** The chief mark of change is to be found in the abandonment of the jupon, formerly so essential a part of a knight's equipment. The armour worn beneath it is therefore now for the first time visible. It consists of :—

i. *Cuirass* of steel, very plain, and rounded in front.

ii. *Taces*, or broad hoops of steel, fastened one to the other, and forming a short skirt. There are usually about six of these.

## IV. Lancastrian Period

We now come to the armour worn by the knights who fought at Agincourt and Orleans. It differed from that of the preceding reigns in being of complete plate, without any admixture of mail, except sometimes a narrow fringe to the lowest tace.

One absolutely new piece of armour came into use. This was the steel *gorget*, encircling the neck, and replacing the camail, which entirely disappears.

The acutely pointed bascinet also fell into disuse, and gave way to a lower and rounder helmet. The gorget was not so deep as the camail had been, involving a lengthening of the épaulières, which now consisted of six or more plates, instead of three only. At the armpits roundels were still used, but gradually gave place to oblong *palettes*, which were sometimes charged with a cross. The coutes at the elbows in most instances became fan-shaped. Below the knee small additional plates were attached to the genouillières. Bawdrics went out with the jupons, and the sword was now kept in position at the left side by a narrow transverse belt ornamented usually with quatrefoils. The misericorde, on the other side, was hooked to one of the taces themselves.

At the close of the French wars came several slight alterations. Two small plates, called *tuilles*, were buckled to the lowermost tace. At first they were hardly deeper than the hoop to which they were attached, but gradually lengthened till they almost touched the genouillières. Pauldrons and placcates now began to make their appearance, but they belong more properly to the next period, to which it is more convenient to leave their description.

## V. The Yorkist Period

The style of armour which was adopted throughout the Wars of the Roses was perhaps the most extraordinary ever invented by mankind.

Its most striking feature is the rapid accumulation of heavy and ungainly steel plates, one upon another, till it is difficult to imagine how any knight could sustain their combined weight. The helmet is but rarely depicted in the

Edward de la Hale, Esq., 1431.  Oakwood, Surrey.
Lancastrian Period of Complete Plate Armour.

brasses of the time, and the hair is worn short at first, and afterwards flowing to the shoulders.

The old armour remains as a foundation, though much of it is greatly changed, chiefly by a process of exaggeration.

The first indications of the coming change are to be seen in the use of :—

i. *Pauldrons*, massive steel plates protecting the upper arms and shoulders. They were at first quite plain, and showed the uppermost plates of the épaulières beneath.

ii. *Placcates*, additional defences to the upper part of the cuirass, one on each side.

iii. *Demi-placcates*, covering the lower part of the cuirass, broad at the bottom, and tapering upwards to a point between the placcates.

iv. *Gardes-de-bras*, sometimes attached to the coutes or gauntlets. Those on the right arm were of different shape to those on the left, the idea being to leave the former freer for action, while the latter was rather for defence.

By the time Edward IV. ascended the throne, in 1461, the armour of the period had reached its utmost development, and continued practically the same till the close of the civil wars.

A collar of mail was now substituted for the gorget, and the pauldrons and coutes had attained to colossal proportions.

i. *The Pauldrons* were worn sometimes on the left shoulder alone, in which case a large garde-de-bras was riveted to the épaulières of the right, and sometimes on both shoulders. They consisted usually of two plates, one above the other, the uppermost being ridged, and having an upturned edge to protect the neck, termed a *pass-guard*.

ii. *The Coutes*, now often called *coudières*, were of immense size, as large as helmets, and often fluted, with escalloped edges.

The skirt of taces was divided transversely into a great number of separate pieces, and was much shortened, while the tuilles increased correspondingly.  Between them appears a short baguette of mail.

The genouillières had extra plates above as well as below. The sword, which had a very short hilt, was hung in front of the body.

## VI. The Early Tudor Period

About the time of the battle of Bosworth, A.D. 1485, we get another complete change, when all the old extravagances were abandoned.  The change must have been sudden as well as complete, for we have scarcely any traces of a state of transition.

The cuirass returns to its simple condition, except that it has a ridge down the centre.  Placcates, demi-placcates, coudières and gardes-de-bras are either abandoned altogether or reduced to the smallest possible dimensions.

Mail collars are retained, and also pauldrons with pass-guards and tuilles, but they are smaller than before.  The latter, as represented on brasses, can now be seen to be four in number.

New features are :—

i.  *Mail Skirt*, the mark of the period.  It appears below the taces, and generally reaches beyond the tuilles.

ii.  *Sabbatons*, or broad-toed shoes, upon the feet instead of pointed sollerets.  A *gusset* of mail is shown at the instep.

iii.  *Spear-rest*, a small hook, occasionally seen screwed to the right-hand side of the breast of the cuirass.

With this style of armour is now frequently seen the *tabard-of-arms*, a most important ornament of knightly equipment.  It was an heraldic coat reaching below the skirt of taces, and charged with the wearer's armorial bearings. It had short sleeves, on each of which the arms were repeated.  The tabard occasionally appears in brasses of the Yorkist period, but did not come into anything like general use till the reigns of Henry VII. and Henry VIII.  It is not seen much later than the middle of the sixteenth century, the last known example being dated 1565.

Sir Humphrey Stanley, 1505.
Westminster Abbey.

**Tudor Knight in Mail Skirt.**

## VII. The Elizabethan Period

Armour now received its last development. The cuirass became long-waisted, and was sharply ridged down the breast.

Pauldrons were discarded, and once more replaced by épaulières, enlarged, having an ornamental edge, and nearly meeting across the cuirass.

The skirt of taces disappeared, and in its stead appendages called *tassets*, or *lamboys*, were buckled immediately to the cuirass. These tassets were a legitimate development of the tuilles, but consisted of many plates, of which the lowest were, except in a few of the earliest examples, rounded off. In some few instances they were fastened to the knee-plates, but did not usually reach quite so low.

Ruffs were always worn round the neck, and generally at the wrists also. At the beginning of Elizabeth's reign the mail skirt was still worn beneath the lamboys, but was speedily abandoned.

The armour of the Stuarts was in all points the same as that of the Elizabethan period. The sword-hilt, however, assumes, with James I., the pattern still in use.

The latest known brasses representing men in armour are to be found at Great Chart, near Ashford, in Kent, A.D. 1680, and Marsworth, Bucks, 1681. The Elizabethan type of armour still holds its ground, and the lamboys are seen covering a large pair of trunk breeches. The ruffs are replaced by a turned-down collar and cuffs.

## BRASSES OF LADIES

Ladies' dress must be taken in close connection with the armour of their husbands, with whom they most usually appear on sculptured tomb or engraved brass. The earliest representations of ladies are to be found on the brasses of Margaret Lady Camoys, at Trotton, Sussex, A.D. 1310; Joan Lady Cobham, at Cobham, Kent, 1320; Alyne Lady Creke, at Westley Waterless, Cambs, 1325; Joan Lady Northwode, at Minster, Sheppey, 1330; and a few more.

The dress is, in all cases, of the most simple character, consisting of a kirtle with tight buttoned sleeves, and over it a loose flowing gown, waistless, and having short sleeves reaching a little below the elbow.

Lady Creke wears also an open cloak or mantle, fastened by a cord across the breast.

A hideous wimple or gorget is worn round the neck, hiding also the chin and sides of the face.

The hair is usually kept in place by a narrow enriched fillet or coronet, while a single plait or curl appears on either side of the forehead.

Upon the head is a veil or coverchef, descending to the shoulders.

This style of dress continued in vogue until the beginning of the camail period among the knights, commencing towards the end of the reign of Edward III.

The changes of fashion may now be marked chiefly by the head-dresses, which are of several distinctive types. The different styles may be briefly enumerated thus :—

1. Reticulated head-dresses, Edward III.-Henry IV.
2. Horned head-dresses, a peculiar development of the first-mentioned, Henry V.-Richard III.
3. Butterfly head-dresses, corresponding to the exaggerated armour of the Yorkist period, Edward IV.-Henry VII.
4. Pedimental head-dresses, corresponding to the mail skirt period of the Tudor knights, Henry VII.-Queen Mary.
5. Paris head-dresses, or Mary Queen of Scots caps, chiefly of the Elizabethan period, Henry VII.-James I.

It will thus be seen that several styles considerably overlap one another, especially the last two, which began almost at the same time, although the one very much outlasted the other.

The first style was subject to a great many variations, and in certain forms is frequently called the *nebule* or *zigzag* head-dress. The hair was enclosed within a thin net, encircling the face, and represented by a series of wavy (nebule) or zigzag lines, from two to six in number. A tress of hair was often allowed to escape on either side, and its end rolled up into a netted ball, of similar construction to the upper net, and resting upon the shoulder (*vide* illus. on p. 79).

The dress worn at the same time was a low-necked closely

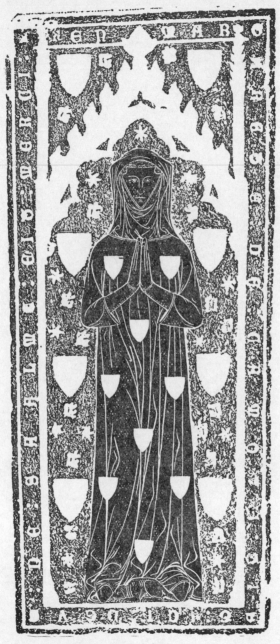

Margaret Lady Camoys, *c.* 1310.    Trotton, Sussex.
The earliest Brass of a Lady, in Kirtle, Gown, Veil and Wimple.

fitting kirtle, with tight sleeves buttoned from the elbow to the wrist. It was frequently buttoned in front as far as the waist, and sometimes had a broad border or trimming of heavy fur. Its chief feature was its simplicity.

Occasionally the kirtle is seen alone, but more frequently another dress is worn over it. This is called a *cote-hardi*, and is almost as simple as the kirtle. Its chief distinction is that its sleeves terminate above the elbows, but have attached to them long and narrow lappets reaching almost to the ground.

A Lady, *c.* 1400. Ore, Sussex.
The Nebule Head-dress, p. 76.

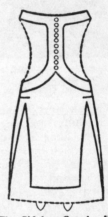

The Sideless Cote-hardi.

It sometimes also has two pockets in front. A very peculiar development of this same dress came quickly into fashion.

It was the *sideless cote-hardi*, a dress as fashionable as it was peculiar. The bodice, or jacket, was absolutely without sides, consisting of a fur trimming which trimmed nothing. To this was attached a short skirt, slit up at the sides, like a Bannockburn warrior's cyclas, and almost resembling a double apron. Over these dresses a mantle was worn, fastened by a cord passed across the breast between two jewelled clasps.

During the reign of Henry V. the most noticeable changes in costume are to be seen in the head-dresses, although it must not be forgotten that the varying styles greatly overlap.

Elena Bernard, 1467.
Isleham, Cambs.
The Horned Head-dress.

The hair is still confined within a net, in a remarkably stiff but handsome manner.

In this *crespine* head-dress, as it is called, the hair is fastened in a net, often jewelled, upon the top of the head, with a bunch or knob, also netted, above each ear. The whole *coiffure* is kept in position by a jewelled band or fillet, and partially covered by a light veil, which hangs down over the shoulders. There are numerous variations of this head-dress, and indeed hardly two brasses can be found in which the hair is done in exactly the same way.

Widows wear a barbe or wimple, and a heavy veil which entirely hides the hair.

The crespine head-dress, however, merely leads up to the style in which the head-dresses assume the *horned* or *mitred* shapes, and which remained in fashion till the close of the Yorkist period.

In it the side nets were increased to a very large size, so as to form a pair of stiff horns. The central part of the hair is usually hidden by the veil, which reaches, as before, to the shoulders.

With the horned head-dress came in a new kind of gown, which commonly, though not always, took the place of the kirtle and mantle. It was plain, and high-waisted, girt under the breast by a narrow but rich band. Its sleeves were extremely wide and loose, but brought together at the wrists. A broad collar was either turned up round the neck, or fell gracefully upon the shoulders.

We now come to one of the most extraordinary erections with which ladies ever burdened themselves. The *butterfly* head-dress came into fashion during the reign of Edward IV., but did not retain its popularity for more than a few years,

Orate p̄ āīa Anne Herward ux̄ Robti herward q̄ obyit
pm̄o die m̄ens Januarij aꝰ dn̄i m̄ ccccl xxxv ꝰ cui aīe ꝑpiciet ꝺeus

Anne Herward, 1485. Aldborough, Norfolk.
The Butterfly Head-dress.

disappearing soon after the accession of Henry VII. It is not seen to advantage in brasses, which always give it an appearance of far greater heaviness than it really possessed. To display its proportions in a brass, it was necessary to turn the figure slightly sideways, and this was invariably done. The hair was brushed straight back from the forehead and enclosed in a net at the back of the head. Upon this was erected a huge framework of wire, covered by a spreading veil. The effect must, at least, have been imposing. The accompanying dress was extremely low in the neck, edged usually with fur, and having tight sleeves and cuffs. To a girdle about the waist a rich charm or ornament was hung by a somewhat lengthy chain. A broad and rich necklace was usually worn. An outer mantle is still often seen. About the same time in which knightly tabards became common, there appeared among the ladies richly embroidered heraldic dresses. A married lady would wear the arms of her own family emblazoned upon her kirtle, and those of her husband on her mantle. The custom continued till the close of the reign of Henry VIII.

Excellent examples of the heraldic kirtle and mantle in connection with the butterfly head-dress may be seen in the brasses of two sisters-in-law at the church of Long Melford, in Suffolk, c. 1480.

The *pedimental* head-dress made its first appearance in the reign of Henry VII. Its shape and style, together with the dress with which it was associated, underwent but little change until the middle of Henry VIII.'s reign. It was exceedingly stiff, and entirely hid the hair. Frontlets of thick velvet, elaborately embroidered, met over the forehead, so as to form a sharp and decided angle, and hung down in lappets on either side of the face, reaching to the shoulders, or lower. Similar lappets, or else a veil, hung behind.

The dress had tight sleeves with fur cuffs, and was cut square at the neck. Its skirt was frequently trimmed with fur. A large embroidered belt, faced with silver, was buckled loosely round the waist, and its end allowed to hang almost to the ground. Three metal roses or clasps were sometimes substituted for the buckle, with a pendent chain attached, generally terminated by a handsome pomander or scent-box.

Several changes were made during the second half of the

bluff king's reign, beginning at about A.D. 1530. The front lappets of the head-dress were frequently pinned up out of the way, and the collar of the dress, no longer cut square, was turned down so as to show the *partlet*, a linen garment drawn together round the neck. The dress sleeves reached only to the elbow, and were very broad, and heavily trimmed with fur. Embroidered under-sleeves, striped longitudinally and slashed beneath, were now rendered visible. A long rosary sometimes takes the place of the chain and pomander.

Elyzth. Perepoynt, 1543.
West Malling, Kent.
The Pedimental Head-dress.

Excellent instances may be seen at Harefield, Middlesex, 1537 and 1540; and at Lullingstone and West Malling, in Kent, 1544, 1533 and 1543 (*vide* illus.).

Throughout the reigns of Edward VI. and Mary, the pedimental head-dress lingered on, but was partially superseded by a new and very different costume.

*The French bonnet, Paris-head,* or *Mary Queen of Scots head-dress*, was a close linen cap with a horseshoe-shaped front, and a short lappet or veil hanging down behind. The outer gown or mantle is frequently straight, without waistband or girdle, and open down the front, though held together by small bows. From its puffed and slashed shoulders false sleeves hang almost to the ground.

Soon after the accession of Queen Elizabeth, false sleeves were abandoned, and true sleeves were cut and slashed from

John Lyndewode and his wife Alice, 1419.
Linwood, Lincolnshire.
Wool Merchant in Tunic and Mantle.

the shoulder to the wrist. A sash was worn round the waist, and below it the gown opened out, showing an elaborately quilted petticoat. Ruffs began to be worn about the neck, and gradually increased in size and stiffness. Towards the end of the reign the centre of the French cap was considerably depressed, and the back lappet turned up upon it. Important changes, which remained in fashion throughout the reigns of James I. and Charles I., now appeared. The embroidered petticoat was still in vogue, but it and the skirt of the dress were gathered up at the waist, often with a flounce, and stuffed out by a large *farthingale*, the precursor of the more modern crinoline. The sash was given up, and the bodice became a long-waisted peaked *stomacher*. A short cloak and a large hood were occasionally worn.

In the reign of James I. and onwards to the Commonwealth, a large broad-brimmed hat is frequently added to the other coverings of the head.

Ladies' brasses of a later date and style to this of the ruff, stomacher and farthingale, are rarely seen, and need not be described.

The latest known brass to a lady, previous to the modern revival, is to be seen in the church of St Mary Cray, in Kent. It commemorates Mrs Philadelphia Greenwood, who died A.D. 1747. She wears a plain gown, with a plaited neckerchief and a long gauzy veil, thrown over her head and falling to the ground.

It must be remembered that in the preceding sketch of female costume, the typical dresses only of the several styles have been mentioned, space forbidding a more complete account. The minute variations and eccentricities of fashion were almost, if not quite, as numerous as they are at the present day.

## BRASSES OF CIVILIANS

The illustrations of civil costume as they appear on brasses do not date back further than the times of Chaucer and Wiclif, and indeed do not become numerous till the reign of Henry VI.

We have, however, quite enough examples from the middle of the reign of Edward III. to show us what sort of dress was worn by the laity when our first great poet sang and our first great reformer preached and wrote.

The extravagances of fashion we must not expect to find. They would be altogether out of place upon the monuments of the dead, and must be looked for rather in illuminated manuscripts, and in the denunciations of sober-minded writers of the day.

## Edward III

Among the earliest civilian brasses, two distinct and contemporary styles of dress may be seen, perhaps distinguishing the wealthier merchant princes from their humbler brethren.

In the simplest of these only one garment is visible, a long loose gown with close sleeves, fastened at the neck by two or three buttons, and furnished with a hood. In range of date it is chiefly confined to the fourteenth century. Good examples are at Great Berkhamstead, Herts, A.D. 1356; St Helen's, Ore, Sussex, c. 1400; and St Michael's, St Alban's, Herts, c. 1400.

The other dress is somewhat more elaborate. Over a very short doublet and tight hose is thrown a tunic, which reaches below the knees. It has no waistbelt, but is made to fit the figure, and is cut open in front towards the bottom, in order to give greater freedom in walking. There are usually two slits for pockets. The sleeves terminate at the elbows, and have long lappets or liripipes attached to them. A tippet and hood are worn over the shoulders.

Examples are to be found at Taplow, Bucks, c. 1350, and in the magnificent foreign brasses at King's Lynn, Norfolk, to Adam de Walsokne, 1349, and Robert Braunche, 1364, and at Newark, Notts, to Alan Fleming, c. 1375.

## Richard II

In the reign of Richard II. several modifications appear. The tunic becomes simpler, without sleeve-lappets, and is girt at the waist by a cord or belt, to which is usually attached an anelace. The anelace is a short sword. Over the tunic is worn a large cloak or mantle, buttoned upon the right

Edw. Courtenay, *c.* 1460. Christ Church, Oxford.
Civilian in Plain Tunic, with Belt and Anelace.

shoulder, and usually gathered up over the left arm. The dress was worn also throughout the reigns of Henry IV. and Henry V.

## Henry VI.—Henry VII

During the greater part of the fifteenth century but few variations appear in the dress of the ordinary civilian. He wears a long tunic, as in the preceding reigns, but it is furnished with exceedingly wide sleeves, narrowing to the wrists. Planché tells us that they were called the devil's receptacles, for whatever could be stolen was dropped into them. The cuffs and the lower edge of the tunic are often edged with fur. The mantle is now discarded by all but certain functionaries, such as judges and mayors. The hair is worn quite short. There remain numberless instances of this style of dress all over England, and the student will find no difficulty in supplying himself with good examples (*vide* illus. on previous page).

## Henry VIII

The next great change came at about the time of the accession of Henry VIII. Reaching to the feet was worn a fur-lined gown, open in front, but kept together by the belt. It is usually turned back a little, so as to show the fur, from the neck to the feet. The sleeves are wide, like those of a surplice. From the belt is usually suspended a gypcière, or purse, and a short rosary. The anelace disappears. Hitherto the shoes have been always sharply pointed, but from this time onwards they are heeled sabots, gradually developing into the modern shoes. The hair is now long, and reaches to the neck.

## Elizabeth

Elizabethan dress is perhaps the most widely represented of any figured on brasses, and is almost always associated in the collector's mind with thin and battered and badly engraved plates, which refuse to yield even fairly good rubbings.

The doublet and hose now worn is too well known to need description, and is, moreover, rarely seen upon a brass. It is almost entirely hidden by the long gown, which differs in many respects from that of the last reign. There is no waistband, and the narrow sleeves hang nearly to the ground. They are, however, intended for ornament, and not for use, the sleeves of the doublet being thrust through slits in their upper parts. Towards the middle of the reign the fur-lining or trimming falls into disuse, and with its disappearance comes the fashion of wearing frills or ruffs round the neck and wrists.

### The Stuarts

The costume of the early years of James I. was in all respects similar to that worn at the close of the last reign, and brasses of later date are of rare occurrence. A passing word will therefore be sufficient before dismissing the subject.

Under Charles I. knee-breeches came into fashion, and with them a short cloak instead of the heavy gown. The ruff was replaced by a wide collar, and jack-boots were sometimes worn, as may be seen at Biddenden, Kent. With the Commonwealth the practice of engraving memorial brasses came to an end, though there are a few isolated examples later. The latest recorded brass commemorates Benjamin Greenwood, A.D. 1773, and lies in the church of St Mary Cray, Kent. During the last fifty years the art has been partially revived, but modern brasses possess little or no originality, and do not fall within the scope of this handbook.

## SHROUD BRASSES

The custom of engraving shrouded figures and skeletons was introduced shortly before the middle of the fifteenth century and continued till the end of the sixteenth. It was a horrible practice, and became most common in the reign of Henry VII., and especially in the eastern counties. The shroud is usually knotted at the head and feet, and sufficiently open to expose the breast and knees of the deceased. These ghastly memorials were frequently laid down during the lifetime of the persons they were intended to commemorate,

Rich. and Cecilie Howard, 1499.  Aylsham, Norfolk.
Husband and wife in shrouds.

93

in order that they might constantly be reminded that they were but mortal. The emaciated corpse is the form most frequently adopted. Skeletons are rarer, but may be seen at Hildersham, Cambs; Weybridge, Surrey; Margate, Norwich and other places.

# IV. Accessories

## BRASSES AND ARCHITECTURE

### CANOPIES

GREAT numbers of brasses are adorned with handsome canopies over and around the figures, and these bear a very close relation to Decorated and Perpendicular Gothic architecture.

In describing them we are at once introduced to a new set of technical terms, which need to be explained to the beginner.

The usual form adopted is that of a Gothic arch springing from a pair af side-shafts, and terminating in a bunch of foliage, called the *finial*. The side-shafts continue beyond the spring of the arch in the form of *pinnacles*. In the earlier examples the upper sides of the arch are quite straight, and give a bold angle at the point to which the finial is affixed. The inner side consists of a pointed or round arch, of which the chief line is called the *soffit*, and is often ornamented with a row of quatrefoils. Its inner surface is diversified by curved and pointed projections, called *cusps*. They are two or more in number, and are sometimes themselves cusped again. The general result is to give the enclosed space the shape of half a trefoil, or half a cinquefoil, as the case may be. The space between the inner and outer arches is occupied by ornamental tracery. The outer edge is ornamented by a row of *crockets* (*i.e.* " little crooks "), which are projecting leaves, as of some creeping plant. They are, however, always placed at regular intervals. The complete gable, with its inner and upper arches and its enclosed tracery, is called the *pediment*.

Straight-sided canopies are comparatively rare in brasses, though they may often be seen in stone or marble tombs of the early part of the fourteenth century.

96

In the brass of Joan de Cobham, Cobham, Kent, *c.* 1320, there is a well-known example of this style of canopy. Its early date is also marked by the characteristic, unknown in later times, of its pediment being made to rest on *corbels* of foliage, from which exceedingly slender shafts descend to the ground.

But the usual shape of the outer arch is that of a graceful curve, which merges into the finial at a considerable height. The side pinnacles reach to about the same altitude.

In detail canopies are usually of great beauty, and their forms and patterns are as multitudinous as they are themselves. The pediments are richly engraved, and frequently enclose within a circle or quatrefoil a flower, a crest, a badge, a shield of arms or some other device. Figures of saints or shields of arms are sometimes substituted for finials and the summits of pinnacles. The whole canopy is often triple, or, if there are two figures below, double, and even doubly triple. In these cases the effect of the clustered pinnacles is very beautiful.

Shields are sometimes hung upon the pinnacles and shafts with admirable effect.

NOTABLE EXAMPLES :—

*Single Canopies.*

The Cobham Series, 1320-1407.
Horsmonden, Kent, *c.* 1330.
Hurstmonceux, Sussex, 1402.
Warbleton, Sussex, 1436.
Others numerous.

*Double Canopies.*

Wymington, Bedfordshire, 1391.
Dartford, Kent, 1402.
Faversham, Kent, 1533.
Common with double figures.

*Triple Canopies.*

Balsham, Cambridgeshire, 1401.
Dartmouth, Devon, 1408.
New College, Oxford, 1417.
Etchingham, Sussex, 1444.
Enfield, Middlesex, 1446.
St Alban's, Hertfordshire, 1451.
Westminster (Abbot Estney), 1498.

In some cases the upper arch alone is present, without any soffit, and supports one or three figures of saints in niches.

G

In the brass of John Bloxham and John Whytton, c. 1420, at Merton College, Oxford, the arches pierce a panelled arcade in a somewhat unique manner. A similar arrangement may be seen in the panelling of the nave walls of the church of Stratford-on-Avon, Warwickshire.

In many canopies, especially those of the end of the fifteenth century, some further work is seen below the soffit and cusps. This is intended to represent vaulting, and exhibits the usual ribs and bosses. It is of course drawn in perspective.

### Embattled Canopies

During the fifteenth century it is not uncommon to find large super-canopies added to those already described, a characteristic of the Perpendicular or Late Gothic style of architecture. The side-shafts are continued upwards beyond their pinnacles, and support a heavy embattled entablature, strengthened by a circular arch, with spandrels on either side.

The pointed canopy is often omitted altogether, and the embattled entablature brought close down to the figure. The shafts are occasionally broadened out into a series of niches, into which the figures of saints are introduced.

*Without saints.*

Lingfield, Surrey, 1420.
Beddington, Surrey, 1432.

After the close of the fifteenth century canopies are rarely met with, and are much debased.

## CROSSES

Crosses were a very favourite form of memorial throughout the fourteenth century, and were often of great beauty. Of

Greek Cross, Fleury.

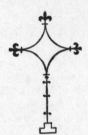

Floriated Quatrefoil Cross.

the large numbers that were then laid down, but few have survived to our day. They were considered " popish " by all zealous Reformers, and ruthlessly torn from the gravestones which they embellished. The despoiled slabs may be seen everywhere in our cathedrals and more important churches. Some few, however, escaped the general destruction of the Tudor and Puritan "crusades," and remain for the most part in a mutilated condition, to indicate the beauty of those we have lost. They may be divided in several classes :—

### 1. Floriated Crosses

(*a*) With a head or demi-figure engraved upon a Greek cross at the intersection of the arms. The floriated extremities or finials are richly worked.

EXAMPLES :—

Richard de Hakebourne, priest, Merton College, Oxford, *c.* 1310.
A priest (head only), Chinnor, Oxon, *c.* 1320.

(*b*) With a quatrefoil head, enclosing a half or full-length figure. Again the finials are richly floriated, and the stem also, where the leaves usually appear in three or four pairs. The base consists of a few steps, or else some animal or religious symbol. This applies to all floriated crosses.

The quatrefoil of the head may itself be drawn within a circle, as at Woodchurch.

**Circle and Quatrefoil Cross.**

EXAMPLES :—

Nichol de Gore, priest, Woodchurch, Kent, *c.* 1330.
Britellus Avenel, priest, Buxted, Sussex, *c.* 1375.

(*c*) With an octofoil head, enclosing a figure or figures. Here we have a series of eight ogee arches, alternately larger and smaller, and terminating with floriated finials both within and without. The under sides of the arches are usually cusped. The stem may be floriated, or else covered with a diaper pattern or inscription.

EXAMPLES :—

John de Bladigdone and wife, East Wickham, Kent, *c.* 1325.
Sir John de Wautone and wife, Wimbish, Essex, 1347.
Nicholas Aumberdene, Taplow, Buckinghamshire, *c.* 1350.
A priest, Merton College, Oxford, 1372.
A civilian, St Michael's, St Alban's, Herts, *c.* 1400.
John Lumbarde, priest, Stone, Kent, 1408.

**Floriated Octofoil Cross.**

(*d*) With a saint or symbol enclosed in the head, and figures kneeling at the foot in an attitude of supplication.

EXAMPLES :—

John Mulsho and wife (with St Faith), Newton-by-Geddington, Northamptonshire, 1400.
Robert Parys and wife (with Holy Trinity), Hildersham, Cambridgeshire, 1408.

## 2. Latin Crosses

(a) Crosses fleury. These differ in many ways
from the Greek crosses described above.
The most noticeable difference is the
entire absence of figures in any part of
the composition. The head is straight
and square, and its arms are usually
terminated each by a *fleur-de-lys*. At
Higham Ferrers, however, the four evangelistic emblems serve as finials. A long
stem rises from a few steps, or, as is the
case in a number of matrices of most
magnificent lost brasses in Ely Cathedral, from the
central finial of a Gothic canopy.

Latin Cross,
Fleury.

EXAMPLES :—

Higham Ferrers, Northants, 1400.
Cassington, Oxon, c. 1415.
Beddington, Surrey, c. 1425.
Broadwater, Sussex, 1445.

(b) Plain crosses. A few small and late brasses are formed
merely by two strips of metal laid across one
another, with an inscription at the foot.

EXAMPLES :—

Hever, Kent, c. 1520. (Henry Bullayen.)
Penshurst, Kent, c. 1520. (Sir Thos. Bullayen.)

## 3. Bracket Brasses

Figures standing upon brackets are not uncommon in the
early part of the fifteenth century. The stem is very much
like a cross, and rises in the same way from steps, or from
some heraldic device or crest. A canopy is frequently added.

EXAMPLES :—

Sir John Foxley and wives, Bray, Berks, c. 1370.
Reginald de Cobham, priest, Cobham, Kent, 1402.
Joan Urban, Southfleet, Kent, 1414.
Bloxham and Whytton, priests, Merton College, Oxford, c. 1420.
Sir Roger L'Estrange, Hunstanton, Norfolk, 1507.

A curious and unique bracket brass occurs at Upper Hardres,
Kent, 1405, in which John Strete kneels at the foot and

prays to St Peter and St Paul, who are represented as standing upon the bracket.

## BRASSES AND HERALDRY

Heraldry plays a very important part in the composition of brasses, and should by no means be neglected. Small shields of arms are commonly let into the slabs towards the corners, and within the border fillet, if there be one. They are engraved with the armorial bearings of the person or persons commemorated, and are of constant use in the identification of these persons when the accompanying inscription happens to be lost. In describing their positions, the heraldic terms *dexter* and *sinister* must always be used. The *dexter* side is that on the right hand of the effigy, and therefore at the spectator's left, and the *sinister* on the effigy's left and spectator's right. The same terms must be used in describing the component parts of each shield.

When a shield is divided down the middle (*party per pale*), with a separate coat on either side, a married couple is implied, the husband's arms being on the dexter side, and the wife's on the sinister. The former is then said to *impale* the latter. If the wife is an heiress, the coats are not impaled, but an *inescutcheon*, or small shield, bearing the wife's arms, is placed upon the centre of those of the husband. Where there are two wives, the husband's arms, on the dexter side, impale the two wives' on the sinister, one above the other.

When a shield is divided into four parts, it is said to be *quartered*, and the quarters are numbered—the upper pair, dexter and sinister, 1st and 2nd, and the lower pair as before, 3rd and 4th. When a man quarters two coats only, the 1st and 4th (identical) are the arms of his father, and the 2nd and 3rd those of his mother, or some more remote ancestress.

There are in heraldry two metals, gold and silver (yellow and white), termed respectively *or* and *argent*. Colours or tinctures are more numerous, but the two most common are blue and red, termed *azure* and *gules*. The others are black, green and purple, termed *sable, vert* and *purpure*. With respect to metals and tinctures, the following rule should be

remembered : a metal is never put upon a metal, nor a colour
upon a colour.  A method of expressing the metals and
colours by dots and lines was invented at the close of the
sixteenth century, but is of no importance in relation to
brasses.  In these memorials the actual colours were always
used in the following manner : the surface of the brass was
cut away, and the cavities filled with coloured enamels or
other perishable substances, of which, in the vast majority
of examples, not a vestige now remains.  Gold was treated
differently, and forms the key to the armorial bearings of
nearly all brasses.  In this case the brazen surface was not
cut away, but was either gilded or left plain, though doubtless polished.  Thus in a rubbing, the parts which appear
black are almost always *or*.  *Argent* was sometimes represented by lead inlaid.

Besides tinctures, two kinds of fur were in constant use.
*Ermine*, white with black spots, with its variants *ermines,*
sable with white spots, and *erminois*, of which the ground
was *or*; the latter may always be determined at a glance.
*Vair*, a blue and white fur, was represented by alternate
pieces in a manner dovetailed together.

For the names of charges and other technical information,
reference must be made to one of the numerous illustrated
manuals and handbooks of heraldry.

But coats-of-arms are not confined to separate shields
unconnected with the designs of brasses.  They appear also
in various parts of the canopies, as finials, or in the spandrels,
or hung from the shafts ; they are sometimes placed half-way
down the sides of border fillets, or on either side of the foot
inscriptions ; they are blazoned on *banners*, as at Felbrigg,
Norfolk, and Ashford, Kent, and on *pennons*, as at Stoke
d'Abernon, Surrey ; they appear on war-shields, as in all
knightly effigies of the reigns of Edward I. and Edward II.,
and on ailettes or epaulettes, as at Trumpington, Cambs ;
they are embroidered on the dress of both knights and their
ladies.

With heraldic dresses knights and ladies must be taken
separately :—

## 1. Knights

*Surcoats* charged with armorial bearings.  A good example may be seen at Chartham, Kent, 1307, where

Sir Robert de Setvans (Septfans) has his surcoat semée (*i.e.* sewn or sprinkled) with *winnowing fans*. Four only appear on his surcoat, but there are two more upon his ailettes and three on his shield.

*Jupons*, at a later date, are usually quite plain, but there are several instances of their being charged with armorial bearings.

EXAMPLES :—

Sir William de Aldeburgh, Aldborough, Yorks, *c.* 1360.
Lord John Harsick, Southacre, Norfolk, 1384.
Sir William Bagot, Baginton, Warwick, 1407.

*Tabards-of-arms* came into use at about the middle of the fifteenth century, and continued till the reign of Elizabeth. Since then they have been worn only by heralds on great public occasions. They were short coats of silk, worn over the body armour, and reaching to the thighs. The wearer's arms were embroidered on the front and on the back, and were repeated on each sleeve.

EXAMPLES :—

William Fynderne, Esq., Childrey, Berks, 1444.
Sir John Say, Broxbourne, Herts, 1473.
Sir Roger l'Estrange, Hunstanton, Norfolk, 1506.
Sir William Gascoigne, Cardington, Beds, *c.* 1540.

## 2. Ladies

Several methods of blazoning ladies' dresses were in vogue. One of the earliest was to embroider the lady's own arms on her kirtle, and her husband's arms on her mantle.

EXAMPLES :—

Two ladies of the Clopton family, Long Melford, Suffolk, *c.* 1480.
Jane and Elizabeth Gascoigne (Pickering and Mowbray), Cardington, Beds, *c.* 1540.

Another was to blazon only the mantle, placing the husband's arms on the dexter side and the lady's on the sinister.

EXAMPLES :—

Joyce, Lady Tiptoft (very fine), Enfield, Middlesex, 1446.
Bridget and Elizabeth Style (Bauldry and Peryn), Beckenham, Kent, 1552.

Sometimes, and especially in late brasses, the husband's arms were omitted, and the lady's embroidered alone on her mantle, as shown in the illustration here given.

Sir Edmund Tame and his two wives, Alice (Greville) and Elizth.
(Tyringham), 1534.
Fairford, Gloucestershire.

Knight in Tabard, and wives in Heraldic Mantles, bearing the arms of
their fathers, as impaled in the shields above.

EXAMPLES :—
Mary Burgoyn, Impington, Cambs, 1505.
Joyce Pekham, Wrotham, Kent, 1525.

*Crests* are frequently given in brasses. The knight pillows his head upon a helmet, and from it, or rather from a *wreath* (of two colours, twisted like a turban), rises the crest. A handsome *mantling*, and *lambrequins*, or ornamental foliage, are frequently added. The helm, wreath, crest and mantling, together with the shield of arms, are sometimes placed apart from and above the figure, making what is called an *achievement.*

*Badges* appear in some few instances, especially in the memorials of crown-keepers and yeomen-of-the-guard, who are distinguished by a rose and crown. There is a good example at East Wickham, Kent, to William Payn, 1568. At Digswell, Herts, a swan is seen embroidered on the collar of Lady Peryent, 1415, a unique usage. A small rectangular, unnamed brass, in the possession of the Surrey Archæological Society, has its field semée of fire-beacons, the badge of the Compton family.

Collars are much worn by knights and ladies of the fifteenth century. The Lancastrian collar of SS., and the Yorkist collar of Suns and Roses, are the most usual.

*The Order of the Garter.* Sir Thomas Bullen, at Hever, wears the full insignia of the order, mantle, collar, hood, badge and garter. In other instances we find only the garter, buckled round the left leg, below the knee.

EXAMPLES :—
Sir Peter Courtenay, Exeter Cathedral, 1409.
Sir Simon de Felbrigge, Felbrigg, Norfolk, 1413.
Lord Camoys, Trotton, Sussex, 1424.
Sir Henry Bourchier, Little Easton, Essex, 1483.
Sir Thomas Bullen, Hever, Kent, 1538.

*Merchants' Marks* are very frequently found engraved upon shields, especially from c. 1450 to c. 1550, in the place of armorial bearing, which, in their case, were granted only to Corporate Companies.

## SAINTS AND THEIR SYMBOLS

As in other monuments, the figures of saints and angels are frequently introduced into the more elaborate brasses. They occur in various positions, especially—

(1) In canopy work : in niches of side-shafts, in the centre of pediments, in super-canopies and at the finials.

(2) In the heads of crosses and upon brackets.

(3) Upon the orphreys of the copes of priests, and upon their morses.

(4) As isolated figures, to whom the persons commemorated are usually offering some invocatory prayer.

*The Holy Trinity.* Most common of all are representations of the Holy Trinity, found in every variety of position. The Father, a venerable figure with long hair and beard, is seated upon a throne, and holds a crucifix between His knees, while the Holy Dove, with outstretched wings, occupies a place behind the head of the cross, or is seated upon its right arm, or is sometimes omitted altogether.

The best early example is at Hildersham, Cambs, 1379, in the head of an octofoil cross. At Balsham, Cambs, 1401, twice at Cobham, Kent, 1405 and 1407, again at Hildersham, 1466, and at Faversham, Kent, *c.* 1480, the Trinity occupies a shrine or tabernacle at the centre finial above a canopy. Shields and isolated plates are very frequent, as at Leigh, Surrey, 1499; Goodnestone, Kent, 1507; Wilne, Derbs, 1513; and Cheam, Surrey, 1542. In the Codrington brass at Bottesford, Leics, 1404, it is engraved on the morse of a cope, upon a very small scale. It is also found, though rarely, in pictorial mural brasses, as at St George's Chapel, Windsor, 1475, and Dauntesey, Wilts, *c.* 1535. In two Kentish examples, Cobham, 1506, and Goodnestone, 1507, the Father wears a triple crown, or papal tiara, and the crucifix rises from an orb.

A small but very typical Trinity may be seen in the illustration on page 105. The three invocatory labels are, however, all addressed to the Saviour, as follows :—

(1) Jesu lord that made us,

(2) & w$^t$ thy blod us bought.

(3) ffor give us our trespas.

*God the Father* is found alone, but only in brasses of foreign workmanship or engraved under foreign influence, always as a venerable figure, enthroned in the centre of a canopy, and preparing to receive the naked soul of the deceased.

Thus five times in the great German brasses at King's Lynn, 1349 and 1364, at St Alban's and North Mimms, Herts, *c.* 1360; twice at Newcastle, 1429, and also at Higham Ferrers, Northants, 1337, and Elsing, Norfolk, 1347, the last on a canopied bracket in connection with the Coronation of the Blessed Virgin Mary.

*The Saviour* alone, with right hand raised to bless, occurs at Diddington, Hunts, 1505; Etwell, Derbs, 1512, and Mereworth, Kent, 1542, the last accompanied by a scroll from the figure of Sir Thos. Nevell :—

Jesus Jesus esto michi Jesus.

At Sibson, Leics, 1532, He is placed above the figure of a priest, and seated, upon a rainbow, with His feet upon an orb, and with his hands raised. At Trinity Hall, Cambridge, 1517, and Tattershall, Lincs, *c.* 1515, He appears in half-effigy rayonnant, on the morse of a cope. At Knebworth, Herts, 1414, in the same position, there is merely the Vernicle, or Sacred Face.

The Resurrection.
Cranleigh, Surrey, 1503.

There are also pictorial representations of the Nativity and the Resurrection, the latter well instanced at Cranleigh, Surrey, in a small plate now set in the chancel pavement. The armour and weapons of the four soldiers should be noticed, of the Yorkist type, a little earlier than the brass itself. A single example of a Pieta may be seen in the Flemish brass at All Hallows Barking, 1535.

## ANGELS

*St Michael.* Represented at Ringwood, Hants, 1416, on the orphrey of a cope, with six wings, shield charged with verbal symbol of the Holy Trinity, and spear thrust into the mouth of a dragon. At Tattershall, Lincs, *c.* 1470, in the shaft of a canopy, attired in amice, alb and dalmatic, and holding scales (illustrated at the end of this section). Also at Balsham, Cambs, 1461, on the orphrey of a cope, associated with

*St Gabriel,* who also frequently appears in representations of the Annunciation.

## SCRIPTURAL SAINTS

*The Blessed Virgin Mary.* Very frequent. Usually enthroned, often crowned and sceptred, and almost invariably accompanied by the Holy Child, except of course in representations of the Annunciation. Her dress varies according to the period of the engraving. Examples too numerous to specify.

*St John Baptist.* Symbol, the Lamb and Banner. Finest example at St Mary de Crypt, Gloucester, 1544, occupying a shrine in pediment of canopy. Others, in canopy work, at Higham Ferrers, Northants, 1337; Newcastle, 1429; Balsham, Cambs, 1461; Diddington, Hunts, 1505; Hereford Cathedral, 1529; in the orphreys of copes, at Balsham, 1401; Bottesford, Leics, 1404; Knebworth, Herts, 1414; Ringwood, Hants, 1416; and as an isolated figure at Aspley Guise, Beds, *c.* 1410.

*St Anne.* (Traditionally the mother of the Blessed Virgin.) Represented with a book in her hand, teaching St Mary to read. Examples at Deerhurst, Glos., 1400; Morley, Derbs, 1470, and Tattershall, Lincs, *c.* 1470, St Mary being a little girl in a kirtle and sideless cote-hardi.

*St Elizabeth.* Also with a book, and teaching St John Baptist, a child with Lamb and Banner. Tattershall, Lincs, *c.* 1470. Both of these are illustrated at the end of the section.

*St Mary Magdalene.* Symbol, the Vase of Ointment. Examples at Balsham, Cambs, 1401, in the orphrey of a cope; Diddington, Hunts, 1505, in canopied niche, and Hereford Cathedral, 1529, in shaft of canopy.

*St Peter.* Symbol, two Keys. The most frequent of all the saints.

*St Paul.* Symbol, a Sword.

*St Peter and St Paul.* The two saints almost always occur together. Examples, Higham Ferrers, 1337; St Alban's, *c.* 1360; North Mimms, Herts, *c.* 1360; Boston, Lincs, *c.* 1400; Balsham, Cambs, 1401; Upper Hardres, Kent, 1405; Knebworth, Herts, 1414; Ringwood, Hants, 1416.

*The Twelve Apostles.* Frequently occupy the side-shafts of a canopy, or the two orphreys of a figured cope. St Paul is usually included amongst the twelve, and St Matthias omitted. The first pair are thus St Peter and St Paul, the second St Andrew and St John, the third St James and St Matthew. The rest vary in order. Good examples may be found,—

(*a*) In canopies, at King's Lynn, 1349, Boston, Lincs, *c.* 1389, and Newcastle, 1429.

(*b*) On copes, at Tattershall, Lincs, *c.* 1515, and Trinity Hall, Cambridge, 1517.

*St Andrew.* Symbol, a Saltire Cross.

*St John Evang.* Symbols, Chalice and Serpent. (See the Tattershall illustration.)

*St James-the-Great.* Symbols, a Scallop Shell and Pilgrim's Staff and Wallet.

*St Matthew.* Symbols, a Book, a Money-box, a Spear or an Axe.

*St Thomas.* Symbols, a Book and a Spear, or a Builder's Rule.

*St Bartholomew.* Symbol, a Butcher's Flaying-knife.

*St Philip.* Symbols, a Cross-headed Staff, a Basket of Bread.

*St James-the-Less.* Symbol, a Fuller's Bat.

*St Simon.* Symbols, a Saw, or one or two Fish.

*St Jude.* Symbols, a Club or Axe, a Cross, a Carpenter's Square.

Several of these also occur separately, especially St John, St James and St Andrew. Tolleshunt Darcy, Essex, has an interesting palimpsest fragment of a large foreign brass, in which each of the twelve Apostles is associated with a particular clause in the Apostles' Creed. There only remain St Philip, St Bartholomew, St James-the-Less and St Thomas.

Head of Cross at Newton, Northants, 1400.
Sancta Fides virgo et martyr.

(The stem and foot of cross, and two kneeling figures, are omitted).

*St Stephen.* Symbol, a Stone and Napkin. Example at Higham Ferrers, Northants, 1337, in niche of canopy-shaft.

## LATER SAINTS

*St Catherine.* Symbols, a Sword and Wheel. One of the most popular saints. Examples in the orphreys of copes, at Balsham, 1401 and 1461; Bottesford, Leics, 1404, and Ring-

H

Matilda Lady Willoughby, 1497 (but engraved *c.* 1470).
Tattershall, Lincolnshire.

wood, Hants, 1416; at Diddington, Hunts, 1505, in a canopied niche; at Hereford Cathedral, 1529, in the shaft of a canopy; and at St George's Chapel, Windsor, 1522, in a pictorial brass.

*St Margaret.* Symbol, a Spear or Cross-staff thrust into the mouth of a Dragon. Often associated with St Catherine, as at Balsham, Bottesford and Ringwood (above). Another interesting example is at Checkendon, Oxon, 1435, on the reverse of a palimpsest inscription.

*St Agnes.* Symbol, a Lamb. Good example at Newcastle, 1429, in central shaft of canopy.

*St Barbara.* Symbol, a Tower. Examples at Ringwood and Newcastle, as above.

*St Faith.* Symbol, an Iron Bed, or Gridiron. Interesting example at Newton-by-Geddington, Northants, 1400, in head of floriated cross. (See accompanying illustration, p. 112.)

*St Nicholas.* Symbols, three Golden Balls, an Anchor. Examples at Balsham, Cambs, 1461, in niche of canopy, and at Knebworth, Herts, 1414, on orphrey of cope.

*St Christopher.* Represented with large staff and bare feet, crossing river with Child upon shoulder. Very popular. There are three interesting examples at Morley, Derbs, 1454, 1470 and *c.* 1525, on separate plates above figures. Also twice at Tattershall, Lincs, *c.* 1470 (see illustration), in shafts of canopies, and at Week, Hants, 1498, on a separate plate.

*St George.* Represented fully armed in armour of the period of the engraving, and slaying the dragon. At Elsing, Norfolk, 1347, in centre of canopy, he is mounted, and killing, not a dragon, but a conventional Satan, with horns and tail. At Cobham, Kent, 1407, he wears bascinet, camail and jupon, and at Tattershall, Lincs, *c.* 1470, an heraldic tabard, charged with a cross.

*St Thomas of Canterbury.* Represented in pontificals, with archbishop's pall and cross-staff. Good examples at Cowfold, Sussex, 1433, on the finial of canopy, with a label, and also at Tattershall, Lincs, *c.* 1470 (here illustrated). Difficult to distinguish from other archbishop saints, as St Nicholas from other bishops.

These are the saints most frequently encountered, though numerous others occur on particular brasses. Thus there are good figures of St Alban and St Oswyn on the brass of

Abbot Delamere, *c.* 1360, in St Alban's Abbey. The Balsham brasses, with their fine canopies and enriched copes, include amongst the rest St Etheldreda, St Wilfrid, St Asaph, St Bridget and St Winifred. Higham Ferrers, 1337, has St Maur and others; Cowfold, St Pancras, as well as St Thos. Cant; and Hereford Cathedral, 1529, St Ethelbert.

In the Tattershall brass, illustrated on page 114, the saints on the dexter side are St Thos. Cant, St John Evang., St Sytha and St Michael; on the sinister side, St Anne and the B.V.M., St Helen, St Christopher and St Elizabeth with St Anne. These are wrongly arranged, the brass having long ago been torn from its slab and the parts displaced. They have lately been refixed in their proper order and in a new slab. St Maurice, St Candidus, St Edmund and St Dorothy also occur in two other brasses in the same church.

## INSCRIPTIONS

Inscriptions vary from century to century quite as much as any other parts of a brass.

There are three kinds of type :—

**1. Lombardic,** called also *Uncial, Longobardic* and *Lombardic-Uncial.* The letters are broad, well-formed, and easily read. They were used in the thirteenth and at the beginning of the fourteenth centuries.

**2. Black Letter,** or Old English.
   (*a*) *Early,* of a round character, being influenced by the Lombardic, which preceded it. Used during the fourteenth century.
   (*b*) *Straight.* The letters all composed more or less of straight lines, which very nearly resemble one another, and are sometimes exceedingly difficult to read. Used during the fifteenth century.
   (*c*) *Tudor.* Again a more rounded type, the letters being much more fanciful, ornamental and easily read. Used during the sixteenth century.

**3. Roman Capitals.** Came into general use in the seventeenth century.

The earliest inscriptions were placed round the edge of the

slab, and every letter was cut out separately, and inserted in its own matrix. Thin fillets of metal were placed above and below the line, in order to protect the letters. At the present time scarcely one remains, but the indents are often sufficiently well marked for the inscription to be read without any great difficulty. In such inscriptions the character was always Lombardic.

A better method was to engrave the inscription upon a single fillet running all round the edge of the slab. In the early part of the fourteenth century these border fillets had plain angles, but towards its close the corners were occupied usually by the four evangelistic symbols, engraved in a quatrefoil projecting from a square set lozenge-wise. Thus we have constantly the angel for St Matthew, the lion for St Mark, the ox for St Luke, and the eagle for St John. At the same time it became customary to add a second inscription, which was written upon a rectangular plate, and placed at the feet of the effigy or effigies.

In the fifteenth century the foot inscription was generally the only one, and was always present, whether there was a border fillet or not. The latter was only retained in the more elaborate brasses. When a brass was raised upon an altar-tomb, the border fillet was commonly placed in *chamfer* —*i.e.* on the sloping verge of the tomb—and was read from outside, instead of from the inside, as was always the case where it was flat.

In the sixteenth century the border fillet was rarely used, and has entirely disappeared by the time that the next century is reached.

Three languages are used—viz. Norman French, Latin and English.

**1. Norman French,** the language of the Court and of the nobility, is commonly used on brasses of the thirteenth and the beginning of the fourteenth centuries.

With a little knowledge of modern French these inscriptions may be easily read, since scarcely any contractions are used. A few simple rules may be given :—

    i. The spelling is more or less phonetic. Thus *c* and *s, s* and *x*, *y* and *i* may be used interchangeably—*e.g.* cis = six, and ycy = ici.

ii. The letter *s* is often inserted before another consonant. Thus aisne or eisne = âiné, fest = fête, fist = fit, gist = git, morust = mourut.

iii. The letter *u* is omitted. Thus cely = celui, gere = guerre, qi or ky = qui, ly = lui.

iv. Malme is written for mon âme, lalme for l'âme, etc.

v. In these and in all other inscriptions, Latin and English, *j* and *v* are almost always represented by *i* and *u*.

The earliest inscriptions are the most simple, giving only the name and a prayer for mercy. The date and other particulars were soon added.

*Stoke d'Abernon, Surrey.* 1277.

Sire : John : Daubernoun : Chiualier : Gist : Icy : Deu : De : Sa : Alme : Eyt : Mercy.

*St Michael's, St Alban's.* *c.* 1330.

John Pecok & Maud sa femme gisont yci dieu de lour almes eit merci amē.

*Cobham, Kent.* 1375.

✠ Icy gist dame Margarete de Cobehm iadis femme a Will Pympe chivalier qe morust le IIII iour de Septembre lan de grace Mil ccc lxxv de qi alme dieu pur sa pite eit mercy Amen.

*All Hallows Barking, London.* *c.* 1400.

✠ Pries p' lalme Willm̄ Tonge q gyt ycy ky dieu de sonn alme eyt mercy.

*Cobham, Kent.* 1407.

✠ De Terre fu fait et fourme
X Et en Terre et a terre suy retourne
X Johan de Cobham foundeur de ceste place qi fu iadys nome
X Mercy de malme eit la seynte Trinite.

**2. Latin.** The language of nearly all inscriptions of the fifteenth century. Both before and after that period it was used more sparingly, dividing the honours, first with French and afterwards with English. The chief difficulties in reading Latin inscriptions are to be found in the various abbreviations which were constantly used. The greater number of them will, however, come under the three heads following :—

i. The syllables *pro, per, prae* are rarely written in full, but are represented merely by their initial letter,

with or without an apostrophe. Thus, p'fectus
for perfectus.

ii. The letters *m* and *n* are always omitted where possible.
A straight line over the next vowel shows their
position. Thus, aīe for animae.

iii. Terminations of all kinds are liable to be cut off
without any other compensation than an apostrophe. Thus, ux' for uxor, ei' for ejus.

Several common words are abbreviated without following
any rule; such as Dñs for Dominus, ecclīa for ecclesia, xp̄s
for christus, Johēs for Johannes. The letter *c* is often written
instead of *t*, as in tercius and eciam for tertius and etiam.

The greater number of inscriptions begin with the words
" Hic jacet "; then follow the name and rank of the
deceased, and the date of his death; all alike end with the
phrase, " Cujus anime propitietur deus, Amen." This is
usually abbreviated to " Cui' aīe ppiciet' de' amē," or sometimes to the bare letters c.a.p.d.a. In Tudor inscriptions
the " Hic jacet " frequently gives place to the alternative
phrase " Orate pro anima." Shortened to " Or' p' aīa."

A second plate, inscribed with elegiac verses, is often
added.

The following are instances :—

*Croydon, Surrey.* 1512.

Silvester Gabriel cuius lapis hic tegit ossa
Vera sacerdotum gloria nuper erat
Legis nemo sacre divina volumina verbis
Clarius aut vita sanctius explicuit
Cominus ergo deū modo felix eminus almis
Qevē pius in scriptis viderat ante videt.

The next takes the form of an address to the reader :—

*Biddenden, Kent.* 1609.

Scire cupis (lector) tumulo quis conditur isto
Accipe : in hoc tumulo foemina virque jacent
Quosq' prius thorus unus amor conjunxerat unus.
Unica defunctos nunc tenet urna duos
Urna quidem corpus tenet hujus & illius una
Unitas animas fulgidus aether habet.

We find also another kind of verses, known as *Leonine*, in
which the lines are made to rhyme. It was at one time
highly fashionable.

*Wymington, Beds.* 1407.

  Hic Margareta : de Brounflet laude repleta.
  Est Edward nata : Seynt Jon chivaler tumula.
  Non lateat te res : Dño Vessy fuit heres.
  Militis in vita : Thome Brounfletq' marita
  Quinq' per hos nat's : una nata generatis.
  In Womyngtona : bona corruit ista patrona.
  Morte die mensis : viceno victa secundo.
  Octobris mundo : puta more ferit necis ensis.
  Annos millenos : C quater suscipe plenos.
  Addenis septenos : domini celestis amenos.
  Nata pater domine : Flamen deus unice t'ne.
  Hanc Margaretam : tibi luce poli cape letam.

The following exhortation was highly popular :—

*East Horsley, Surrey.* 1478.

  Quisquis eris qui transieris sta plege plora
  Sum q$^d$ eris fuerāq' q$^d$ es : pro me precor ora.

This also :—

*Temple Church, Bristol.* 1396.

  Es testis xp̄e : qd' non jacet hic lapis iste
  Corpus ut ornet' : sp̄e ut memoret'
  Huic tu qui transis : magnus medius puer an sis
  Pro me funde preces : dabit michi sic venie spes.

The translation of titles is in many cases perfectly obvious. The following, however, do not at first sight suggest their English equivalents :—

| | | | |
|---|---|---|---|
| Miles | = Knight | Prepositus | = Provost |
| Armiger | = Esquire | Decanus | = Dean |
| Generosus | = Gentleman | Capellanus | = Chaplain |
| Comes | = Earl | Elemosinarius | = Almoner |
| Consul | = Counsellor | Domicella | = Maid of Honour |
| Camerarius | = Chamberlain | Pannarius | = Draper |
| Pincerna | = Cup-bearer | Pelliparius | = Tanner |

**3. English.** Here we have several difficulties to overcome, such as obsolete words and form, random spelling, and arbitrary abbreviations. The dialect and spelling of the earlier inscriptions is in the main that of Chaucer and Wiclif, and may be best mastered by reading the " Canterbury Tales," which might, in costume as well as in language, be illustrated throughout by brasses; or the Holy Scriptures according to the quaint Saxon translation of the Oxford Schoolman. When once the dialect is familiar, the abbreviated words can be filled out with the greatest ease.

Before the Reformation the great majority of English

inscriptions began with the words, "Of your charity pray for the soul of," or more simply, "Pray for the soul of," and ended "On whose soul Jesus have mercy. Amen." The concluding phrase was often amplified by the addition, after "On whose soul," of "and all Christian souls." Sometimes it was still further amplified, as at Stifford, Essex, 1504, "Of your charite pray for the soulle of Johñ Ardalle . . . and for his fader soulle and his moder soulle and all crystyn soullys on whose soullys ihū have mercy amen." Or more explicitly, "Of whose soul of your charity say a paternoster and an ave."

In cases where the brass was laid down before the person's death, the date of decease was necessarily omitted, and we frequently find blank spaces which have never been filled up. Some of these inscriptions to the living substitute "good estate " for " soul."

It is exceedingly common to find that the opening and concluding clauses have been totally or partially erased, especially in and near London. This was probably done at the Reformation by the children of the persons commemorated, in order that the Royal Commissioners might not tear up the brasses as "Popish."

Verses are often found in addition to, or instead of, the ordinary prose inscription :—

*Holm-next-the-Sea, Norfolk.* c. 1405.

Herry Notyngham & hys wyffe lyne here
yat madeñ this chirche stepull & quere
two vestments & belles they made also
crist hem saue therfore ffro wo
ande to bringe her saules to blis at heuen
sayth pater & aue with mylde steuen.

*Ash, Kent.* c. 1460.

Prey for the sowle of Jane Keriell
Ye ffrendis alle that forth by pass
In endeles lyff perpetuell
That god it grawnte m'cy and grace
Roger Cletherowe hir fadir was
Thowgh erthe to erthe of kynde reto'ne
Prey that the sowle in blisse sojo'ne.

*Cople, Bedfordshire.* c. 1500.

What can myght powr or auncyet bloode avayll
Or els ryches, that men cownte felicite
What can they helpe, ferfull dethe to assayll

Certes nothynge, and that is p(ro)vyd by me
That had thos yistis rehersid w<sup>t</sup> all plente
Nev̄thelesse yit am I leyd lowe in clay
That whylom was squyer called thos g'y.    (Gray.)
Benet my wyf eke is fro this world past
yit We trust to be had in memory
As longe as the paryshe of Coople shall last
For our benefitis don to it largely.
As witnesse xx<sup>ti</sup> pownd wt other yistis many
Wherfor all cristen men that goo by this way
P'y for y<sup>e</sup> soulis of Benet and Thōs gray.

*Romney, Kent.* 1510.

Of yo<sup>r</sup> charite pray for me
Thomas lamberd of Romeney
Which dyed the xxiiii day of August
In lyke wyse so alle ye must
for dethe is sure to Alle mankynde
therfore have my soule in mynde
Which ended M<sup>t</sup> V<sup>c</sup> X
I y<sup>e</sup> yeres of hym y<sup>t</sup> dyed for alle men.

From these examples it will be seen that not only is the spelling peculiar, but the versification faulty, and that to an extreme degree.

A glossary of the more common archaic words will probably be useful :—

| | | | |
|---|---|---|---|
| almys | = alms | mede | = merit |
| auncynt | = ancient | moder | = mother |
| aungeles | = angels | o<sup>r</sup> | = our |
| awtere | = altar | pish | = parish |
| bles | = bliss | pson | = parson |
| certes | = surely | quere | = choir or chancel |
| cheyffe | = chief | redecion | = redemption |
| crysten | = christian | sowlys | = souls |
| deptyd | = departed | steven | = staves of music |
| eke | = also | s'teyne | = certain |
| erchdiakn | = archdeacon | thred | = third |
| eyre | = heir, heiress | twey | = two |
| fadyr | = father | vestment | = a set of vestments |
| ffro | = from | wen | = think |
| halud | = hallowed | whylom | = once |
| hem | = them | wot | = know |
| her | = their | yat | = that |
| maden | = made (and similarly other verbs) | ys | = this |
| | | yistis | = gifts |
| mci | = mercy | | |

After the Reformation the prayers for the soul of course disappeared. Inscriptions began, " Here, or under this stone, lyeth the body of," and occasionally ended with,

" To whom God grant a joyful resurrection." The old simplicity and piety often gave place to lengthy and fulsome flatteries of the deceased person, and the character of the composition at last reached as low an ebb as the art of engraving to which it ministered. But the change was gradual, and many of the inscriptions remain of the highest interest.

The two following will supply examples of the kind of prose inscriptions in vogue after the Reformation :—

*Biddenden, Kent.* 1598.

John Evrenden beinge of the age of threescore yeares havinge passed the tyme of his pilgrimage with good and godly report hath finished his mortall days. His wives were two, Jone and Jane. With the first he lived twentye-five yeares and had issue William Ferdinando Isabell and Phebe; with the other seven yeares and had noe issue and now lyeth under this marble stone who was buried the thirteenth day of Aprill 1598.

*Headcorn, Kent.* 1636.

Here lyeth the body of John Byrd sonn of William Byrd of this parish of Headcorn, who was borne the 10th of May 1629, and in the time of his sicknesse delivered many Godly exhortations to his parents, taking his leave of them with such unexpected expressions as are not common in so young a child he departed this life on the 31st of January, anno 1636.

Verse inscriptions abound, and are of all kinds ; the two examples below have little in common with one another :—

*Lydd, Kent.* 1572.

As nature breath & lyfe doth yelde,
So drawes on death by kynde
And yet through fayth in Chryste by deathe
Eternall lyfe we fynde.
Behold a profe by me that dyd,
Enjoye my vitall breath ;
Full thre skore yeres & twelve thereto,
And then gave place to death
A Juratt of thys Towne was I,
And Thomas Bate by name,
Leke the I was, and now am dust
As thow shalt be the same
Fower Chyldren now my place supplye
My soule it ys wyth Chryst,
Who sende to them and the good lyfe,
And eke in hym to rest.

*Rye, Sussex.* 1607.

Loe Thomas Hamon here enterd doth lye
Thrice burgesse for the parliament elected

> Six times by freemens choyce made maior of Rye
> And Captaine longetime of the band selected
> Whose prudent courage justice gravitie
> Deserves a monument of memorye.

At Stifford, Essex, we have a curious instance of one inscription imitating another, a mother having died some three years after her daughter. The two brasses are quite distinct, and the epitaphs run as follows :—

*Ann Lathum, daughter of Thos. Lathum.* 1627.

> Behold in me the life of man
> Compar'd by David to a span
> Who in my strength death cal'd away
> Before the middle of my daye
> Let freinds and parents weepe no more
> Her's all the odds I went before
> And let them sone their lives amend
> That death may be a welcombe freind.

*Elizth. Lathum, wife of Thos. Lathum.* 1630.

> Yet once Againe behold and see
> The frayletie of this life in me
> And as t'was sayd to me before
> Let freinds and parents weepe no more
> So I may now the phrase returne
> Let children all forbeare to mourne
> And let them all in love remayne
> And be prepar'd heaven to attayne.

Punning is frequently resorted to, as well in Latin as in English. Two very similar examples will suffice :—

*Thos. Hylle, New College, Oxford.* 1468.

> Mons in valle jacet : quem tu deus erige rursum
> Ut valeat montem cristā p'fingere sursum

*Thos. Grenhill, Beddington, Surrey.* 1634.

> Hee once a Hill was fresh & Greene
> Now wither'd is not to bee seene
> Earth in Earth shoveld up is shut
> A Hill into a Hole is put.

*Scrolls* are seen issuing from the mouths or hands of fifteenth and sixteenth century figures, and curving upwards over the head. They are inscribed for the most part with pious sentences, ejaculatory prayers, and are usually in the Latin language.

They may be divided into several classes :—

*Invocations of the Holy Trinity.*

Sancta Trinitas unus deus miserere nobis.

O beata Trinitas { libera nos
justifica nos
salva nos

*Invocations of God the Father.*

Pater de celis deus miserere nobis.
Miserere mei deus.
Deus propicius esto mihi peccatori.
Sit laus deo.
Cor mundum crea in me deus.

*Invocations of God the Son.*

Jhū fili dei miserere mei.
Domine Jhū secundum actum meum noli me judicare.
Vulnera xpē tua mihi dulcis sint medicina.
Virginis atque dei fili crucifixe redemptor Humani
    generis : xpē memento mei.
Exultabo in deo Jhū meo
In domino confido.

Credo quod { redemptor meus vivit.
de terra surrecturus sum
in carne mea videbo deum salvatorem meum.

*Invocations of God the Holy Ghost.*

Spiritus sancte deus miserere nobis.

*Invocations of the Blessed Virgin Mary.*

Sancta Maria ora pro nobis.
Mater dei memento mei.
O virgo virginum ora pro nobis tuum filium.

Occasionally they appear in English :—

*Bexley, Kent.* 1513.

What so ever my dedys have bee
of me allmyghty Jhū have mercy.

*Carshalton, Surrey.* 1524.

O blyssyd lady of pite pȳ for me
y my soule savyd may be.

With the Reformation their character completely changed.
Scrolls still continued sparingly in use, though the reason
for their existence was gone—viz. as vehicles of invocatory
prayers.

A few examples will show the change :—

> Taedet animam meam vitae meae.
> Cupio dissolvi et esse cum Christo.
> Vive pius moriere pius.
> Dns dedit dns abstulit.
> I know that my redeemer liveth.
> I rejoice only in the Lord.

On some few brass slabs of the fifteenth century small scrolls are scattered about on each side of the figure, and inscribed with one or two words only. These words are usually " Jhu," " Mercy," " Grace," " Misericordia," " Jesu mercy," or " Lady helpe." The two last are perhaps the most common.

Thos. de Horton, Priest, *c.* 1360, N. Mimms, Herts.
Engraving of Foreign Workmanship, probably N. German.

128

# V. Additional Classes

## BRASSES OF FOREIGN WORKMANSHIP

AMONG brasses of more than usual interest are those engraved by foreign artists. A number of these exist in England, and form a class by themselves. They closely resemble the brasses of North Germany and Flanders, and differ in style very materially from those commonly used at home. In most cases they are rectangular in shape, the figures being engraved upon a background of diaper work beneath splendid canopies. Figures alone, without canopy or background, rarely occur, but may be recognised by minor differences in style, and by comparison with Continental examples, nearly all of which are illustrated in Mr Creeny's fine volume of photo-lithographs, catalogued below in the Bibliographical section of this book.

In our own country the examples fall naturally into several groups. First come three great brasses, the largest as well as the most elaborate in all England. They commemorate as many wealthy merchants, and were perhaps engraved in Lubeck, a city which carried on a considerable trade with King's Lynn and other parts of the east coast, through the operations of the Hanseatic League.

Adam de Walsokne and wife Margaret. 10 ft. by 5 ft. 7 in. A.D. 1349.
Robert Braunche and two wives. 8 ft. 8 in. by 5 ft. 5 in. A.D. 1364.
    Both at *King's Lynn, Norfolk.*
Alan Fleming. 9 ft. 4 in. by 5 ft. 7 in. A.D. 1361, but engraved *c.*
    1375. *Newark, Nottinghamshire.*

They are remarkable, not only for their size, but for boldness of design, great elaboration of detail and for the large number of subsidiary figures, with saints and angels enshrined in canopy work. Similar brasses exist at Lubeck, 1356, Stralsund in Pomerania, 1357, and Thorn in Prussian Poland, 1361.

A second group, of ecclesiastical brasses, includes that of Abbot Delamere at St Alban's, another great memorial, measuring 9 ft. $3\frac{1}{2}$ in. by 4 ft. $3\frac{1}{2}$ in., engraved in the Abbot's lifetime and under his own superintendence, a practice which was in all probability exceedingly common. Other brasses, apparently by the same engraver, are to be found at Schwerin in Mecklenberg, 1347, to two bishops, at Lubeck, 1350, also to two bishops, and at Ringstead, Denmark, 1319 (but certainly engraved later), to King Eric and Queen Ingeborg. All these are of enormous size, and have the same characteristics as the St Alban's brass.

Abbot Thomas Delamere, *c.* 1360. *St Alban's Abbey, Hertfordshire.*
Simon de Wensley, priest, *c.* 1360. *Wensley, Yorkshire.*
Thomas de Horton, priest, *c.* 1360. *North Mimms, Hertfordshire.*

Of the two parish priests, the former consists of a figure only, but so engraved that there is not the smallest doubt of its foreign origin. The priest is nearly life-size, and is attired in eucharistic vestments, all the apparels of which are beautifully diapered. The principal lines are very broad, and cut with great boldness, exhibiting a characteristic feature of foreign workmanship. At North Mimms the figure is much smaller, but in style not unlike that at Wensley. A canopy is added (see illustration), which is of the same general character as in the larger brasses, but is cut away round the figure itself. A fragment of another work of the same school is preserved in the British Museum. It shows the mitred head of an abbot or bishop, with part of the surrounding canopy and groundwork, and bears a similarity to the corresponding parts of the Delamere brass. It was obtained from some Continental church by Mr A. G. Pugin.

Other foreign brasses in England are of a more miscellaneous character :—

Ralph de Knevyngton, Esq., 1370. *Aveley, Essex.* In armour ; small ; canopy plain.
Thomas de Topclyff, and wife, 1391. *Topcliffe, Yorkshire.* 5 ft. 9 in. by 3 ft. 1 in. Canopy with saints and angels.
Roger Thornton, and wife, 1429. *All Saints', Newcastle.* 7 ft. 6 in. by 4 ft. 3 in. Canopy with saints and angels.
Ludowic Cortewille, and wife, 1504. *South Kensington Museum.* 6 ft. 8 in. by 3 ft. 6 in. Brought from the chapel of the ruined castle of Cortville, near Liege.
Margaret Hornebolt, 1529. *Fulham, Middlesex.* Lozenge-shaped mural plate ; demi-figure in shroud.
Thomas Pownder, and wife, 1525. *St Mary Quay, Ipswich.*
Andrew Evyngar, and wife, *c.* 1535. *All Hallows Barking, London.*

Henry Oskens, priest, 1535. *South Kensington Museum.*
Nicolas le Brun, 1547. *British Museum.*
Dr Duncan Liddel, 1613. *St Nicholas, Aberdeen.*

Each is the representative of a type, and deserves careful
study, and indeed a considerable literature has gathered round
all of them. The Topcliffe brass is of the same general
character as the first great citizen brasses, but smaller and
simpler. At Newcastle the same tradition is carried on, with
certain changes of style due to its later date. But a wholly
different character is exhibited in the brass of Ludowic Cortewille, an armed figure, and his lady, in which the Gothic
spirit has given place to that of the Renaissance, and where
the style is distinctly Flemish, instead of apparently North
German. A very similar memorial remains in the cathedral
at Bruges, to Jehan de Likerke and his wife ,1518. Margaret
Hornebolt is of less interest than the rest, but the Pow_nder
and Evyngar brasses, though of comparatively small size, are
excellent examples of the Flemish Renaissance. The Oskens
brass at South Kensington is German, and came originally
from Nippes, near Cologne. It is probably the most beautiful piece of Renaissance work amongst existing brasses, containing within an elaborate canopy a figure of the Blessed
Virgin, some fourteen inches high, standing upon a crescent,
and surrounded by a glory of fiery rays. Below are St Peter
and the Emperor St Henry, and the kneeling figure of the
priest. Nicolas le Brun is again wholly different, and is
our only example of a French brass. It is extremely small,
measuring only about twenty-five by fifteen inches, and includes a symbolic rendering of the Crucifixion, after the
manner of the book-engravings of the period. The Aberdeen
brass was engraved at Antwerp, and is again a fine example
of another distinct style.

Besides the above-mentioned, there are many English
brasses, nearly fifty in number, which, on being detached
from their stone matrices, have been found to have been cut
from older plates of foreign workmanship, whose engravings
appear upon the reverse side. These are reckoned amongst
the palimpsests mentioned below.

In the sixteenth and seventeenth centuries the use of small
mural, rectangular plates became common in this country,
and care must be taken to distinguish them from foreign

brasses. One of the earliest, representing a man in armour, wife and children (c. 1500), was once in Netley Abbey, and is now in the possession of the Surrey Archæological Society. Its history is a curious one, and for some years it did duty as the back of a cottage fireplace, where it was discovered by the incumbent of a neighbouring parish. Fortunately it remains uninjured. Boutell has actually set it down as Flemish, but without sufficient reason.

## FOREIGN INFLUENCE

There are a few well-known brasses which differ considerably from the usual English types, and which, though not actually foreign, have probably been produced under foreign influence. The chief of these are as follows :—

Sir Robt. de Setvans, 1306. *Chartham, Kent.*
Sir John de Northwode and lady, c. 1330. *Minster, Isle of Sheppey.*
Laurence de St Maur, priest, 1337. *Higham Ferrers, Northants.*
John de Grovehurst, priest, c. 1340. *Horsmonden, Kent.*
Sir Hugh Hastings, 1347. *Elsing, Norfolk.*
Wm. de Rothewell, priest, 1361. *Rothwell, Northants.*

All of them present certain peculiarities which are difficult to explain except under some such hypothesis.

## PALIMPSEST BRASSES

The term palimpsest is applied to those brasses which have been laid down a second time, in memory of some person other than the one for whom the plate was originally engraved. Its primary application was to a certain class of *manuscripts*, from which the first writings were scraped or sponged out, in order that the somewhat costly parchment might be used by another writer. The best-known instance perhaps is that of the New Testament Codex Ephraemi, of the fifth century, now at Paris ; in it the theological works of Ephraem the Syrian are written over the partially erased text of the New Testament.

Palimpsest brasses are usually of a date subsequent to the dissolution of the lesser and greater monasteries, 1536-1539, when great numbers of plates found their way from the abbeys and priories to parish churches.  In these cases new figures were engraved and cut from the older memorials, which were turned over and made to do duty once more as new brasses.  Out of the comparatively small number of brasses which have in modern times become detached from their slabs, a remarkably large proportion of those of the latter part of the sixteenth century have been found to be palimpsest.  Earlier examples also occur, but much more rarely.  Over 200 are already known, and others are constantly being discovered.  They may be divided into several classes :—

(1) *Palimpsests where the reverse is found to be part of an earlier brass of English type*

These are the most usual, and may be found in all parts

Palimpsest Evang. Symbol, British Museum.

of the country.  A single example may here suffice to explain their character.

At Hedgerly, Bucks, the brass of Mary Bulstrode, 1540, is entirely made up of palimpsest fragments, brought apparently from Bury St Edmund's, in Suffolk.  On the reverse of the figure is an early inscription in English verse; on that of the Bulstrode inscription, another to Thomas de Totyngton, Abbot of St Edmund's, 1301-1312; on that of a plate of children, part of the figure of an abbot, *c.* 1530, showing his chasuble, dalmatic and crozier; and finally, on the reverse of a shield, a representation of the Resurrection. The great Abbey of St Edmund's was only delivered up to the king in November 1539, a few months before the death of Margaret Bulstrode.

The accompanying illustration shows on the obverse

the symbol of St Mark, from one of the angles of a border fillet, and on the reverse part of a shield or coat-of-arms. It is now preserved at the British Museum, but nothing is known of its origin.

(2) *Palimpsests where the reverse is found to be part of an earlier brass of foreign workmanship*

Special interest attaches to these brasses, and they appear to be either spoilt or stolen plates which had somehow come into the hands of exporters, who sent them over to the English engravers as cheap or second-hand stock. A majority of them are Flemish and Dutch, with the English obverse later in date than the great sack of the Netherland churches by the Calvinists, which took place in 1566. About fifty fragments are known, and should be compared with our few complete examples of foreign workmanship, referred to in the preceding section. They have all been described, and most of them illustrated, by Mr Mill Stephenson in the Transactions of the Monumental Brass Society.

(3) *Palimpsests where parts of an earlier brass have been appropriated to later use without reversing the plate*

This practice seems to have been not uncommon. An inscription of the later date would be added, and if there were shields-of-arms in the composition, they would have to be removed, and others substituted, as at Okeover, Staffordshire, where a large brass of Lord Zouch and his two wives, 1447, was appropriated to the use of Humphrey Oker, Esq., and his wife, in 1538.

Simpler examples are frequent. At Ticehurst, Sussex, Sir John Wyborne, 1510, is represented by the figure of a knight which was engraved, *c.* 1370, and in this case his two wives have been added; they are placed on either side of the original effigy, and, being only half its size, look supremely ridiculous. In these cases of misappropriation warriors seem to have been the chief offenders, as at Laughton, Lincs, *c.* 1400 and 1549; Bromham, Beds, *c.* 1430 and 1535; and Isleworth, Middlesex, *c.* 1450 and 1544. At Weybridge, Surrey, three skeletons, *c.* 1520, are made to represent the three children of Sir John Trevor, the last of whom died in 1605. In many of these instances the Dissolution of the Monasteries may once more give an explanation.

(4) *Palimpsests where alterations have been made in a single commemoration*

This type is rare, and may be exemplified by the brass of Laurence de Wardeboys, Burwell, Cambs. This man was the last Abbot of Ramsay, in the Huntingdonshire fens, and had his brass laid down during his abbacy, 1508-1539, representing him in mitre and full vestments. Then came the Dissolution, and he was forced to resign his office, dying about three years later. The figure was altered to that of a priest in canonicals, cassock, surplice, almuce and hood, in the following way :—The lower part was turned over and re-engraved, and an entirely new head and shoulders were added. Traces of the original matrix remain, especially the cutting for the mitre. The canopy of this brass is also palimpsest, but of the ordinary type. Part of it is cut from the figure of a deacon, and shows on the reverse his fringed plain dalmatic and his maniple.

(5) *Palimpsests where alterations have been made in the actual engraving*

Again a single example may best serve to explain, in a well-known example at Waterpery, Oxon, which commemorates Walter Curzon, Esq., and his wife, 1527. The figures of a knight and lady of the middle of the previous century have been adapted to the more modern style of dress. To the male effigy a new head and shoulders have been given, while the skirt of taces has been altered to one of mail; other changes of less importance have been made in the other parts of the armour. The upper half of the lady is entirely new, and the lower part has been shaded and slightly altered.

# VI. Selected Bibliography

## A. Books on Brasses in General

### PRIMARY

Haines, Herbert. *A Manual of Monumental Brasses, comprising an introduction to the Study of these Memorials, and a List of those remaining in the British Isles*, 2 vols., 1861. Still the chief text-book on the subject. Vol. II contains a list of brasses which has been entirely superseded by the following work.

Stephenson, Mill. *A List of Monumental Brasses in the British Isles*, 1926. An austere book running to over 700 pages, unrelieved by any commentary. Inscriptions are not quoted.

Giuseppi, M. S., and Griffin, Ralph. *An Appendix to a List of Monumental Brasses in the British Isles by Mill Stephenson*, 1938. Including 112 pages of additions.

Macklin, H. W. *The Brasses of England*, 1907. A more discursive treatise by the author of the present work, intended for the more advanced student.

Monumental Brass Society. *Transactions*, Vol. I (Cambridge University Association of Brass Collectors), 1887–91. Vol. II, 1892–6. Vol. III, 1897–9. Vol. IV, 1900–3. Vol. V, 1904–9. Vol. VI, 1910–32. Vol. VII, 1934–40. Vol. VIII, 1943–49 (publication continuing). *Portfolios*. Vols. I–V (publication continuing).

### SECONDARY

Cambridge Camden Society. *Illustrations of the Monumental Brasses of Great Britain*, 1840–6. With essays by various authors.

Boutell, Chas. *Monumental Brasses and Slabs: an historical and descriptive notice of the Incised Monumental Memorials of the Middle Ages*, 1847. *The Monumental Brasses of England, a Series of Engravings upon Wood, with brief descriptive notices*, 1849. An elaborate appendix to the preceding work.

Waller, J. G. and L. A. R. *A Series of Monumental Brasses from the thirteenth to the seventeenth century*, 1842–64. 62 coloured plates, drawn and engraved by the authors.

Oxford University Brass Rubbing Society. *Oxford Journal of Monumental Brasses*. Vol. I, 1897–9; Vol. II, 1900. *Oxford Portfolio of Monumental Brasses*, 1898–1901.

Ward, J. S. M. *Brasses*, 1912. An elementary introduction.

Suffling, Ernest R. *English Church Brasses from the* 13th *to* 17th *century*, 1910.

Crossley, F. H. *English Church Monuments*, 1921. Including a very brief account of brasses.

Gawthorp, W. E. *The Brasses of Our Homeland Churches*, 1923. An elementary introduction.

Victoria and Albert Museum. *Catalogue of Rubbings of Brasses and Incised Slabs*, 2nd ed., 1929. With an introduction by Muriel Clayton. An extremely handy reference book, copiously illustrated.

## B. Costume in Brasses

(*M.B.S.* = *Transactions of the Monumental Brass Society*)

Druitt, Herbert. *A Manual of Costume as illustrated in Monumental Brasses*, 1906. A large proportion of the illustrations are reproductions of direct photographs of brasses.

Clayton, H. J. *The Ornaments of the Minister as shown in English Monumental Brasses*. Alcuin Club Collections, XXII, 1919.

Beaumont, E. T. *Academical Costume; illustrated by ancient monumental brasses*, 1928.

Edwards, Lewis. *Professional costume of lawyers illustrated principally by monumental brasses*. *M.B.S.*, VII, 1936–8.

## C. Authorities for Separate Counties

Nearly all the old county histories contain references to brasses but their names must be excluded for lack of space. For the same reason notes on brasses in individual churches are omitted unless in book form. Readers will also find useful *The Reports of the Royal Commission on Historical Monuments*, *The Victoria County History* and Methuen's *Little Guides*.

*Bedfordshire.*

Addington, H. *The Brasses of Bedfordshire, Archæological Journal*, XL, 1883.

Sanderson, H. K. St J. *The Brasses of Bedfordshire, M.B.S.*, II–III, 1893–7.

Isherwood, Grace. *Monumental Brassses in Bedfordshire Churches*, 1906.

*Berkshire.*

Morley, T. H. *Monumental Brasses of Berkshire*, 1924.

*Cambridgeshire.*

Cave, C. J. P., Charlton, O. J., and Macalister, R. A. S. *The Brasses of Cambridgeshire*. *M.B.S.*, II–V, 1893–1905 (not completed).

Benton, G. Montagu. *Monumental Brasses now existing in Cambridgeshire (excluding Cambridge)*, 1902.

*Cheshire.*

See Lancashire.

*Cornwall.*

Dunkin, E. H. W.   *The Monumental Brasses of Cornwall*, 1882.

*Cumberland.*

Bower, R.   *Brasses in the Diocese of Carlisle, Cumberland and Westmorland Antiquarian and Archæological Society*, 1894.

*Derbyshire.*

Field, H. E.   *The Monumental Brasses of Derbyshire, M.B.S.*, III and V, 1898–1904.

*Devon.*

Crabbe, W. R.   *The Monumental Brasses of Devon, Transactions of the Exeter Diocesan Architectural Society*, 1854.

Rogers, W. H. W.   *The Ancient Sepulchral Effigies and Monumental and Memorial Sculpture of Devon*, 1877.

*Essex.*

Chancellor, F.   *Ancient Sepulchral Monuments of Essex*, 1890.

Christy, Miller; Porteous, W. W., and Smith, Bartram.   *The Monumental Brasses of Essex*, edited by R. H. D'Elboux, 1952; *Memorials of Old Essex*, 1908.

*Gloucestershire.*

Davis, Cecil T.   *Monumental Brasses of Gloucestershire*, 1899.

*Hampshire.*

Cave, C. J. P.   *Monumental Brasses of Hampshire, M.B.S.*, V–VI, 1907–11.

*Isle of Wight.*

Lewis, R. W. M.   *Complete List of the Monumental Brasses of the Isle of Wight, M.B.S.*, II, 1892.

*Herefordshire.*

Haines, Herbert.   *The Monumental Brasses of the Cathedral and County of Hereford, British Archæological Association Journal*, XXVII, 1871.

Davis, Cecil T.   *The Monumental Brasses of Herefordshire and Worcestershire, Transactions of the Birmingham and Midland Institute*, 1884–5.

*Hertfordshire.*

Andrews, W. F.   *Memorial Brasses in Hertfordshire*, 2nd ed., 1903.

*Huntingdonshire.*

French, Valpy.   *The Brasses of Huntingdonshire, The Antiquary*, IV, 1881.

Macklin, H. W.   *The Brasses of Huntingdonshire, M.B.S.*, III, 1898.

*Kent.*

Belcher, W. D.    *Kentish Brasses,* I, 1888; II, 1905.

Griffin, R., and Stephenson, Mill.    *Monumental Brasses in Kent,* 1923.

*Lancashire.*

Thornely, J. L.    *The Monumental Brasses of Lancashire and Cheshire,* 1893.

*Lincolnshire.*

Jeans, G. E.    *A List of existing Sepulchral Brasses in Lincolnshire,* 1895. *The Sepulchral Brasses of Lincolnshire* in *Memorials of Old Lincolnshire,* 1911.

*Middlesex.*

Stephenson, Mill.    *Notes on the Monumental Brasses of Middlesex, Transactions of the St Paul's Ecclesiological Society,* IV, 1900.

Beloe, E. M., jun.    *The Monumental Brasses of Westminster Abbey,* 1898.

*Norfolk.*

Cotman, John Sell.    *Engravings of the most Remarkable of the Sepulchral Brasses in Norfolk,* 1819.    *Engravings of Sepulchral Brasses in Norfolk and Suffolk,* 2 vols., 2nd ed., 1839.    Includes essays by several early authorities.

Beloe, E. M., jun.    *The Monumental Brasses of Norfolk,* 1890–1 (25 lithographs without text).

Farrer, E.    *A List of the Monumental Brasses remaining in the County of Norfolk,* 1890.

*Northamptonshire.*

Hartshorne, C. H.    *An Endeavour to classify the Sepulchral Remains in Northamptonshire,* 1840.

Hudson, Franklin.    *The Brasses of Northamptonshire,* 1853.

*Nottinghamshire.*

Briscoe, J. P., and Field, H. E.    *The Monumental Brasses of Nottinghamshire,* Pt. I, 1904 (all issued).

*Oxfordshire.*

See above *Oxford Journal of Monumental Brasses.*

*Somerset.*

Connor, A. B.    *Monumental Brasses in Somerset, Proceedings of the Somerset Archæological and Natural History Society,* LXXVII–XCII, 1931–46 (not yet completed).

*Suffolk.*

Cotman, John Sell.    *Engravings of the most Remarkable of the Sepulchral Brasses in Suffolk,* 1819.    See also Norfolk.

Farrer, E.    *A List of the Monumental Brasses remaining in the County of Suffolk,* 1903.

*Surrey.*

Stephenson, Mill. *Monumental Brasses in Surrey, Transactions of the St Paul's Ecclesiological Society*, III, 1895.

Fairbank, F. R. *Monumental Brasses in the County of Surrey in Memorials of Old Surrey*, 1911.

*Sussex.*

Macklin, H. W. *Sussex Brasses in Memorials of Old Sussex*, 1909.

Mosse, H. R. *Monumental Effigies of Sussex*, 2nd ed., 1933.

Davidson-Horston, Mrs C. E. D. *Sussex Monumental Brasses*, Sussex Archæological Collections, LXXVI–VII, 1935.

*Warwickshire.*

Badger, E. W. *The Monumental Brasses of Warwickshire*, 1895.

*Wiltshire.*

Kite, E. *The Monumental Brasses of Wiltshire*, 1860.

*Yorkshire.*

Stephenson, Mill. *Monumental Brasses in the East Riding, Yorks. Archæological Journal*, XII, 1893; *Monumental Brasses in the West Riding*, XV, 1900; *Monumental Brasses in the North Riding*, XVIII, 1903; *Monumental Brasses in the City of York*, XVIII, 1905; *Additions*, XX, 1909.

## D. Foreign Brasses

The works here listed are not recommended as covering the whole range of brasses on the Continent. The aim has been rather to enable the reader:

1. To obtain a general view of the industry.
2. To appreciate better the foreign brasses in England.

Creeny, W. F. *A Book of Fac-similes of Monumental Brasses on the Continent of Europe*, 1884.

Eichler, Hans. *Die Gravierten Grabplatten aus Metall im XIVᵉ Jahrhundert und ihre Vorstufen*, Cologne, 1933. *Flandrische gravierte Metallgrabplatten des XIVᵉ Jahrhunderts, Jahrbuch des preussischen Kunstsammlungen*, LIV, 1933.

Collon-Gevaert, Suzanne. *Histoire des Arts du Metal en Belgique*, 2 vols., Brussels, 1951. Gives by far the best introduction to the Flemish brass industry of which the manufacture of monumental brasses formed part.

# E.  Technical

Cameron, H. K.  *The Metals used in Monumental Brasses, M.B.S.,* VIII, 1946.

Collon-Gevaert, Suzanne, *vide supra.*


# F.  Artists

Esdaile, Mrs A. J. K.  *The Scuptor and the Brass, M.B.S.,* VII, 1935.

Esdaile, Mrs A. J. K., and D'Elboux, R.  *An alphabetical list of Post-Reformation Brasses of known authorship, M.B.S.,* VIII, 1944.


## ADDITIONS TO THE BIBLIOGRAPHY

# B.  Costume in Brasses

Kent, J. P. C.  *Monumental Brasses, a new classification of military effigies* in *Journal of the British Archaeological Association,* XII, 1949, p. 70–97.


# D.  Foreign Brasses

Belonje, J. and Greenhill, F. A.  *Some Brasses, in Germany and the Low Countries* in *M.B.S.,* IX, 1955–62, pp. 213–20, 290–6, 379–87, 447–59, 493–508.

Cameron, H. K.  *Brasses at Lübeck,* in *M.B.S.,* IX, 1952, pp. 72–6.

Norris, N. W.  *The schools of Monumental Brasses in Germany* in *of the British Archaeological Association,* XXII, 1959, pp. 34–52.

# VII. County Lists

BRASSES are widely distributed, and are to be found in every county in England, being most numerous in East Anglia, the Home Counties and the Valley of the Thames. Kent, Norfolk, Essex and Suffolk contain the largest numbers, and are followed by Oxon, Bucks, Herts, Berks and Surrey.

The following lists are intended to include, in a very abbreviated form, the whole series of figure-brasses to be found in the churches of the United Kingdom, together with a few inscriptions of exceptional interest, and most of those which are accompanied by coats-of-arms. The general principle followed is to allow one line to each place, and to insert as much information as possible. Every date implies a separate brass, and where there are many brasses, little more can be given. Where there are only one or two, it is often possible to give the surname, or even the full name of the principal person commemorated. Children and accessories, except canopies, cannot usually be noted. Even so the lists extend to many pages, and include nearly 4000 brasses. These numbers should be compared with those of Haines' lists, which embrace 3200 figure-brasses and 1200 inscriptions, and occupy 240 pages. If all known inscriptions were added, the total would probably rise to at least 8000 brasses. It has not been found possible here to include brasses in private possession or in museums, or the matrices of lost brasses, however important. The dates are usually those to be found upon the brasses themselves, unless they were evidently engraved later, when the approximate dates are given of the actual engraving. The note Palimpsest implies only that some part of a brass is of that character, the later date, of the obverse, being alone mentioned. The word Priest, without anything further, means one in the eucharistic or mass vestments, alb, amice, chasuble, etc., while a bishop or abbot, unless otherwise stated, is understood to be in pontificals.

143

The principal abbreviations used are as follows :—

| | | | |
|---|---|---|---|
| acad. | =academical dress, usually cassock, surplice or tabard, tippet and hood | for. | =foreign, of foreign workmanship |
| alm. | =almuce | her. | =heraldic, in heraldic dress, of either sex |
| arm. | =a man in armour, of whatever rank, knight, esquire or gentleman | inscr. | =inscription |
| | | kng. | =kneeling |
| | | l. | =lady |
| | | mutil. | =mutilated |
| arms. | =a shield or coat of arms | palimp. | =palimpsest, some part re-engraved or re-used |
| *c.* | =*circa*, about | pecul. | =peculiar |
| can. | =canopy, or canopied | pr. | =priest |
| chal. | =chalice | qd. pl. | =quadrangular plate |
| civ. | =a man in civilian dress, of whatever rank | shr. | =shroud, a figure in a shroud |
| | | skel. | =skeleton |
| demi. | =demi-figure, half-effigy | sm. | =small |
| | | tab. | =tabard-of-arms |
| eccles. | =ecclesiastic, usually post-Reformation | trip. | =triple |
| | | w. | =wife, or with |
| Fr. | =French | ws. | =wives |

A few of the best or most interesting brasses in each county are indicated by an asterisk (*) in the margin. The brasses of Ireland, Scotland and Wales, which are very few in number, follow those of England. None are known in the Channel Islands, nor in the Isle of Man, save a late inscription at Peel.

## BEDFORDSHIRE

*Ampthill.* Wm. Hicchecok, woolman & w., 1450. Lady, 1485. Civ. & w., 1506. Sir Nich. Harvey, arm., 1532.
*Arlesey.* Inscriptions, 1638, 1759, 1761, 1768, all with coats-of-arms.
*Aspley Guise.* Priest & St John Bapt., *c.* 1410. Arm., *c.* 1490.
*Barford, Great.* Arm. & wife, *c.* 1525.
*Barford, Little.* Thos. Perys, civ. & wife, 1535.
*Barton-in-the-Clay.* Priest, demi, 1396. Civ., *c.* 1400.
*Bedford, St Mary.* Civ. (covered), 1627. Lady, qd. pl., 1663. Arms, 1671.
*Bedford, St Paul.* Sir Wm. Harper, arm. & wife, 1573.
*Biddenham.* Civ. & w., *c.* 1490. 2 shrouds, *c.* 1530. L., qd. pl., 1639.
*Biggleswade.* Wm. Halsted, civ. & 2 ws., 1449. Fragments, 1481.
*Blunham.* Rich. Maulaye, civ. & wife, 1506.
*\*Bromham.* Arm. & 2 wives, canopy, large, 1435 (approp. to 1535).
*Caddington.* Civ. & wife, 1505. Civ. & 2 wives, 1518.
*Campton.* Rich. Carlyll, civ. & wife, 1489.
*Cardington.* Arm. in tabard & 2 ws., heraldic, *c.* 1540. Arm. & w., 1638.
*Clifton.* John Fisher, arm. & wife, 1528.
*Cople.* Serjeant-at-law & w., *c.* 1410. Arm., *c.* 1415. Arm. & w., 1435, *c.* 1520, 1556. Judge & w., 1544, 1563.

*Dean.* Thos. Parker, priest in almuce, 1501.
*Dunstable.* Civ. & w., 1516. 2 civs. & w., 1640. Many fragments.
*Eaton Bray.* Jane, Lady Bray, kng., qd. pl., 1558.
*Eaton Socon.* Civ. & w., *c.* 1400. Lady, *c.* 1450.
*Elstow.* Margery Argentine, 1427. Elizth. Herwy, abbess, 1524.
*Eyworth.* Rich. Gadburye, civ. & w., 1624.
*Felmersham.* Civ. & wife, *c.* 1610.
*Flitton.* Lady, 1434, 1544. Harry Gray, arm., 1545. Civ., 1628.
*Goldington.* Rich. Fyssher, civ., 1507. Robt. Hatley, arm., 1585.
*Gravenhurst, Lower.* An inscr., 1362. Civ. & 3 ws., 1606.
*Hatley Cockayne.* Arm., *c.* 1430. L., *c.* 1480. Arm. & ws., 1515, 1527.
*Haynes.* Anth. Newdegate, civ., qd. pl., 1568.
*Higham Gobion.* Jane Cason, 1602. Kath. Brown, 1603.
*Holwell.* Chalice & 2 wild men, to Robt. Wodehowse, priest, 1515.
*Houghton Conquest.* Arm., w. & arm., 1493. Arm. & w., 1500.
*Houghton Regis.* Priest, demi, 1410. Priest, 1506.
*Husborne Crawley.* John Carter, civ. & w., 1600.
*Kempston.* Wm. Carter, civ. & w., qd. pl., 1605.
*Langford.* Thos. Hundon, priest, 1520.
*Leighton Buzzard.* 3 civs., qd. pl., 1592. Civ. & w., qd. pl., 1636.
*Lidlington* (old church). Civ. & w., *c.* 1495.
*Luton, St Mary.* Civ., *c.* 1425. L. & trip. can., *c.* 1490. Pr. in cap & almuce, *c.* 1510. Arm. & 2 ws., 1513. L., 1515. Many fragments.
*Marston Morteyne.* Walter Papley, pr., demi, 1420. Thos. Reynes, arm. & w., 1451. Inscr. & arms, Reynes, 1506.
*Maulden.* Rich. Faldo, arm. & w., 1576. Anne Faldo, 1594.
*Meppershall.* Mepertyshale, arm., 1440. Boteler, arm. & w., 1441.
*Poddington.* John Howard, civ., 1518.
*Pottesgrove.* Civ. & w., 1535. Ditto, foreign palimp., 14th cent., 1563.
*Pulloxhill.* Geo. Fitz, arm. & w. (covered), 1603. Inscr. & arms, 1700.
*Renhold.* Edm. Wayte, civ. & w., small, 1518.
*Salford.* John Peddar, civ. & w., 1505.
*Sharnbrook.* Cobbe, 2 civs. & w., 1522. Inscr. & arms, 1618.
*Shillington.* Priest in cope, large, 1400. Pr. in cope, 1485.
*Souldrop.* John Hanger, civ., qd. pl., 1608.
*Stagsden.* John Cocke, arm., qd. pl., 1617.
*Stevington.* Thos. Salle, arm., 1422.
*Sutton.* A Latin cross fleury, 1516.
*Thurleigh.* John Harvye, arm., *c.* 1420. Inscr. & arms, 1490.
*Tilbrook.* Civ. & wife, *c.* 1400.
*Tingrith.* Robt. Hogeson, civ., qd. pl., 1611.
*Toddington.* Arms & fragments, *c.* 1475.
*Totternhoe.* John Warwekhyll, priest w. chalice, 1524. A child, 1621.
*Turvey.* Civ., *c.* 1480. Pr. in almuce, *c.* 1500. Lady, 1606.
*Wilshamstead.* Wm. Carbrok, priest, demi, *c.* 1425.
*Woburn.* Canopy & inscr., 1394.
*Wymington.* Civ. & w., canopy, good, 1391. Lady, 1407. Sir Thos. Brounflet, arm., large, 1430. Pr. in cope, w. chalice, 1520.
*Yelden.* Priest, 1433. Ecclesiastic, 1617. Civ., qd. pl., 1628.

## BERKSHIRE

*Abingdon, St Helen.* Barbur, civ., demi, 1417. Priest in acad., 1501.
*Aldermaston.* Arms & inscriptions, *c.* 1425, 1574, 1638.
*Appleton.* John Goodryngton, in shroud, 1518.

K

*Ashbury.* Civ., demi, *c.* 1360. Priest in cope, 1409. Ditto, 1448.
*Binfield.* Priest in cope, demi, 1361. Palimp. inscr., 1558.
*Bisham.* Crekett, civ., 1517. Brinckhurst, civ. & 2 ws., 1581.
*\*Blewbury.* John Balam, priest, 1496. Arm. & 2 ws., *c.* 1515. Sir John
 Daunce, arm. in tab. & w., 1523, 1548.
*\*Bray.* Foxley, arm. & 2 ws., heraldic, bracket, 1378. A judge, 1475
 Civ. & 2 ws., *c.* 1490. Civ. & w., qd. pl., 1610. Ditto, 1620.
*Brightwell.* Pr. w. chalice, 1507. Civ. & w., 1509. Ditto, 1512.
*Buckland.* John Yate, civ. & w., 1578.
*Burghfield.* Nich. Williams, arm. & w., 1568.
*\*Childrey.* Fynderne, arm. in tab. & w., canopy, 1444. Pr., *c.* 1480.
 Civ. & w., *c.* 1480. Pr. w. chalice, *c.* 1490. L. in shroud, 1507.
 Arm. & w., 1514. Civ. & w. in shrouds, 1516. Civ. & w., *c.* 1520.
 Pr. in acad., 1529.
*Cholsey.* John Mere, priest w. chalice, 1471.
*Ccmpton.* Rich. Pygott, civ. & w., 1520.
*Cookham.* Civ. & w., 1458, 1503, 1577. Arm. & w., 1510, 1527.
*Coxwell, Great.* Wm. Morys, civ., 1509. Lady, *c.* 1510.
*Cumnor.* Arm. & w., 1572. Lady, 1577. Civ. & w., 1599.
*Dencheworth.* Hyde, arm. & w., 1516. Ditto. 1562. Ditto, 1567.
*Farringdon.* Civ. & w., 1485. Pr., 1505. Arm. in tab. & 2 ws., 1547.
*Fawley.* Mary Gunter, qd. pl., 1621.
*Finchampstead.* Elizth. Blighe, 1635.
*Hagbourn, E.* Hugh Keate, civ. & w., qd. pl., 1627.
*Hampstead, E.* Thos. Berwyk, civ., demi, 1443.
*Hanney, W.* Pr., large, *c.* 1370. Arm., 1557, 1599. Civ. & 2 ws., 1592.
 Arm. & 2 ws., 1602. Civ. & w., 1611.
*Harwell.* John Jennens, civ. & w., 1599.
*Hatford.* Francis Pigott, shields & inscr., 1614.
*Hendred, E.* Hen. Eldysley, civ., 1439. John Eyston, arm. & w., 1589.
*Hurst.* Civ. & w., 1574. Lady in bed, qd. pl., *c.* 1600.
*Kintbury.* John Gunter, civ. & w., 1626.
*Lambourn.* Civ. & w., demi, 1406. 2 civs., demi, *c.* 1410. Arm. in
 tabard, *c.* 1485. Civ. & w., 1619.
*Langford.* Walter Prunes, civ. & w., 1609.
*Letcombe Regis.* Lady, *c.* 1440.
*Locking, E.* Edw. Keate, civ. & w., 1624. Lady, 1628.
*Longworth.* Priest, demi, 1422. Shrouds, 1500. Lady, 1566.
*Newbury.* Civilian & wife, 1519.
*Reading, St Giles.* John Bowyer, civ. & w., 1521.
*Reading, St Laurence.* Civ. & w., *c.* 1415, 1584. Civ., palimp., 1538.
*Remenham.* Arm., 1591. Pastor, 1622.
*Sandhurst.* Rich. Geale, civ. & w., 1608.
*Shefford, Little.* John Fetyplace, arm. & w., 1524.
*\*Shottesbrooke.* Priest & civ., canopy, *c.* 1370. Lady, 1401. Arm., 1511.
 Civ. & 3 ws., 1567.
*Sonning.* Laurence Fyton, arm., 1434. Civ. & w., 1549. Lady, 1575,
 1589. Child, sm., 1627.
*\*Sparsholt.* Priest in cross, 1353. Civ., *c.* 1495, 1602. Lady, *c.* 1510.
*Stanford-Dingley.* Margt. Dyneley, 1444. Civ., 1610.
*Stanford-in-the-Vale.* Roger Campedene, priest, demi, 1398.
*Steventon.* Civ. & w., small, 1476. Arm. & w., 1584.
*Stratfield-Mortimer.* Rich. Trevet, arm., 1441. Lady, 1441.
*Streatley.* Civ., sm., 1583. Lady, 1570. Civ. & w., 1603.
*Swallowfield.* Lady, sm., 1466. Christopher Lytkott, arm. & w., 1554.

*Tidmarsh.* Margt. Wode, 1499. Leyneham, arm. in tabard, **1517.**
*Tilehurst.* Gauwin More, civ. & w., 1469.
*Upton Nervet.* Wm. Smith, civ. & w., sm., 1627.
*Waltham, Bright.* John Newman, civ., sm., 1517.
*Waltham, White.* Lady, 1445. Lady, small, 1506.
*Wantage.* Pr., demi, *c.* 1360. Arm., large, 1414. Pr. in acad., sm., 1512. Civ. & 2 ws., 1522. Lady, 1619.
*Welford.* Pr. in acad., sm., *c.* 1490. Civ., sm., *c.* 1530.
*Windsor, Old.* Humfrey Michell, civ. & w., 1621.
*\*Windsor, St George's Chapel.* Canopy, etc., 1380. Arm. & w., heraldic, qd. pl., 1475. Pr. in almuce, qd. pl., 1522. Child in cradle, 1630. Ditto, 1633.
*Winkfield.* A yeoman-of-the-guard, demi, qd. pl., 1630.
*Wittenham, Little.* Pr., 1433. Civ., sm., 1454. L., 1472. Civ., 1483. Civ. & w., *c.* 1585. Arm., 1588. Child, qd. pl., 1683.
*Wokingham.* Civ. & w., *c.* 1520. Ditto, *c.* 1610.
*Wytham.* Man in armour & w., *c.* 1455.

## BUCKINGHAMSHIRE

*Amersham.* Civ. & w., 1430, 1439, 1521. Civ., *c.* 1450. Child, 1623.
*Astwood.* John Chibnale, civ. & 2 ws., 1534.
*Beachampton.* Civ., 1600. Lady, small, 1611.
*Beaconsfield.* John Waren, civ. & w., 1609.
*Bledlow.* Wm. Hern, priest, small, 1525.
*Bletchley.* Thos. Sparke, priest, a bust in oval, qd. pl., 1616.
*Bradenham.* A priest, 1521.
*Burnham.* Civ. & w., *c.* 1500, 1563. Civ. & 3 ws., 1581.
*Chalfont St Giles.* Pr., sm., *c.* 1470. Lady, *c.* 1510. Civ. & 2 ws., *c.* 1540. Arm. & w., 1558. Arm. & 2 ws., 1570.
*Chalfont St Peter.* Arm. & w., *c.* 1446. Ditto, 1446. Pr., palimp., 1545.
*Chearsley.* John Frankeleyn, civ. & w., 1462.
*Chenies.* Civ. & 2 ws., 1469. Arm. & w., canopy, 1484. Pr., sm., 1494. Lady, heart & canopy, 1510. Lady, 1511, 1524.
*Chesham Bois.* Lady, 1516. Arm., 1552. Chrysom, *c.* 1520.
*Chicheley.* Arm. & w., 1558. Skel. in shroud, qd. pl., sm., *c.* 1560.
*Claydon, Middle.* Lady, 1523. Pr., demi, w. chalice, 1526. Roger Gyffard, arm. & w., 1542.
*Clifton Reynes.* Reynes, arm., 1428. Man & w. in shrouds, *c.* 1500.
*Crawley.* John Garbrand, parson, qd. pl., 1589.
*Crendon, Long.* John Canon, civ. & w., 1468.
*Datchet.* Hanbery, civ. & w., qd. pl., 1593. Arms & inscr., 1559.
*\*Denham.* Arm. & 2 ws., 1494. Abbess, *c.* 1540. Lady, palimp., reverse a friar, 1545. Priest, 1560.
*Dinton.* Arm. & w., 1424, 1539, 1628. Civ. & w., 1486, 1558. Arm., 1551.
*\*Drayton Beauchamp.* Arm., 1368, 1375. Pr. w. chalice, sm., 1531.
*Dunton.* Civ. & w., sm., *c.* 1420. Lady, sm., *c.* 1510.
*Edlesborough.* Arm. & 3 ws., 1540. Civ. & w., 1592.
*Ellesborough.* Thos. Hawtrey, arm. & w., 1544.
*Emberton.* John Mordon, priest, *c.* 1410.
*\*Eton College Chapel.* Vice-provost, in cap & almuce, sm., 1489. Provost in alm., triple can., 1503. Fellow, w. chalice, sm., 1509. Arm., 1521. Pr. in cope, 1522. Fellow, 1525. L., 1528. Pr. w. chalice, 1535. Provost, 1535. Vice-prov. in hood, palimp., 1545. Lady, 1560. Fellow, kng., 1636, and 11 inscrs.

*Haddenham.* Priest in cope, *c.* 1420. Pr., demi, 1428.
*Halton.* Henry Bradshawe, chief baron of exchequer, & w., 1553.
*Hambledon.* Civ., 1457. Civ. & w., 1497, *c.* 1600. L., kng., 1500.
   Civ. & 2 ws., qd. pl., 1634.
*Hampden, Gt.* Arm. & w., *c.* 1525. Arm. & 2 ws., 1533.
*Hanslope.* Mary Birchemore, child, 1602.
*Hardmead.* Francis Catesby, civ., 1556.
*Haversham.* Lady, 1427. Skeleton, qd. pl., 1605.
*Hedgerley.* Robt. Fulmer, civ. & w., sm., 1498. Lady, palimp., 1540.
*Hitcham.* Thos. Ramsey, arm. & w., 1510. Nich. Clarke, arm., 1551.
*Hitchendon.* Robt. Thurloe, priest, 1493.
*Horwood, Gt.* Hen. Upnore, priest in acad., em., 1487.
*Iver.* Rich. Blount, arm. & w., 1508.
*Ivinghoe.* French inscr., Fallywolle, 1368. Civ. & w., 1517. Civ., 1531,
   1576, 1594.
*Langley Marsh.* John Bowser, civ., 1608.
*Lillingstone Dayrell.* Paul Dayrell, arm. & w., 1491. Priest, sm., 1493.
*Linford, Gt.* Civ. & w., 1473. Ditto, 1536. Ditto, 1611.
*Linslade.* Civ. & 3 ws., *c.* 1500.
*Loughton.* Hugh Parke, priest, demi, 1514.
*Ludgershall.* 3 ladies, *c.* 1600.
*Marlow, Little.* Alice Ledewich, 1430.
*Marston, N.* Rich. Sanders, civ., qd. pl., 1602.
*Marsworth.* Nich. West, judge, arm., 1586. Mary West, 1606. **Edm.**
   West, serjeant-at-law, arm. & w., qd. pl., 1681.
*Milton Keynes.* Adam Babyngton, priest, 1427.
*Missenden, Gt.* A crest, *c.* 1450. Lady, *c.* 1510.
*Missenden, Little.* John Style, civ., 1613.
*Moulsoe.* Rich. Ruthall, arm. & w., 1528.
*Nettleden.* Sir Geo. Cotton, arm., 1545.
*Newport Pagnell.* Civ., mutil., large, *c.* 1440.
*Penn.* L. in shroud, 1540. Arm. & w., 1597, 1638, 1641. Lady, 1640.
*Quainton.* L., demi, *c.* 1360. Pr. in cassock, kng., sm., 1422. Pr. in
   cope, 1485. Lady, 1509, 1593. Civ., 1510.
*Risborough, Monks.* Robt. Blundell, priest, 1431. Civ. & w., demi, *c.*
   1460. Children, *c.* 1520.
*Saunderton.* Isabella Saunterdon, demi, *c.* 1430.
*Shalston.* Dame Susan Kyngeston, vowess, 1540.
*Slapton.* Priest, demi, 1462. Yeoman-of-crown & 2 ws., 1519.
*Soulbury.* John Turney, civ. & w., 1502. John Mallet, civ., 1516.
*Stoke Poges.* Sir Wm. Molyns & w., 1425. Hampdyn, civ. & w., 1577.
*Stone.* Wm. Gurney, in shroud, & w., 1472. Civ., palimp., 1520.
*Stow.* Alice Saunders, sm., 1479. Child, sm., 1592.
*Swanbourn.* Thos. Adams, yeoman, & w., 1626.
*Taplow.* Cross & civ., *c.* 1350. Civ., lady & shroud, 1455. Arm. & 2
   ws., palimp., 1540.
*Thornton.* Robt. Ingylton, arm. & 3 ws., canopy, 1472. Lady, 1557.
*Tingewick.* Erasm. Williams, rector, demi, qd. pl., 1608.
*Tyringham.* Arm., 1484. Mary Catesby, 1508.
*Turweston.* Priest, *c.* 1450. Civ. & 2 ws., sm., *c.* 1490.
*Twyford.* Priest, demi, 1413. Thos. Giffard, arm., 1550.
*Upton.* Agnes Bulstrode, in shroud, kng., sm., 1472. Edw. Bulstrode,
   arm. & 2 ws., 1517. Arm. & w., 1599.
*Waddesdon.* Priest, 1543. Pr. in shroud, 1548. Arm., 1490. Arm. &
   w., *c.* 1560.

*Wendover.* Wm. Bradschawe, civ. & w., kng., sm., 1537.
*Weston Turville.* Civilian, *c.* 1580.
*Weston Underwood.* Elizth. Throkmarton (under organ), 1571.
*Whaddon.* Thos. Pygott, serjeant-at-law, & 2 ws., 1519. Lady, 1612.
*Winchendon, Nether.* Arm., *c.* 1420. Civ. & w., 1487.
*Winchendon, Over.* An Austin Canon, 1502. Arms and inscr., 1558.
*Wing.* Civ. & w., 1489, *c.* 1490. A porter, qd. pl., 1648.
*Winslow.* Thos. Fige, civ. & w., sm., 1578.
*Wooburn.* Civ., 1488. Civ. & w., *c.* 1500. Priest in cope, 1519.
    Shroud, *c.* 1520. Child, qd. pl., sm., 1642.
*Wootton Underwood.* Edw. Greneville, civ. & w., 1587.
*Worminghall.* Philip King, civ. & w., 1592.
*Wyrardisbury.* Arm., *c.* 1500. Civ., sm., 1512. Arms, etc., 1561.


# CAMBRIDGESHIRE

*Abingdon Pigotts.* Civilian, *c.* 1470.
*Balsham.* Priest in cope, canopy, 1401. Ditto, 1462. Arm., *c.* 1480.
*Barton.* John Martin, civ. & w., *c.* 1600.
*Bassingbourn.* Edw. Turpin, civ. & w., 1683.
*Burwell.* Laurence de Wardeboys, abbot, in almuce, palimp., 1542.
*Cambridge—*
    *St Benet.* Dr Billingford, in acad., kng., 1432.
    *St Mary the Great.* Arms, etc., Lorkin, 1591. Ditto, Scott, 1617.
    *St Mary the Less.* Pr. in acad., 1440. Ditto, demi, *c.* 1480.
    *Caius Coll.* Arm., *c.* 1500.
    *Christ's Coll.* Arm. & w., 1516. Pr. in acad., *c.* 1540.
    *Jesus Coll.* Arms, etc., Duckett, 1603.
    *St John's Coll.* Pr. in acad., canopy, 1414. Pr., *c.* 1430.
    *King's Coll.* Provost in acad., 1496. Ditto, 1507. Provost in almuce,
        1528. Ditto, 1558. Arms, etc., 1559.
    *Queens' Coll.* Pr. in cope, *c.* 1480. Pr. in acad., *c.* 1535. Civ., 1591.
    *Trinity Hall.* Pr. in cope, 1517. Pr. in acad., *c.* 1530. Civ., 1598.
        Arms, etc., 1611, 1645, 1659.
*Croxton.* Edw. Leeds, Master of Clare, in gown, 1589.
*Dry Drayton.* Hutton, arm. & w., *c.* 1530.
*Elm.* Arms & inscr., Fincham, 1667.
*Eltisley.* Arms & inscr., Marshall, 1640.
*Ely Cathedral.* Bp. Goodrick, 1554. Dean Tyndall, 1614. Arms, etc.,
    Wagstave, 1616.
*Fordham.* Wm. Cheswryght, civ. & w., 1521.
*Fulbourn.* Pr., *c.* 1390. Pr. in cope, canopy, 1391. Pr., 1477. Lady, *c.*
    1480, 1490.
*Girton.* Priest in cope, 1492. Ditto, 1497.
*Haddenham.* Canopy, 1405. Civ. & w., 1454.
*Hatley, E.* A lady, *c.* 1520.
*Hatley St George.* Sir Baldwin Seyntgeorge, arm., 1425.
*Hildersham.* Cross & figs., Robt. de Paris, civ. & w., kng., 1379.
    Arm. & w., 1427. Arm., canopy, 1466. Shroud, *c.* 1530.
*Hinxton.* Sir Thos. de Skelton & 2 ws., 1416.
*Horseheath.* Sir John d'Argentine, arm., 1382. Civilian, 1552.
*Impington.* John Burgoyn, arm. in tabard & w., 1505.
*Isleham.* Sir John Bernard, arm. & w., can., 1451. Thos. Peyton, arm.
    & 2 ws., can., 1484. Civ. & w., 1574.

*Kirtling.* Edw. Myrfin, civ., kng., 1553.
*Linton.* Henry Paris, arm., 1427. Arms, etc., 1538, 1558, 1577.
*March.* Civ. & w., 1501. Arm. in tab. & w., kng., sm., 1517.
*Milton.* Wm. Coke, judge, & w., 1553. Civ. & w., 1660.
*Quy.* John Ansty, arm., sons in tabards, *c.* 1465.
*Sawston.* Civ., *c.* 1420. Arm., *c.* 1480. Shrouds, *c.* 1500. Priest w. chalice, sm., 1527.
*Shelford, Gt.* Pr. in cope, canopy, 1418. Arms, etc., Risley, 1511.
*Shelford, Little.* Arm. & w., 1405, *c.* 1405. Pr. in acad., *c.* 1480.
*Stapleford.* Wm. Lee, priest, qd. pl., sm., 1617.
*Stretham.* Joan Swan, 1497.
*Swaffham Prior.* John Tothyll, arm & w., sm., 1462. Civ. & w., 1515, 1521, *c.* 1530. Civ., 1638.
*\*Trumpington.* Sir Roger de Trumpington, 1289.
*\*Westley Waterless.* Sir John de Creke & w., *c.* 1325.
*Weston Colville.* Arm. & w., *c.* 1420. Eccles. & w., kng., qd. pl., 1636.
*Wicken.* Margt. Peyton, sm., 1414. Civilian, sm., *c.* 1520.
*Wilbraham, Little.* Wm. Blakwey, priest in acad., kng., sm., 1521.
*Wilburton.* Priest in cope, can., 1477. Civ. & w., 1506. Ditto, 1516.
*Wimpole.* Priest in cope, 1501. Civ., *c.* 1500. Lady, *c.* 1535.
*Wisbech.* Thos. de Braunstone, arm., 1401.
*Wood Ditton.* Henry Englissh, arm. & w., 1393.


## CHESHIRE

*Chester Cathedral.* Thos. Madock & w., 1792.
*Chester, St Peter.* Civilian, *c.* 1460.
*\*Macclesfield.* Roger Legh, civ., 1506, and Mass of St Gregory.
*Middlewich.* Elizth. Venables, qd. pl., 1591.
*Over.* Hugh Starky, arm., *c.* 1510.
*\*Wilmslow.* Sir Robt. del Bothe, arm. & w., 1460.
*Wybunbury.* Ralf Dellvys, arm. & w., 1513.


## CORNWALL

*Anthony, E.* Margery Arundell, canopy, 1420.
*Blisland.* John Balsam, priest, 1410.
*St Breock.* Civilian & wife, *c.* 1510.
*St Budock.* John Killigrew, civ. & w., 1567.
*\*Callington.* Nich. Assheton, justice, & w., 1465.
*Cardynham.* Thos. Awmarle, priest, sm., *c.* 1400.
*Colan.* Francis Bluet & w., 1572. Coswarth & w., 1573.
*St Columb Major.* John Arundel, arm. & 2 ws., 1545. Ditto & w., *c.* 1630, 1633.
*Constantine.* Rich. Geyrveys, civ. & w., qd. pl., palimp., 1574. John Pendarves, civ. & w., qd. pl., 1616.
*Crowan.* St Aubyn, *c.* 1420. Civ. & w., *c.* 1490. Ditto, mutil., *c.* 1550.
*St Erme.* Robt. Trencreeke, civ. & w., 1596.
*Fowey.* 2 civs. & w., *c.* 1450. Civ., 1582. Lady, 1602.
*St Gluvias.* Thos. Kyllygrewe & w., 1484
*Gorran.* Lady, kng., *c.* 1510.
*Grade.* Jas. Eryssy, arm. & w., 1522.
*Helston.* Thos. Buggins, civ. & w., 1602.

*Illogan.* Jas. Bassett, arm. & w., 1603
*St Ives.* Agnes Trevnwyth, kng., 1462.
*St Just.* Priest in plain cope, *c.* 1520.
*Landrake.* Edw. Cowrtney, arm., sm., 1509.
*Landulph.* Inscr. to Theodore Paleologus, 1636, & 2 others.
*Lanteglos-by-Fowey.* Mohun, arm. & w., *c.* 1440. Ditto & w., 1525.
*Launceston.* Lady, sm., *c.* 1620.
*Lostwithiel.* Tristram Curteys, arm., 1423.
*Madron.* John Clies, civ. & w., 1623.
*\*Mawgan-in-Pyder.* Pr. in cope, *c.* 1420. Lady, 1578. Civ., *c.* 158c.
Lady, palimp., *c.* 1580, & inscrs.
*St Mellion.* Peter Coryton, arm. & w., 1551.
*Minster.* Robt. Hender, arm. & w., kng., 4 sm. plates, 1602.
*St Michael Penkevil.* Arm., 1497. Pr. in acad., 1515. Civ., 1619.
Arm., qd. pl., *c.* 1640. Lady, 1622.
*St Minver.* Roger Opy, 1517.
*Probus.* John Wulvedon, civ. & w., 1514.
*Quethiock.* Roger Kyngdon & w., 1471. Rich. Chiverton & w., 1631.
*St Stephens-by-Saltash.* Fragments, *c.* 1480. Inscr., 1613.
*Stratton.* Sir John Arundell, arm. & 2 ws., 1561.
*Tintagel.* Joan Bon, demi, *c.* 1430.
*Truro Cathedral.* Civ., *c.* 1580. Ditto, 1630. Inscr., 1567.
*Wendron.* Pr. in cope, mutil., 1535. Civ. & w., mutil., *c.* 1580.


## CUMBERLAND

*Bootle.* Sir Hugh Askew, arm., sm., 1562.
*\*Carlisle Cathedral.* Bishop Bell, trip. can., 1496. Bp. Robinson, qd.
pl., 1616.
*Crosthwaite.* Sir John Ratclif, arm. & w., 1527.
*Edenhall.* Wm. Stapilton, arm. in tabard & w., 1458.
*Greystoke.* Pr. in almuce, demi, 1526. Lady, *c.* 1540, 1547. Civ., 1551.


## DERBYSHIRE

*Alfreton.* Inscr. to John Ormond, Esq., & w., effs. lost, 1507.
*Ashborne.* Dedication inscr., 1241. Francis Cockayne, serjt.-at-law
in tab. & w., trip. can., 1538.
*Ashover.* James Rolleston, arm. & w., 1507. Priest, *c.* 1510.
*Bakewell.* Arms & inscr., 1628, 1653, 1658, 1732.
*Chesterfield.* Lady, 1451. Arm. & w., restored, 1519. Ditto, 1529, and
inscrs.
*Crich.* Child in swaddling-clothes, qd. pl., 1637, and inscrs.
*Dronfield.* Thos. & Rich. Gomfrey, priests, 1399. Civ. & w., 1578, and
inscrs.
*Edensor.* John Beton, arm., small, 1570.
*Etwall.* Lady, 1512. Sir John Porte & 2 ws., heraldic, 1557.
*Hathersage.* Eyre, arm. & w., 1463. Ditto, heraldic, *c.* 1500, *c.* 1560.
*Hope.* Henry Balguy, civ., qd. pl., 1685.
*Hucknall.* Inscr. to Rich, Pawson, vicar, 1537.
*Kedleston.* Rich. Curzon, arm. & w., 1496.
*Longstone.* Rowland Eyre, civ. & w., kng. w. crucifix, qd. pl., 1624.

*Morley*. Stathum, arm. & w., kng., 1454. Ditto & 2 ws., 1470. Ditto & 3 ws., 1481. Sacheverell, arm. & w., *c.* 1525. Ditto, 1558.
*Mugginton*. Nich. Kniveton, arm. & w., *c.* 1475.
*Norbury*. Sir Anthony Fitzherbert, Justice of Comm. Pleas, & w., heraldic, palimp., 1538.
*Sawley*. Bothe, arm. & w., 1467. Ditto, 1478. Shylton & w., 1510.
*Staveley*. Frecheville, arm. in tab., *c.* 1480. Arm. & w., kng., 1503.
*Taddington*. Rich. Blackwall, civ. & w., 1500.
*Tideswell*. Holy Trin., etc., for Sir Sampson Meverell, 1462. Civ. & w., 1483. Bp. Pursglove, in pontif., 1579.
*Walton-on-Trent*. Robt. Morley, priest, w. chalice, 1492.
*Wilne*. Hugh Wylloughby, arm. & son, in tabards, & w., kng , 1513.
*Winksworth*. Thos. Blakewall, civ. & w., 1525. Civ. & w., 1510.
*Youlgrave*. A lady, *c.* 1600.


## DEVONSHIRE

*Atherington*. Sir Arthur Basset, arm. & 2 ws., *c.* 1540.
*Allington, E.* John Fortescue, arm. & w., 1595. Lady, kng., *c.* 1600.
*Bickleigh*. Inscr. to Nich. Slannyng, 1568.
*Bigbury*. Lady, *c.* 1440. Elizth. Burton, *c.* 1460.
*Blackhauton*. Nich. Forde, civ. & w., 1582.
*Braunton*. Elizth. Chechester, kng., palimp., 1548.
*Chittlehampton*. John Coblegh & 2 ws., 1480.
*Clovelly*. Cary, arm., 1540, *c.* 1540. Inscr., w. skel. & spade, 1655.
*Clyst St George*. Julian Osborne, lady, qd. pl., 1614.
*Dartmouth, St Petrock*. Roope, civ., 1609. Lady, 1610. Ditto, 1614.
*Dartmouth, St Saviour*. John Hauley, arm. & 2 ws., canopy, 1408. Lady, *c.* 1470. Civ., *c.* 1600.
*Ermington*. Wm. Strachleigh, civ. & w., kng., 1583.
*Exeter Cathedral*. Sir Pet. Courtenay, canopy, 1409. Canon Langeton, pr. in cope, kng., 1413.
*Filleigh*. Rich. Fortescue, arm., qd. pl., 1570.
*St Giles-in-the-Wood*. Lady, 1430. Ditto, 1592. Ditto, 1610.
*Haccombe*. Carew, arm., 1469, 1568. Lady, 1589, 1611. Civ. & w., qd. pl., 1656.
*Harford*. Thos. Williams, arm., 1566. Civ. & w., qd. pl., 1639.
*Kentisbeare*. Inscr. to Lady Mary Carew, 1558.
*Loxhore*. Cross-inscr. to Rich. Carpenter, rector, 1627.
*Monkleigh*. Arm., kng., *c.* 1580. Angels and scroll, 1509.
*Otterton*. Rich. Duke, civ., 1641. Sarah Duke, 1641.
*Ottery St Mary*. John, Wm. & Rich. Sherman, *c.* 1620.
*Petrockstow*. Henry Rolle, arm. & w., qd. pl., 1591.
*Powderham*. Arms & inscr., Smyth, 1698.
*Sampford Peverell*. Margt. Poulet, 1602.
*Sandford*. Mary Dourich, lying on tomb, 1604.
*Shillingford*. Sir Wm. Huddersfield & w., heraldic, qd. pl., 1516.
*Staverton*. John Rowe, civ., demi, 1592.
*Stoke Fleming*. John Corp, civ. & granddau., canopy, 1391.
*Stoke-in-Teignhead*. Priest, *c.* 1370. Inscr. on heart, 1641.
*Tawstock*. Arms & inscr., Pagett, 1648.
*Tedburn St Mary*. Edw. Gee, parson, & w., 1613.
*Tiverton*. John Greenway, civ. & w., 1529.

*Tor Mohun.* Wilmota Cary, 1581.
*Washfield.* Henry Worth, civ. & w., 1606.
*Yealmpton.* Sir John Crokker, arm., 1508. Palimp. inscr., 1580.


## DORSETSHIRE

*Bere Regis.* John Skerne, civ. & w., kng., 1596.
*Bryanston.* Inscrs. below matrices, 1528 & 1566.
*Compton Valence.* Thos. Maldon, priest, demi, *c.* 1440.
*Corfe Mullen.* Rich. Birt, civ., 1437.
*Dorchester, St Peter.* Scroll & inscr. to Joan More, 1436.
*Evershot.* Wm. Grey, priest w. chalice, 1524.
*Fleet.* Mohun, arm. & w., 1603. Ditto, 1612.
*Knowle.* John Clavell, arm. & 2 ws., 1572.
*Litton Cheney.* Palimp. inscr., 1486, & 2 others.
*Lytchett Matravers.* Thos. Pethyn, priest in shroud, *c.* 1470.
*Langton.* John Whitewod, civ. & 2 ws., 1467.
*Melbury Sampford.* Sir Giles Strangwayes, arm. in tab., 1562. Several arms & inscrs.
*Milton Abbey.* Sir John Tregonwell, arm. in tabard, kng., 1565. Inscr. & several good matrices.
*Moor Crichel.* Isabel Uvedale, 1572.
*Moreton.* Jas. Frampton, arm, 1523.
*Pimperne.* Dorothy Williams, qd. pl., 1694.
*Puddlehinton.* Thos. Browne, parson, sm., qd. pl., 1617.
*Puddletown.* Civ., demi, 1517. Arm. in tab., qd. pl., 1524. Arm, 1595.
*Puncknowle.* Wm. Napper, arm., *c.* 1600.
*Purse Caundle.* Arm., 1500. Lady, 1527. Priest, sm., 1536.
*Rampisham.* Thos. Dygenys, civ. & w., 1523.
*Shapwick.* Maria Oke, *c.* 1395.
*Sturminster Marshall.* Henry Helme, vicar, 1581.
*Swanage.* Wives of Wm. Clavell, *c.* 1470.
*Swyre.* Arms & inscr., Russell, 1505. Ditto, 1510.
*Thorncombe.* Sir Thos. Brook, civ. & w., 1436.
*Wimborne Minster.* Half-effigy of St Ethelred, engr. *c.* 1440.
*Woolland.* Mary Argenton, 1616.
*Wraxall.* Arms & inscr., Elizth. Lawrence, 1672.
*Yetminster.* John Horsey, arm. & w., 1531.


## DURHAM

*Auckland, St Andrew.* A canon, *c.* 1400. Cross on qd. pl., sm., 1581.
*Auckland, St Helen.* Civilian & wife, mutil., *c.* 1450.
*Billingham.* Robt. Brerely, priest in almuce, 1480.
*Brancepath.* Rich. Drax, priest in acad., demi, 1456.
*Chester-le-Street.* A lady, perhaps 1430.
*Greatham..* Marginal inscr., *c.* 1350.
*Hartlepool.* Jane Bell, 1593.
*Houghton-le-Skerne.* Dorothy Parkinson, qd. pl., 1592.
*Houghton-le-Spring.* Margery Belassis, qd. pl., 1587.
*Sedgefield.* A lady, *c.* 1340. Two skeletons in shrouds, *c.* 1470.
*Sockburn.* Arms & inscr., Conyers, 1433.

## ESSEX

*Althorne.* B.V.M., etc., to Margt. Hyklott, 1502. Crucifixion, etc., to Wm. Hyklott, 1508.
*Arkesden.* Rich. Fox, arm., 1439.
*Ashen.* Arm. & wife, small, *c.* 1440.
*Aveley.* Arm., qd. pl., foreign, sm., 1370. Child, sm., 1583. Arms & ch., *c.* 1520. Inscr., palimp., 1584. Two children, 1588.
*Baddow, Gt.* Jane Paschall, 1614.
*Bardfield, Gt.* Alionora Bendlowes, 1584.
*Barking.* Pr. in acad., w. chalice, *c.* 1480. Pr., demi, 1485. Civ. & w., 1493, 1596. Children, *c.* 1530. Arms & inscr., Merell, 1598.
*Belchamp St Paul.* Arms, etc., Golding, 1591. Wm. Golding, arm., *c.* 1595.
*Bentley, Little.* Sir Wm. Pyrton, arm. & w., 1501.
*Berden.* Wm. Turnor, civ. & 2 ws., 1473. Thompson, civ. & w., *c.* 1610.
*Blackmore.* Civ., mutilated, *c.* 1450.
*Bocking.* John Doreward, arm. & w., 1420. Oswald Fitch, civ., 1613.
*Boreham.* Alse Canceller, 1573.
*Bowers Gifford.* Sir John Giffard, arm., mutil., 1348.
*Bradfield.* Joan Rysby, 1598.
*Bradwell-juxta-mare.* Margt. Wyott, 1526.
*Braxted, Little.* Wm. Roberts, arm. & 2 wives, 1508.
*Brightlingsea.* Civ. & w., 1496. L., 1505, 1514. Civ. & 2 ws., 1521. Civ. & w., 1525. 2 ladies on earlier bracket, 1536. Civ., 1578.
*Bromley, Gt.* Wm. Byschopton, priest, canopy, 1432.
*Canfield, Gt.* John Wiseman, arm. & w., kng., 1518. Lady, *c.* 1525. Thos. Fytche, civ., 1588.
*Canfield, Little.* 2 ladies, 1578. Ann Pudsey, 1593.
*Chesterford, Gt.* Lady, *c.* 1530. John Howard, child, sm., 1600.
*Chesterford, Little.* Isabel Langham, 1462.
*Chigwell.* Civ. & w., 1620. Archbishop Harsnett, in cope, 1631.
*Chrishall.* Sir John de la Pole, arm. & w., trip. can., *c.* 1370. Lady, sm., *c.* 1450. Civ. & w., kng., *c.* 1480.
*Clavering.* Civ. & w., kng., sm., *c.* 1480. Civ. & w., 1591, 1593.
*Coggeshall.* 2 ladies, *c.* 1490. Civ. & w., *c.* 1500, *c.* 1540. Civ., 1580.
*Colchester, St James.* John Maynard, civ., *c.* 1584. His wife, 1584.
*Colchester, St Peter.* Civ. & w., kng., qd. pl., 1530. 2 civs. & w., 1553; civ., 1563; civ. & 2 ws., 1610, all ditto. Civ. & w., kng., 1572.
*Corringham.* Rich. de Beltoun, pr., demi, *c.* 1340. Civ., sm., *c.* 1460.
*Cressing.* Dorcas Musgrave, 1610.
*Dagenham.* Sir Thos. Urswyk, judge, civ. & w., 1479.
*Dengie.* Lady, *c.* 1520.
*Donyland, E.* Nich. Marshall, civ., 1621. Mary Gray, 1627
*Dunmow, Gt.* A lady, *c.* 1580.
*Easter, Good.* Margaret Norrington, 1610.
*Easton, Little.* Robt. Fyn, pr., *c.* 1420. Henry Bourchier, K.G., Earl of Essex, arm. & w., 1483.
*Eastwood.* Thos. Burrough, civ., 1600.
*Elmdon.* Civ. & 2 ws., *c.* 1530.
*Elmstead.* Two hands holding heart, with scroll, *c.* 1500.
*Elsenham.* Dr Tuer, vicar, 1616. Anne Fielde, 1615. Alice Tuer, 1619.
*Epping.* Thos. Palmer, barrister, 1621.
*Fambridge, N.* Wm. Osborne, civ. & w., 1607.

*Faulkbourn.* Henry Fortescue, arm., 1576. **Mary Darell, 1598.**
*Felstead.* Cristina Bray, demi, 1420. Arm., *c.* 1420.
*Finchingfield.* John Berners, arm. & w., heraldic, 1524.
*Fingringhoe.* John Alleyn, civ., inscr. palimp., *c.* 1610.
*Fryerning.* Lady, palimpsest, *c.* 1560, and fragments.
*Goldhanger.* Audrey Heyham, 1531. Arms, etc., Heyham, 1540.
*Gosfield.* Thos. Rolf, lawyer, in acad., 1440.
*Halstead.* Bartholomew, Lord Bourgchier, & 2 ws., 1409. Lady, 1604.
*Ham, E.* Hester Neve, 1610. Elizth. Heigham, 1622.
*Ham, W.* Thos. Staples, civ. & 4 ws., 1592.
*Hanningfield, W.* Isabel Clonvill, demi, 1361.
*Harlow.* Arm. & w., sm., *c.* 1430. Civ., 1559, 1602, 1615. Civ. & w., *c.* 1480, 1518, 1582, *c.* 1585, *c.* 1630. Civ. & 2 ws., 1636.
*Hatfield Peverel.* John Alleyn, civ. & w., 1572.
*Hempstead.* Civ., *c.* 1475, *c.* 1480. Civ. & w., *c.* 1470, 1492, 1518, *c.* 1530.
*Henny, Gt.* Wm. Fisher, civ. & w., *c.* 1520.
*Heybridge.* John Whitacres, civ., 1627.
*\*Horkesley, Little.* Sir Robt. & Sir Thos. Swynborne, arm., canopies, 1412. Shroud, 1502. 2 arm. & w., heraldic, 1549.
*Hornchurch.* Civ. & w., 1591, 1604. 2 ladies, 1602. Many fragments.
*Horndon, E.* Anne Tyrell, *c.* 1480. Arm., sm., kng., mutil., *c.* 1520.
*Hutton.* Arm. & w., *c.* 1525.
*Ilford, Little.* Thos. Heron, schoolboy, 1517. Anne Hyde, 1630.
*Ingrave.* Margt. Fitz Lewis, 1466. Rich. Fitz Lewis & 4 ws., heraldic, 1528.
*Kelvedon Hatch.* Lady, *c.* 1560.
*Laindon.* Priest w. chalice, *c.* 1480. Ditto, *c.* 1510.
*Lambourne.* Robt. Barfott, civ. & w., 1546.
*Latton.* Sir Peter Arderne, judge, arm. & w., 1467, *c.* 1485. Priest w. chalice, *c.* 1520. Lady, *c.* 1560, 1604. Civ. & w., *c.* 1600.
*Laver, High.* Edw. Sulyard, arm. & w., *c.* 1500.
*Layer Marney.* Arm., *c.* 1430.
*Leigh.* Rich. & John Haddok, civs. & ws., 1453. Rich. Chester, civ. & w., 1632. Price, ditto, 1640.
*Leighs, Gt.* Ralph Strelley, priest, demi, mutil., 1414.
*Leyton, Low.* Ursula Gasper, 1493. Tobias Wood, civ. & w., *c.* 1620.
*Lindsell.* Thos. Fytche, civ. & w., 1514.
*Littlebury.* Civ., *c.* 1480, *c.* 1520. Pr. w. chalice, *c.* 1510. Civ. & w., *c.* 1510. Lady, 1578, 1624.
*Loughton.* Civ. & w., 1541. Arm. & w., *c.* 1560, 1637. Civ., 1594.
*Margaretting.* Arm. & w., curious, *c.* 1550.
*Matching.* John Ballett, civ. & w., 1638.
*Messing.* Lady, *c.* 1530.
*Nettleswell.* Thos. Laurence, civ. & w., 1522. Civ. & w., 1607.
*Newport.* Thos. Brond, civ. & w., 1515. Nightingale, ditto, 1608.
*Norton, Cold.* A lady, *c.* 1520.
*Ockendon, N.* Wm. Poyntz, arm. & w., 1502. Thomasyn Ardall, 1532.
*\*Ockendon, S.* Sir Ingelram Bruyn, canopy, large, 1400. Lady, 1602.
*Ongar, High.* A civilian, *c.* 1510.
*Orsett.* A civilian, sm., kng., *c.* 1535. Fragments, etc.
*Parndon, Gt.* Rowland Rampston, civ., 1598.
*\*Pebmarsh.* Sir Wm. Fitzralph, cross-legged, canopy, large, *c.* 1320.
*Rainham.* A lady, *c.* 1475. Civilian & wife, *c.* 1500.
*Rawreth.* Edm. Tyrell, arm. & w., kng., 1576.

*Rayleigh.* A civilian and wife, mutil., *c.* 1460.
*Rayne.* Arms & inscr., Capell, 1573.
*Rettendon.* Civ. & 2 ws., *c.* 1540. Civ., 1605. Ditto, 1607.
*Rochford.* Maria Dilcok, sm., 1514.
*Roydon.* Thos. Colte, arm. & w., 1471. John Colte, arm. & 2 ws.,
    heraldic, 1521. Civ., *c.* 1580. Lady, 1589.
*Runwell.* Eustace Sulyard, arm. & w., kng., 1587.
*Saffron Walden.* Priest, *c.* 1430. 2 ladies, *c.* 1480. Lady, *c.* 1495, *c.*
    1530. Civ. & w., *c.* 1510, *c.* 1530. Civ. *c.* 1530.
*Sandon.* Patrick Fearne, parson, & w., 1588. Fragments.
*Shopland.* Thos. Stapel, serjeant-at-arms, arm., mutil., 1371.
*Southminster.* Civ. & 2 ws., *c.* 1565. Civ., 1634. Arms, etc., 1556.
*Springfield.* Thos. de Coggeshall, arm., *c.* 1420.
*Stanford Rivers.* Chrysom, 1492. Borrow, arm. & w., 1503. Arm. &
    w., *c.* 1540.
*Stapleford Tawney.* Arms & marginal inscr., Scott, 1505.
*Stebbing.* Lady, large, *c.* 1390.
*Stifford.* Pr., demi, *c.* 1375. Shroud, *c.* 1480. Civ. & w., 1504, 1622.
    Lady, 1627, 1630.
*Stisted.* Elizth. Wyseman, kng., 1584.
*Stock.* Rich. Twedye, arm., 1575.
*Stondon Massey.* Carre, civ. & w., 1570. Civ. & w., palimp., for., 1573.
*Stow Maries.* Mary Browne, 1602.
*Strethall.* Priest in acad., *c.* 1480. Palimp. inscr., 1539.
*Terling.* Wm. Rochester, civ. & w., 1558. Civ. & 2 ws., 1584.
*Thaxted.* Priest in acad., *c.* 1450.
*Theydon Gernon.* Priest in cope, 1458. Ellen Braunche, 1567.
*Thorington.* A lady.
*Thurrock, Grays.* Two ladies, *c.* 1510.
*Thurrock, West.* Humphrey Heies and son, 1585. Kath. Redinge, 1591.
*Tillingham.* Edw. Wiot, civ., kng., 1584.
*Tilty.* Arm. & w., 1520, 1562. Margt. Tuke, 1590.
*Tollesbury.* Civilian & wife, 1517.
*Tolleshunt Darcy.* Arm. & w., palimp. (foreign), 1419. Arm., 1540.
    Palimp. inscr., 1559.
*Toppesfield.* John Cracherowd, civ. & w., 1534.
*Twinstead.* Isaac Wyncoll, civ. & w., 1610.
*Upminster.* L., heraldic, 1455. Civ., palimp., *c.* 1540, 1545. Lady, *c.*
    1555, 1626. Arm., 1591. Fragments.
*Waltham Abbey.* Stacy, civ. & w., qd. pl., 1565. Colte, civ. & w., 1576.
*Waltham, Great.* Rich. Everard, civ., 1617. Civ. & 2 ws., *c.* 1600.
*Waltham, Little.* John Maltoun, arm., 1447.
*Walthamstow.* Monox, civ. & w., 1543. Hale, civ. & w., palimp., 1588.
*Warley, Little.* Anne Hamner, demi, 1592.
*Weald, N.* Walter Larder, civ. & w., 1606.
*Weald, S.* Fragments of ten brasses, *c.* 1450-1634.
*Wendens-Ambo.* Wm. Loveney, arm., *c.* 1410.
*Wenden-Lofts.* Wm. Lucas, civ. & w., *c.* 1450.
*Widdington.* A civilian, *c.* 1445.
*Willinghale Doe.* Thos. Torrell, arm., *c.* 1442. Lady, 1582, 1613.
\*Wimbish.* Sir John de Wautone & w., sm., in head of cross, 1347.
*Woodham Mortimer.* Dorothie Alleine, child, 1584.
*Writtle.* Arm. & w., *c.* 1500. 2 ditto, 1513. Civ. & 4 ws., *c.* 1510. Lady,
    1524, 1592. Civ. & w., 1567, 1606, 1616.

*Wyvenhoe.* Viscount Beaumont, arm., canopy, 1507. Pr. w. chalice, 1535. Elizth., Countess of Oxford, heraldic, canopy, 1537.
*Yeldham, Gt.* Rich. Symonds, civ. & w., *c.* 1611.

## GLOUCESTERSHIRE

*Abbenhall.* Rich. Pyrke, civ. & w., 1609.
*Berkeley.* Wm. Freme, civ., holding a heart, 1526.
*Bisley.* Kath. Sewell, 1515.
*Bristol—*
  *St James.* Henry Gibbes, civ. & w., 1636.
  *St John.* Thos. Rowley, civ. & w., 1478.
  *St Mary Redcliff.* Chief Justice Sir John Juyn, 1439. Arm. in tab. & 2 ws., qd. pl., 1475. Civ. & w., canopy, 1480. Serjt.-at-law & w., 1522.
  *St Peter.* Robt. Lond, priest w. chalice, 1461.
  *St Werburgh.* Wm. Gyttyns, civ. & w., qd. pl., 1586.
  *Temple Church.* Civ., demi, 1396. Priest in cope, palimp., *c.* 1460.
  *Trinity Almshouses.* John Barstaple, civ., 1411. Lady, *c.* 1411.
  *Grammar School.* Nich. Thorne, civ. & 2 ws., *c.* 1570.
*Cheltenham, St Mary.* Sir Wm. Greville, judge, & w., 1513.
*Chipping Campden.* Wool-merchant & w., can., 1401. Civ. & w., 1450, 1467. Civ. & 3 ws., 1484.
*Cirencester.* Arm. & w., can., 1438. Pr. w. chalice, 1478. Pr. in cassock, *c.* 1480. 12 brasses of civs. (wool-merchants) & ws., *c.* 1400, 1440, 1442, 1462, *c.* 1470, *c.* 1480, 1497, *c.* 1500, *c.* 1500, *c.* 1530, 1587, 1626, and fragments.
*Clifford Chambers.* Hercules Raynsford, arm. & w., 1583. Lady, 1601.
*Deerhurst.* Sir John Cassy, judge, & w., can., 1400. L., *c.* 1520, 1525.
*Dowdeswell.* Priest in cope, *c.* 1520.
*Dyrham.* Sir Morys Russel & w., canopy, large, 1401.
*Eastington.* Elizth. Knevet, heraldic, 1518.
*Fairford.* Tame, arm. & w., 1500. Ditto & 2 ws., heraldic, 1534.
*Gloucester, St John Bapt.* John Semys, civ. & 2 ws., 1540.
*Gloucester, St Mary de Crypt.* John Cook, civ. & w., can., 1544.
*Gloucester, St Michael.* Alys & Agnes Henshawe, 1519.
*Kempsford.* Walt. Hichman, civ. & w., 1521.
*Lechlade.* Civ. & w., 1450. Civ., *c.* 1510.
*Leckhampton.* Wm. Norwoodd, civ. & w., qd. pl., 1598.
*Micheldean.* Margery & Alice Baynham, *c.* 1485.
*Minchinhampton.* Civ. & w., *c.* 1500, 1519. Ditto in shrouds, *c.* 1510.
*Newent.* Roger Porter, arm., sm., 1523.
*Newland.* Arm. & w., *c.* 1445.
*Northleach.* 7 brasses of civs. (wool-merchants) & ws., *c.* 1400, 1447, 1458, *c.* 1485, *c.* 1490, 1501, 1526. Pr. in surplice, kng., *c.* 1530.
*Olveston.* Morys & Sir Walt. Denys, arm. in tabards, 1505.
*Quinton.* Joan Clopton, vowess, canopy, *c.* 1430.
*Rodmarton.* John Edward, lawyer, 1461.
*Sevenhampton.* John Camber, civ., 1497.
*Thornbury.* Avice Tyndall, 1571.
*Todenham.* Wm. Molton, civ. & w., 1614.
*Tormarton.* John Ceysyll, civ., 1493.
*Weston-upon-Avon.* Greville, arm. in tabard, 1546. Ditto, 1559.

*Weston-sub-Edge.* Wm. Hodges, civ., 1590.
*Whittington.* Rich. Coton, civ. & w., 1560.
*Winterbourne.* A lady, *c.* 1370.
*Wormington.* Anne Savage, in a bed, 1605.
*Wotton-under-Edge.* Thos. Lord Berkeley & w., large, 1392.
*Yate.* Alex. Staples, civ. & 2 ws., 1590.

# HAMPSHIRE

*Aldershot.* Arms & inscr., Sir John Whyte, *c.* 1573.
*Alton.* Lady, *c.* 1510. Several frags. & inscrs.
*Andover.* Arms & inscr., Nich. Venables, 1602.
*Basingstoke.* Robt. Stocker, civ. & w., 1606. Child, 1621.
*Bramley.* Wm. Joye, civ., 1452. Gwen Shelford, 1504. **Civ. & w.,** sm., 1529.
*Bramshott.* John Weston, civ. & w., *c.* 1430. *Nr Headley.*
*Candover, Brown.* Civilian & wife, *c.* 1520. *nr Winchester*
*Candover, Preston.* Kath. Dabrigecort, 1607.
*Chilbolton.* Arms & inscr., Thos. Tutt, *c.* 1610.
*Christchurch.* Many empty matrices to priors and monks, etc.
*Crondall.* Nich. de Kaerwent, priest, large, 1381. John Gyfford, arm., kng., sm., 1563. Skeleton, qd. pl., 1641.
*Dogmersfield.* Anne Sutton, qd. pl., 1590.
*Dummer.* Wm. at Moore, civ., kng., *c.* 1580.
*Eling.* Arms & inscr., Wm. Pawlet, 1596.
*Eversley.* Large cross to Rich. Pendilton, 1502.
*Fareham.* Arms & inscr., Constance Riggs, 1653.
*Farlington.* Arms & inscr., Antony Pounde, 1547.
*Fordingbridge.* Wm. Bulkeley, arm. & w., kng., qd. pl., 1568.
*Froyle.* John Lighe, civ., 1575.
*Hale.* Arms & inscr., Sir John Penruddocke, 1600.
*Hartley Wespall.* Arms & inscr., John Waspaill, 1452.
*Havant.* Thos. Aileward, priest in cope, 1413.
*Headbourne Worthy.* John Kent, civ., sm., 1434. *Nr. Winchester*
*Headley.* Civilian & wife, sm., *c.* 1510. *Nr Bramshott*
*Heckfield.* Elizth. Hall, 1514. Several inscrs.
*Hinton Ampner.* Arms & inscr., Stewkeley, 1642. Several inscrs.
*Itchen Stoke.* Joan Batmanson, 1518. *Nr. Winchester*
*Kimpton.* Robt. Thornburgh, arm. & 2 ws., kng., 1522.
*Kingsclere.* Wm. Estwood, priest, sm., 1519. Lady, sm., 1503.
*Lymington.* Arms & inscr., Joan Guidott, 1668.
*Mapledurwell.* John Canner, civ. & w., sm., *c.* 1525.
*Monxton.* Alice Swayne, kng., sm., 1599.
*Mottisfont.* Arms & inscr., Sir Wm. Sandys, 1628.
*Nursling.* Arms & inscr., Andrew Mundy, 1632.
*Oakley, Church.* Robt. Warham, civ. & w., 1487.
*Odiham.* Civ. & w., *c.* 1480. Pr., 1498. Lady, 1504, 1522. Civ., *c.* 1535. Arm., *c.* 1540. Child, 1636.
*Prior's Dean.* John Compton, civ. & w., 1605.
*Ringwood.* John Prophete, priest in cope, w. saints, can., 1416.
*Sherborne St John.* Civ. & w., demi, *c.* 1360. Arm. in tab., kng., 1488. Arm., kng., sm., 1492. Arm. & 2 ws., sm., 1492. Arm., kng., sm., *c.* 1540.

*Sherfield-on-Loddon.* Lady, qd. pl., 1595. Civ., kng., sm., *c.* 1600.
*Sombourne, King's.* Two civilians, *c.* 1380.
*Southampton, God's House.* Priest in cope, *c.* 1500.
*Southwick.* Arm. & w., sm., *c.* 1520, appropriated palimp.
*Stoke Charity.* Wayte, arm., 1482. Hampton, arm. & w., 1483.
*Sutton, Bishops.* Arm. & wife, *c.* 1520.
*Thruxton.* Sir John Lysle, canopy, *c.* 1425.
*Tytherley, W.* Anne Whittehede, 1480.
*Wallop, Nether.* Dame Mary Gore, prioress, 1436.
*Warnborough, S.* Robt. Whyte, arm., kng., sm., 1512.
*Weeke.* Fig. of St Christopher, for Wm. Complyn & w., 1498.
*Whitchurch.* Rich. Brooke, civ. & w., 1603.
*Winchester College, Chapel & Cloisters.* Facsimiles of lost originals, 3
   wardens & 8 fellows, some demi, 5 in euch., 1 in almuce, 4 in cope,
   1 in acad., 1413-1559. Civ., 1498. Palimp., 1559, and many inscrs.
*Winchester, St Cross.* John de Campeden, pr. in cope, 1382. Pr. in
   alm., 1493. Pr., 1518, & inscrs.
*Winchester, St Maurice.* Children in swaddling-clothes, 1612.
*Winchfield.* Arms & inscr., Rudyerd, 1652 & 1659.
*Yateley.* Civ. & w., 1517, 1532. Lady, mutil., 1578. Civ., *c.* 1590.

## HEREFORDSHIRE

*Brampton Abbotts.* Joan Rudhale, sm., 1506.
*Burghill.* John Awbry, civ. & w., qd. pl., 1616.
*Clehonger.* Arm. & w., *c.* 1470.
*Colwall.* Anth. Harford, arm. & w., qd. pl., *c.* 1590.
*Hereford Cathedral.* Bp. Trilleck, canopy, 1360. Priest in cope, in
   head of cross, *c.* 1360. Pr. in cope, *c.* 1430, 1434, *c.* 1480. Dean
   Frowsetoure, in cope, canopy, 1529. Arm. & w., can., large, 1435.
   Arm. & 2 ws., 1514. Fragments.
*Ledbury.* Pr. in acad., kng., *c.* 1410. Arm., 1490. Arm., qd. pl., 1614.
*Ludford.* Wm. Fox, arm. & w., 1554.
*Marden.* Margt. Chute, 1614.

## HERTFORDSHIRE

*Albury.* Arm. & w., *c.* 1475. Civ. & w., 1588. Arm. & w., qd. pl.,
   1592.
*Aldbury.* Verney, arm. in tab. & w., heraldic, 1547. Civ., sm., 1478.
*Aldenham.* 9 civ. brasses, w. ladies, *c.* 1520-*c.* 1535, 1608. Shroud, 1547.
*Amwell, Gt.* A friar, *c.* 1450. Civ. & 2 ws.
*Ardeley.* Philip Metcalff, priest, 1515. Thos. Shotbolt, civ. & w., 1599.
*Aspenden.* Civ. & w., 1500. Clyfford, arm. in tab. & w., kng., 1508.
*Aston.* John Kent, civ. & w., 1592.
*Baldock.* L., *c.* 1410. Civ. & w., *c.* 1420, *c.* 1480. Shrouds, *c.* 1480.
*Barkway.* Robt. Poynard & 2 ws., 1561.
*Barley.* Andrew Willet, minister, 1621.
*Bayford.* Arm. & w., *c.* 1550. Arm., *c.* 1610.
*Bennington.* A Canon of Windsor, in cope, mutil., *c.* 1450.
*Berkhamstead, Gt.* Civ. & w., 1356. Arm., *c.* 1365. Lady, *c.* 1370.
   Pr., demi, *c.* 1400. Civ., 1485. Lady in shroud, sm., 1520.
*Braughing.* Barbara Hanchett, 1561.
*Broxbourn.* Pr. w. chalice, *c.* 1470. Arm. in tab. & w., heraldic, 1473.
   Pr. in acad., *c.* 1510. Serjeant-at-arms, 1531.

*Buckland.* Lady, 1451. Pr. in cope, w. chalice, 1478. Civ., 1499.

*Cheshunt.* Canopy, etc., for Nich. Dixon, pr., 1448. Civ. & w., 1499. Lady, 1453, *c.* 1500, 1609.

*\*Clothall.* John Wynter, pr., 1404. Pr. w. chalice, 1519. Pr. in cope, 1541. Lady, 1572. Ecclesiastic, 1602.

*Datchworth.* Device & inscr., 1622.

*\*Digswell.* Arm. & w., large, 1415. Arm., 1442. Shrouds, 1484. Civ. & w., 1495, *c.* 1530.

*Eastwick.* Joan Lee, 1564.

*Essendon.* Wm. Tooke, civ. & w., kng., 1588. Arms, etc., *c.* 1600.

*Flamstead.* Priest in cope, 1414. Civ. & w., *c.* 1470

*Gaddesden, Gt.* Wm. Croke, civ. & w., 1506. Civ. & w., sm., *c.* 1525.

*Hadham, Gt.* Priest in acad., demi, *c.* 1420. Civ. & w., 1582. Civ. & 2 ws., 1610.

*Hadham, Little.* Pr. in cope, sm., *c.* 1470. Arm. & w., *c.* 1485.

*Harpenden.* Anabull, civ. & w., 1456. Cressye, civ. & w., 1571.

*Hatfield.* Arms & inscr., Fulke Onslow, 1602.

*Hemel Hempstead.* Robt. Albyn, arm. & w., *c.* 1400.

*Hinxworth.* Ward, civ. & w., 1481. Lambard, civ. & w., 1487.

*Hitchin.* 6 civ. brasses w. ladies, 1421–*c.* 1550. 4 shroud brasses, *c.* 1480-1490. Priest in cope, 1498. A heart, 1474.

*Hunsdon.* Lady in shroud, 1495. Jas. Gray, park-keeper, w. Death, etc., qd. pl., 1591.

*Ickleford.* Thos. Somer, civ. & w., demi, *c.* 1400.

*Ippolyts.* Ryce Hughes, civ. & w., qd. pl., 1594.

*Kelshall.* Rich. Adane, civ. & w., 1435.

*Kimpton.* A lady, *c.* 1450.

*Knebworth.* Priest in cope, w. saints, 1414. Arm. & 2 ws., 1582.

*Langley, Abbot's.* 2 ladies, sm., 1498. Civ. & 2 ws., 1607.

*Langley, King's.* Lady, 1528, *c.* 1600. Civ. & 2 ws., 1588.

*Letchworth.* Civ. & w., demi, *c.* 1400. Priest w. heart & scrolls, 1475.

*\*Mimms, N.* Priest, foreign, *c.* 1360. L., 1458. Arm., 1488. Civ. & w., *c.* 1490. Child, 1531. Arm. & w., *c.* 1560.

*Newnham.* Civ. & 2 ws., *c.* 1490. Lady, 1607.

*Offley.* Samwel, civ. & 2 ws., 1529. Civ. & 3 ws., *c.* 1530.

*Pelham, Brent.* Two ladies, 1627.

*Pelham, Furneux.* Civ. & w., canopy, *c.* 1420. Arm. & w., 1518.

*Radwell.* Civ. & w., 1492. Civ. & 2 ws., 1516. Lady, 1602.

*Redbourn.* Pecok, civ., 1512. Rede, arm. & w., kng., 1560.

*Rickmansworth.* Thos. Day, civ. & 2 ws., 1613.

*Royston.* Pr. in acad., canopy, 1432. Cross, w. heart & wounds, *c.* 1450. Civ. & w., *c.* 1500.

*\*St Alban's, Abbey.* Abbot Delamere, *c.* 1360. Palimp. frag. of abbot *c.* 1400. 4 monks, *c.* 1450, *c.* 1470, *c.* 1470, 1521. Arm. & w., *c.* 1465, 1519. Arm., 1480. Civ. & w., 1411. Civ., *c.* 1465, *c.* 1470, and fragments.

*\*St Alban's, St Michael.* John Pecok, civ. & w., *c.* 1380. Arm., *c.* 1380. Civ. in cross, *c.* 1400.

*St Alban's, St Peter.* Roger Pemberton, civ., 1627.

*St Alban's, St Stephen.* Wm. Robins, arm. & w., 1482.

*Sandon.* John Fitz-Geffrey, arm. & w., 1480.

*Sawbridgeworth.* Arm. & w., 1433, *c.* 1600. Civ. & 2 ws., 1470. Shrouds, 1484. Lady, 1527, *c.* 1600.

*Standon.* Civ., *c.* 1460. Civ. & arm., 1477. Arm., 1557.

*Stanstead Abbots.* Arm., *c.* 1480. Civ. & w., *c.* 1540. Ditto, 1581.

*Stevenage.* Steph. Hellard, priest in cope, *c.* 1500.
*Tewin.* Thos. Pygott, civ., 1610.
*Walkerne.* Civ. & w., *c.* 1480. Ditto, 1583. Ditto, 1636.
*Ware.* Lady, *c.* 1400. Ditto, 1454. Civ. & 2 ws., *c.* 1470.
*Watford.* Sir Hugh de Holes, judge, & w., large, 1415. 3 civs., qd. pl., 1613.
*Watton.* Arm., canopy, 1361. Pr. in cope, can., *c.* 1370. Civ., *c.* 1450, *c.* 1470. Lady, 1455. Arm., 1514. Lady, *c.* 1550.
*Wheathamstead.* Civ. & w., *c.* 1450, *c.* 1510. Arm., much mutil., *c.* 1500. John Heyworth, arm. & w., 1520.
*Willian.* Rich. Goldon, priest w. heart, 1446.
*Wormley.* Civ. & w., 1479. Ditto, *c.* 1490. Ditto, 1598.
*Wyddiall.* John Gille, civ. & w., 1546. Margt. Plumbe, demi, 1575.


## HUNTINGDONSHIRE

*Broughton.* Laurence Martun, civ., mutil., *c.* 1490.
*Diddington.* Wm. Taylard, arm. & w., kng., w. saints, 1505. Lady, 1513.
*Gidding, Little.* Arms & inscr., 1656, 1657, 1717, 1719.
*Godmanchester.* Civilian, *c.* 1500.
*Offord Darcy.* Arm. & 2 ws., *c.* 1440. Priest in acad., kng., *c.* 1530.
*Sawtry All Saints'.* Wm. Le Moigne, arm. & w., 1404.
*Somersham.* Priest, *c.* 1530.
*Standground.* Arms & inscr., Elias Petit, 1634.
*Stilton.* Rich. Curthoyse, civ. & w., 1606. 2 civs., 1618.
*Stukeley, Little.* Civilian, *c.* 1590.


## ISLE OF WIGHT

*Arreton.* Harry Hawles, arm., mutil., *c.* 1430.
*Calbourne.* Arm., *c.* 1380. Time, Death, etc., to Daniel Evance, rector, 1652. Arms & inscr., Price, 1638.
*Carisbrooke.* Arms, Keeling, 1619.
*Freshwater.* Adam de Compton, arm., 1367.
*Kingston.* Rich. Mewys, civ., 1535.
*Shorwell.* Rich. Bethell, pr. in cassock & scarf, 1518. Wives of Barnabas Leigh, qd. pl., 1619. Arms, etc., Leigh, 1621. *REV. WAKEFIELD.*


## KENT

*Acrise.* Mary Heyman, 1601. Arms, etc., Hamon, 1613.
*Addington.* Arm., demi, 1378. Arm. & w., canopy, 1409. Arm., *c.* 1425, *c.* 1460. Arm. & w., 1470. Priest, demi, w. chalice, *c.* 1470.
*Aldington.* Arm. & w., *c.* 1470. Fragment, 1475.
*Ash, near Sandwich.* Lady, mutil., can., *c.* 1440. L., *c.* 1460. Civ. & w., sm., 1525. Arm. & w., 1602. Civ. & w., 1642.
*Ash, near Wrotham.* Rich. Galon, priest, demi, 1465.
*Ashford.* Lady, mutil., canopy, 1375. Several fragments.

L

*Aylesford.* Cosyngton, arm. & w., 1426. Palimp. inscr., Savell, 1545.
*Beckenham.* Arm. in tabard & 2 ws., heraldic, kng., 1552. Lady, 1563.
*Bethersden.* Wm. Lovelace, civ., 1459. Thos. Lovelace, civ., sm., 1591.
*Bexley.* A hunting-horn, etc., c. 1450. Civ., sm., 1513.
*Biddenden.* 2 civs. & w., sm., c. 1520. Arm. & w., kng., 1566. Civ.,
    1593. Civ. & w., 1628, 1641, 1685. Civ. & 2 ws., 1584, 1598, 1609.
*Birchington.* Civ., 1449, 1459. Lady, 1518, 1528, 1533. John Heynys,
    priest w. chalice, 1523.
*Birling.* Walter Mylys, civ., 1522.
*Bobbing.* Arm. & w., c. 1420. Arm., mutil., can., 1420. L., 1496.
*Borden.* Civilian, c. 1460. Priest in almuce, 1490.
*Boughton Malherbe.* Civ. & w., kng., sm., 1499. Arm. & w., 1529.
*Boughton-under-Blean.* Civ. & w., 1508, 1591, and 1591. Arm., 1587.
*Boxley.* Wm. Snell, priest in acad., 1451. Arm., 1576.
*Brabourn.* Arm., canopy, 1434. Lady, 1450, 1528. Arm., 1527.
*Bredgar.* Thos. Coly, priest in acad., w. chalice, 1518.
*Brenchley.* Civilian & 3 ws., c. 1500. Civ. & w., c. 1540.
*Bromley.* Rich. Thornhill & 2 ws., 1600.
*Brookland.* Thos. Leddes, priest, sm., 1503.
*Canterbury—*
    *St Alphege.* Priest in acad., 1523. Arms, etc., Prude, c. 1510.
    *St George.* John Lovelle, priest in cope, without almuce, 1438.
    *St Margaret.* John Wynter, civ., 1470.
    *St Martin.* Civ. & w., 1587. Arm., 1591, and inscrs.
    *St Mary Northgate.* Raff Brown, civ., c. 1540.
    *St Paul.* Geo. Wyndbourne, civ. & w., 1531.
*Capel-le-Ferne.* John Gybbis, civ. & w., sm., 1526.
*Challock.* Thos. Thorston, civ. & w., sm., 1508.
*Chart, Great.* Notary, c. 1470. Civ. & w., 1485, 1500, 1565. **Civ. &**
    5 ws., 1499. Arm. & 2 ws., 1513. Civ., kng., 1680.
*Chart, Little.* Arms & inscr., Darell, 1438.
*\*Chartham.* Sir Robt. de Setvans, 1306. Priest in cope, 1416, 1454.
    Priest in almuce, 1508. Lady, sm., 1530.
*Chelsfield.* Crucifix, etc., mutil., to Robt. de Brun, priest, 1417. Priest,
    sm., 1420. Lady, c. 1480, 1510.
*Cheriton.* Priest in acad., 1474. Child, 1502. Lady, 1592.
*Chevening.* Arms & inscr., Lennard, 1556. Civ. & wife, 1596.
*Chiddingstone.* Arms, etc., Birchensty, 1537, and other inscrs.
*Chislehurst.* Alan Porter, priest, demi, 1482.
*Cliffe.* Thos. Faunce, civ. & w., 1609. Civ. & 2 wives, 1652.
*\*Cobham.* Lady, c. 1320, 1375, 1380, 1395. Arm., 1354, c. 1365, 1367,
    1405, 1407, all large w. fine canopies. Priest in almuce, demi, 1418.
    Pr. in cope, c. 1450, 1498. Ditto on bracket, c. 1420. Cross, mutil.,
    1447. Arm., demi, 1402. Lady, 1433. Lady, canopy, 1506. Arm. &
    w., 1529.
*Cooling.* Feyth Brooke, sm., 1508, and inscrs.
*Cranbrook.* Civ. & chrysom, c. 1520. Civ. & w., kng., c. 1640.
*Cray, St Mary.* Civ. & 3 ws., 1508. L., 1544. Civ. & w., 1604. l..,
    qd. pl., 1747. Civ., qd. pl., 1775.
*Cudham.* Alice Waleys, 1503.
*Cuxton.* Palimpsest inscrs., 1500, 1545.
*Dartford.* Civ. & w., can., 1402. Lady, 1454, 1464, c. 1590, and 1612.
    Civ. & w., 1496. Civ., 1508. Civ. & 2 ws., 1590, and inscrs.
*Davington.* Civ. & w., kng., qd. pl., 1613. Lady, kng., qd. pl., 1613.
*Deal, Upper.* Civ. & w., 1508. Arm., kng., 1562. Chrysom, 1606.

*Denton.* Arms & inscr., John Boys, 1543.
*Ditton.* Rowland Shakerley, arm., mutil., 1576.
*Dover, St James.* Vincent Huffam, eccles. & w., c. 1600.
*Dover, St Mary.* Wm. Jones, civ. & w., 1636.
*Downe.* Civilian, sm., c. 1420. Civ. & w., c. 1420. Civ. & w., 1607.
*Eastry.* Thos. Nevynson, arm. & w., 1590.
*Edenbridge.* John Selyard, civ., 1558.
*Elmsted.* Lady, c. 1510, and several inscriptions.
*Erith.* Civ., sm., 1425. Civ. & w., 1435, 1511. Lady, 1471. Edw.
    Hawte, arm. & w., 1537.
*Farningham.* Priest, demi, 1451. Lady, sm., 1514. Civ., kng., 1517.
    Thos. Sibill, arm. & w., 1519.
*Faversham.* Civ., mutil., can., 1414. Pr. in cope, can., c. 1480. Pr.
    w. chalice, 1531. Civ., c. 1500, c. 1580, 1610. Civ. & w., can.,
    1533. Civ. & 2 ws., 1533, and many fragments, arms and inscrs.
*Fordwich.* Aphra Hawkins, 1605.
*Gillingham.* Arms & inscr., Wm. Beaufitz, 1433.
*Goodnestone.* Civilian and wife, 1507, 1558 and 1568.
*Goudhurst.* Arm., canopy, 1424. Ditto, c. 1490. Arm. & w., c. 1520.
*Graveney.* Lady & son, demi, c. 1370. Rich. de Feversham, arm.,
    1381. John Martyn, judge, & w., can., 1436.
*Halling.* Silvester Lambarde, in a bed, qd. pl., 1587.
*Halstead.* Wm. Burys, arm., 1444. Wm. Petley, civ. & w., 1528.
*Halstow, High.* Wm. Palke, minister, & w., sm., 1618.
*Hardres, Upper.* John Strete, pr. in acad. & bracket, 1405. Arms &
    inscrs., Hardres, 1533 and 1575.
*Harrietsham.* Susanna Parthericke, kng., qd. pl., 1603.
*Harty.* Habram Fare, civ., mutil., 1515. Arms & inscr., Haward, 1610.
*Hawkhurst.* John Roberts, civ. & w., c. 1495.
*Hayes.* Priest, demi, c. 1460. Priest, sm., c. 1470. Ditto, 1523.
*Headcorn.* John Byrd, child, kng., qd. pl., 1636.
*Herne.* Arm. & w., c. 1420. Pr. in acad., c. 1450. Lady, 1470, 1539.
    Civ. & 2 ws., 1604.
*Hever.* Lady, 1419. Sir Thos. Bullen, K.G., 1538. Eccles., kng., 1585.
*Higham.* Arms & inscr., Boteler, 1615.
*Hoath.* Lady, c. 1430. Civilian & w., palimp., sm., 1532.
*Hoo, All Hallows.* Wm. Copinger, arm., kng., 1594.
*Hoo, St Werburgh.* Pr., demi, c. 1410. Pr., large, 1412. Civ., c. 1430.
    2 civs., 1446. Arm. & w., 1465. Lady, 1615. Civ. & w., 1640.
*Horsmonden.* Priest, large, can., c. 1340. Lady, 1604.
*Horton Kirby.* Lady, c. 1470. Civilian & wife, 1595.
*Hunton.* Civilian, c. 1510. Arms, etc., Francis Fane, 1651.
*Ightham.* Clement, arm. in tabard & w., 1528. Lady, 1626, and inscrs.
*Iwade.* Simon Snellyng, civ. & w., c. 1450.
*Kemsing.* Thos. de Hop, priest, demi, c. 1320.
*Kingsnorth.* Humf. Clarke, & wife, c. 1550. Arms & inscr., 1579.
*Langdon, E.* A lady, small, c. 1570.
*Lee.* Lady, sm., 1545. L., 1582. Nich. Ansley, arm., kng., 1593.
*Leeds.* Kath. Lambe, sm., 1414. Wm. Merden, civ. & w., sm., 1509.
*Leigh.* Lady in a tomb, qd. pl., sm., c. 1580, and several inscriptions.
*Lenham.* Arms, etc., Codd, 1631.
*Linstead.* Lady, c. 1570. Civ. & w., 1621. Arms, etc., 1637, 1642.
*Luddesdown.* Man in armour, mutilated, c. 1440.
*Lullingstone.* Arms, etc., Rokesle, 1361. Sir Wm. Pecche, arm., 1487.
    Alice Baldwyn, sm., 1533. Elizth. Hart, 1544.

*Lydd.* Priest in acad., 1420. Civ. & w., canopy, 1430. Civ., 1429, *c.* 1510, *c.* 1530, 1570, 1597, 1608, 1613. Civ. & w., 1557, 1566, and *c.* 1590.

*Maidstone, All Saints.* Thos. Beale, civ. & w., qd. pl., 1593. Civ. & w., qd. pl., 1640.

*Malling, E.* Selby, civ. & w., 1479. Pr. in almuce, w. chal., sm., 1522.

*Malling, W.* Civilian, sm., 1497. Ditto, 1532. Lady, mutilated, 1543.

*\*Margate, St John.* Civ., 1431. Heart & scrolls, 1433. Civ. & w., 1441. Civ., 1442. Arm., 1445. Skeleton, 1446. Priest, sm., 1515. Palimp. inscr., foreign, 1582. Arm., 1638.

*Mereworth.* John de Mereworth, arm. & canopy, mutil., 1371. Civ. & w., 1479. Civ., kng., 1542.

*Mersham.* Priest, *c.* 1480, and several inscriptions.

*Milton-next-Sittingbourne.* Arm., *c.* 1470. John Norwood, arm. in tabard & w., 1496. Margt. Alese, 1539.

*\*Minster-in-Sheppey.* Sir John de Northwode & w., *c.* 1330.

*Monkton.* A priest, *c.* 1460.

*Murston.* John Eveas, arm. & w., 1488.

*Newington.* Two civs., 1488. Lady, 1580, 1600. Civ. & 2 ws., 1581.

*Newington-juxta-Hythe.* Lady, mutil., *c.* 1480. Civ. in shroud & w., 1501. Priest w. chal., sm., 1501. Civ. & 3 ws., 1522. Civ. *c.* 1600. Arm. & w., 1630, and seven inscriptions.

*Northfleet.* Priest, large, 1375. Pr., demi, 1391. Arm. & w., 1433.

*Orpington.* Arms, etc., Gulby, 1439. Priest in cope, 1511.

*Otham.* Thos. Hendley, civ. & 3 ws., kng., qd. pl., 1590.

*Otterden.* Man in armour, 1402, 1502, 1508. Lady, 1487, *c.* 1630.

*Peckham, E.* A civilian & wife, small, *c.* 1525.

*Peckham, W.* Elizth. Culpepir, 1460.

*Pembury.* Elizth. Rowe, child, 1607.

*Penshurst.* Small cross, *c.* 1520. Civ. & w., 1514, and many arms & inscriptions.

*Pluckley.* Arm., 1440. Arm. & w., *c.* 1510. Lady, 1526. Arm., *c.* 1600. Ditto, qd. pl., *c.* 1600. Arm. & w., kng., qd. pl., *c.* 1630. Arm. in tabard, ditto, *c.* 1630.

*Preston, near Faversham.* Arm. & w., 1442. Arm., 1459. Lady, 1615.

*Rainham.* Lady, *c.* 1500. Civ., 1529. Civ. & w., *c.* 1580.

*Ringwould.* Lady, mutil., sm., 1505. Civ., sm., 1530.

*Ripple.* Arms & inscr., Warren, 1591, 1612.

*Rochester, St Margaret.* Thos. Cod, priest in cope, palimp., 1465.

*Romney, New.* Arms & inscr., 1375. Civ., 1510. Civ. & w., 1610.

*Romney, Old.* John Ips, civ. & w., sm., *c.* 1520.

*St Laurence, Thanet.* Arm., 1444. Lady, *c.* 1490. Arms & inscr., 1610.

*St Mary-in-the-Marsh.* Matilda Jamys, 1499. Wm. Gregory, civ., 1502.

*St Nicholas, Thanet.* Two civs., Edvarod & Parramore, & w., 1574.

*St Peter, Thanet.* Rich. Colmer, civ. & w., 1485. Nich. Esstone, civ. & w., sm., 1503.

*Saltwood.* Priest, demi, *c.* 1370. Arm. & w., 1437. Angel & heart, etc., for Anne Muston, 1496.

*Sandwich, St Clement.* Civ., can., *c.* 1490. Arms & inscr., 1583, 1597.

*\*Seal.* Lord Wm. de Bryene, arm., 1395.

*Selling, near Faversham.* A civilian, *c.* 1530. Fragments, *c.* 1530.

*Sheldwich.* Arm. & w. & canopy, 1394. Arm. & w., 1426. Joan Mareys, in shroud, demi, 1431.

*Shorne.* Civ. & w., demi, 1457. Lady, *c.* 1470, 1583. Chalice, 1519.

*Snodland.* Civ., sm., 1441. Ditto, 1486. Civ. & w., 1487. Civ. & 2 ws., 1541.

*Southfleet.* Joan Urban, on bracket, 1414. Civ. & w., 1420. Priest in cope, demi, 1457. Shroud, *c.* 1520. Civ. & w., *c.* 1520.

*Staple.* A civilian, *c.* 1510.

*Staplehurst.* A lady, *c.* 1580.

*Stockbury.* Hooper, civ. & w., qd. pl., *c.* 1630. Lady, qd. pl., 1648.

*Stoke.* Wm. Cardiff,, priest, 1415. Arms, etc., Williams, 1577.

*\*Stone.* Priest in head of cross, 1408. Arms & inscr., 1574.

*Stourmouth.* Thos. Mareys, priest in acad., 1472.

*Sundridge.* Roger Isly, arm., 1429. Civ., *c.* 1440. Arm. & w., 1520.

*Sutton, E.* Sir Edw. Filmer, arm. & w., qd. pl., 1638.

*Teynham.* Arm., 1444. Civ., 1509. Ditto, sm., 1533. Civ. & w., 1639.

*Thannington.* Thos. Halle, arm., 1485.

*Tilmanstone.* Rich. Fogg, civ. & w., kng., qd. pl., *c.* 1600.

*Trotterscliffe.* Wm. Crofton, civ. & w., 1483.

*Tunstall.* Priest, 1525. Lady, *c.* 1590, and several inscriptions.

*Ulcombe.* Arm. & canopy, 1419. Arm. & w., 1470.

*Upchurch.* Civilian & wife, demi, *c.* 1340.

*Westerham.* Civ. & w., 1529. Civ., 1531. Civ. & 2 ws., 1533. Two civs., *c.* 1545. Civ. & 2 ws., 1557, 1566. Wm. Dye, parson, 1567, and inscriptions.

*\*Wickham, E.* John de Bladigdone, civ. & w., demi, in head of cross, *c.* 1325. Yeoman of the Guard & 3 ws., 1568.

*Wickham, W.* Wm. de Thorp, pr., sm., 1407. Stokton, ditto, 1515.

*\*Woodchurch.* Priest in head of cross, *c.* 1320. Civ. & w., 1539.

*Wrotham.* Civ. & w., 1498. Civ., *c.* 1500. Arm. & w., 1512. Ditto, heraldic, 1525. Arm., *c.* 1530. Arm. & w., 1611. Lady, 1615.

*Wye.* Two civs., John Andrew and Thos. Palmere, & w., *c.* 1440.


## LANCASHIRE

*Childwall.* Henry Norris, arm. & w., heraldic, 1524.

*Eccleston.* Priest in cope, *c.* 1485.

*Flixton.* R. Radclyffe, civ. & 2 wives, *c.* 1580.

*Lancaster, St Mary.* Thos. Covell, civilian, 1639.

*Manchester Cathedral.* Arm. & w., much mutil., *c.* 1465. Stanley, Bishop of Ely, 1515. Arm. & w., palimpsest, 1548. Civ. & w., qd. pl., 1607. Ditto, 1630.

*Middleton.* Priest w. chalice, 1522. Arm. & w., *c.* 1530. 2 arm. & w., 1531. Assheton, civ. & w., 1618. Ditto, arm. & w., 1650.

*Newchurch.* Children & inscr., Ratclyff, 1561.

*Ormskirk.* Arm. in tabard, Scarisbrick, *c.* 1500.

*Preston.* Seath Bushell, civ., 1623.

*Rufford.* Sir Robt. Hesketh, arm., inscr., palimpsest, 1543.

*Sefton.* Margt. Bulcley, canopy, 1528. Sir Wm. Molineux, arm. & 2 ws., 1568. Ditto, *c.* 1570.

*Ulverstone.* Myles Dodding, civ. & w., 1606.

*Walton-on-the-Hill.* Thos. Beri, civilian, 1586.

*Whalley Abbey.* Raffe Caterall, arm. & w., 1515.

*\*Winwick.* Peers Gerard, arm. in tab., w. canopy, 1492. Sir Peter Legh, arm. w. chasuble over, & w., 1527.

## LEICESTERSHIRE

*Aylestone.* Wm. Heathcott, parson, 1594.
*Barwell.* John Torksay, eccles. & w., qd. pl., 1614. Civ. & w., 1659.
*Bosworth, Husband's.* Rice Jem, rector, 1648.
*\*Bottesford.* Henry de Codyngtoun, priest in cope, w. saints & canopy, 1404. John Freman, pr. in cope, *c.* 1440.
*Bowden, Gt.* Inscr., Wolstonton, foreign palimp., 1403.
*\*Donington, Castle.* Robt. Staunton, arm. & w., w. canopy, 1458.
*Hinckley.* Civilian & wife, *c.* 1490.
*Hoby.* Man in armour & w., mutil., *c.* 1490.
*Leicester, Wigston's Hospital.* Priest in shroud, *c.* 1540.
*Loughborough.* Civ. & w., inscr., palimp., 1441. Civ. & w., 1480, and fragments.
*Lutterworth.* John Fildyng, civ. & w., 1418. Civ. & w., *c.* 1470.
*Melton Mowbray.* A large inscribed heart and inscr., 1543.
*Packington.* Priest in almuce, *c.* 1480.
*Queeniborough.* A lady, 1634.
*Saxelby.* A lady, 1523.
*Scalford.* A civilian, kng., *c.* 1520, and inscriptions.
*Sheepshed.* Thos. Duport, arm. & w., qd. pl., 1592.
*Sibson.* John Moore, priest in almuce, & Saviour, 1532.
*Stapleford.* Francis Sherard, arm. & w., 1492.
*Stokerston.* John Boville, arm. & w., 1467. Arm. & w., *c.* 1490.
*Swithland.* Agnes Scot, *c.* 1455.
*Thurcaston.* John Mershden, priest in cope, 1425.
*Wanlip.* Sir Thos. Walsch, arm. & w., 1393.
*Wymondham.* Margery Barkeley, 1521.

## LINCOLNSHIRE

*Algarkirk.* Nich. Robertson, civ. & 2 wives, 1498.
*Althorpe.* Wm. de Lound, priest, *c.* 1370.
*Asgarby-by-Sleaford.* Arms & inscr., Butler, 1603.
*Ashby Puerorum.* Lytleburye, arm. & w., *c.* 1560. Ditto, *c.* 1560.
*Barholm.* Arms & inscr., Fordham, 1641.
*Barrowby.* Nich. Deen, civ. & w., 1479. Margt. Deen, heraldic, 1500.
*Barton-on-Humber, St Mary.* Lady, demi, *c.* 1380. Seman, civ., 1433.
*Bigby.* Elizth. Skypwith, *c.* 1520. Nayler, rector, & w., qd. pl., 1632.
*\*Boston.* Civ., canopied, 1398. Pr. in cope, *c.* 1400. Civ. & 2 ws., bracket & can., mutil., *c.* 1400. Lady, palimp., *c.* 1460. Civ. & w., *c.* 1480. Civ., 1659, and many fragments and matrices.
*Broughton.* Sir Hen. Redford & w., canopied, *c.* 1370.
*Burton Coggles.* Cholmeley, arm., 1590. Ditto, civ. & w., 1620.
*Burton Pedwardine.* Mary Horsman, 1631.
*\*Buslingthorpe.* Sir Rich. de Boselyngthorpe, arm., demi, *c.* 1290.
*Conisholme.* John Langholme, arm. & w., kng., 1515.
*Corringham.* Civ. & w., kng., qd. pl., 1628. Arms & inscr., 1631.
*Cotes-by-Stow.* Butler, arm. & w., 1590. Ditto, kng., 1602.
*Cotes, Great.* Isabella Barnardiston, *c.* 1420. Arm. & w., kng., 1503.
*Covenham, St Bartholomew.* John Skypwyth, arm., 1415.
*\*Croft.* Man in armour, demi, *c.* 1300.
*Driby.* Jas. Prescot, civ. & w., kng., 1583.

*Edenham.* An archbishop, small, *c.* 1500.
*Evedon.* Dan. Hardeby, civ. & w., kng., 1616.
*Fiskerton.* Priest in cope, *c.* 1490.
*Gedney.* A lady, *c.* 1390.
*Glentham.* Elizth. Tourney, demi, 1452.
*Grainthorpe.* A large cross, *c.* 1380.
*\*Gunby.* Massyngberd, arm. & w., can., *c.* 1405, with later inscr. Wm.
    Lodyngton, justice, can., 1419.
*Hainton.* John Henege, civ. & w., 1435. Sir Thos. Henneage, arm. &
    w., heraldic, 1553.
*Hale.* Arms & inscr., Cawdron, 1625.
*Halton Holgate.* Bridgett Rugeley, qd. pl., 1658.
*Harpswell.* Arm. & w., kng., *c.* 1480.
*Harrington.* Margt. Copledike, 1480. Copledike, arm. & w., 1585.
*Holbeach.* Arm, *c.* 1420. Johanna Welby, 1488.
*Horncastle.* Sir Lionel Dymoke, arm., palimp., also in shroud, 1519.
*Ingoldmells.* Wm. Palmer, w. a " stylt," 1520.
*Irnham.* Sir Andrew Luttrell, canopied, 1390. Arm., *c.* 1430.
*Kelsey, South.* Arm. & w., *c.* 1410.
*Laughton.* Arm., canopied, w. later inscr., *c.* 1400.
*Leadenham.* Lady Elizth. Beresforde, qd. pl., 1624.
*Lincoln, St Mary-le-Wigford.* Cross & inscr., Horn, 1469
*Lincoln, Cathl. Ch. of B.V.M.,* Bp. Wm. Smyth, *c.* 1495 (replica).
*\*Linwood.* John Lyndewode, woolman & w., canopied, 1419. Woolman,
    canopied, 1421.
*Mablethorpe St Mary.* Elizth. Fitz William, 1522.
*Northope.* Francis Yerburgh, civ. & 2 ws., 1595.
*Norton Disney.* Wm. Disney, arm. & w. and arm. & 2 ws., palimp., 1578.
*Ormsby, South.* Lady, *c.* 1420. Skypwyth, arm. & w., can., 1482.
*Pinchbeck.* Margt. Lambart, w. 27 shields, qd. pl., 1608.
*Rand.* Lady, *c.* 1590, and several fragments.
*Rauceby.* Wm. Styrlar, priest, 1536.
*Scampton.* Arms, etc., Fitzwilliam, 1581. Bolles, 1644, 1648.
*Scotter.* Marmaduke Tirwhit, civ. & w., kng., qd. pl., 1599.
*Scrivelsby.* Sir Robt. Demoke, arm., 1545.
*Sleaford.* Geo. Carre & w., 1521, and inscrs.
*Somerby.* Arms & inscr., Bradshaw, 1673.
*Somersby.* Geo. Littlebury, civ., kng., 1612.
*Spalding, Johnson Hospital.* Civ. & w., kng., qd. pl., 1597.
*Spilsby.* Margt. de Wylughby, 1391. Lord Willoughby d'Eresby & w.,
    canopied, *c.* 1410.
*Stallingborough.* Ayscugh, arm. & w., heraldic, 1541. Lady, *c.* 1600.
*\*Stamford, All Saints.* Woolman & w., 1460. Ditto, canopied, *c.* 1460.
    Lady, 1471. Civ. & w., 1475. Ditto, *c.* 1490. Pr. in cope, 1508.
*Stamford, St John.* Civ. & w., 1489. Priest, 1497.
*Stoke Rochford.* Hen. Rochforth, arm. & w., 1470.
*\*Tattershall.* Civ., 1411. Ralph, Lord Cromwell, canopied, 1455
    Priest, 1456. Lady, can., 1479. Ditto, 1497. Pr. in cope, *c.* 1510.
    Priest, 1519.
*Theddlethorpe, All Saints.* Robt. Hayton, arm., 1424.
*Waltham.* Joan Waltham, son & dau., demi, 1420.
*Welton-le-Wold.* Arms & inscr., Dyon, *c.* 1600.
*Wickenby.* Arms & inscr., Millner, 1635.
*Winterton.* Two ladies, 1504.
*Winthorpe.* Rich. Barowe, civ. & w., 1505. Robt. Palmer, 1515.

*Witham, North.* Wm. Misterton, civ., mutil., 1425.
*Witham, South.* Arms & inscr., Harington, 1597.
*Wrangle.* John Reed, civ. & w., 1503.


# MIDDLESEX

*Acton.* Humfrey Cavell, civ., 1558.
*Ashford.* Civilian & w., 1522.
*Bedfont.* Civilian & lady, 1631.
*Brentford, New.* Hen. Redmayne, civ. & w., 1528.
*Chelsea.* Lady Jane Guyldeford, heraldic, 1555. Sir Arthur Gorges, arm. & w., 1625.
*Clerkenwell, St James.* John Bell, Bp. of Worcester, 1556.
*Cowley.* Walter Pope, civ. & w., inscr. palimp., 1502.
*Drayton, West.* Civ., sm., *c.* 1520. Lady, 1529. Jas. Good, M.D. & w., 1581.
*Ealing.* Rich. Amondesham, civ. & w., *c.* 1490.
*Edgware.* Anth. Childe, in swaddling-clothes, 1599.
*Edmonton.* Civs., Asplyn, Askew & w., *c.* 1500. Nich. Boone, civ. & w., *c.* 1520. Edw. Nowell, civ. & w., 1616.
*\*Enfield.* Joyce, Lady Tiptoft, heraldic, can., *c.* 1470. Civ. & w., 1592.
*Finchley.* Lady, 1487. Civ. & w., 1609. Lady, 1609. Civ. & 3 ws., qd. pl., 1610.
*Fulham.* Margt. Saunders, demi, on lozenge plate, Flemish, 1529.
—— *Greenford, Great.* Priest, demi, *c.* 1450. Lady, *c.* 1480. Pr., *c.* 1515. Civ., 1544.
—— *Greenford, Little.* Hen. Myllet, civ. & 2 ws., 1500. Civ., *c.* 1590.
*Hackney.* Christopher Urswic, priest in cope, 1521. Arm., 1545. Arm. & 4 ws., 1562. Vicar, in pulpit or pew, 1618.
*Hadley.* 2 ladies, 1442. Civ. & w., 1500. Lady, *c.* 1504. Civ. & w., 1518, 1614.
*Harefield.* Lady, 1444. Serjeant-at-law, 1528. Arm. & w., 1537, *c.* 1540. Civ. & w., 1545.
*Harlington.* Priest, demi, 1419. Lovell, arm. & w., 1445.
*\*Harrow.* Arm. on canopied bracket, *c.* 1370. Arm., *c.* 1390. Priest in cope, 1442. Pr. in acad., demi, *c.* 1460. Pr. in cope, 1468. Civ. & 3 ws., 1488. Inscr. & verses, palimp., 1574. Arm. & w., 1579. Civ. & w., 1592. Civ., 1603.
*Hayes.* Priest, *c.* 1370. Arm., 1456. Arm. & w., 1576.
*Hendon.* John Downner, civ., 1515.
*Heston.* Lady in childbed, qd. pl., *c.* 1580.
*\*Hillingdon.* Lord Le Strange & w., can., 1509. Arm., 1528. Civ. & w., 1579. Civ., 1599.
*Hornsey.* John Skevington, child in shroud, *c.* 1530.
*Ickenham.* Civ., *c.* 1580, 1582. Edm. Shorditche, arm. & w., 1584.
—— *Isleworth.* Arm., *c.* 1450. Palimp. inscr., 1544. A nun, sm., 1561. Civ., *c.* 1590.
*Islington, St Mary.* Arm. & w., *c.* 1535. Ditto, 1546.
*Kingsbury.* John Shephard & 2 ws., 1520.
*Littleton.* Inscr. and roses, 1553.
*London—*
    *\*All Hallows Barking, Tower Hill.* Woolman & w., 1437. Civ. & w., 1477. The Resurrection, *c.* 1510. Civ., 1498. Civ. & 2 ws.,

*London—*
>   1518. Civ. & w., qd. pl., Flemish, 1533. Arm. & w., 1546. Ditto, qd. pl., 1560. Civ., 1591.

*St Andrew Undershaft.* Nich. Leveson, civ. & w., 1539. Simon Burton, civ. & 2 ws., qd. pl., 1593.

*St Bartholomew-the-Less.* Wm. Markeby, civ. & w., 1439.

*St Cath., Regent's Park.* Wm. Cutinge, civ. & w., 1599.

*St Dunstan-in-the-West.* Hen. Dacres, civ. & w., 1530.

*Great St Helen, Bishopsgate.* Civ. & w., c. 1465. Priest in acad., 1482. Civ. & w., 1495. Pr. in acad., c. 1500. Arm., 1510, 1514. Lady, heraldic, c. 1535.

*Holy Trin., Minories.* Constantia Lucy, child, 1596.

*St Martin, Ludgate.* Thos. Berrie, civ., qd. pl., 1586.

*St Olave, Hart Street.* 2 ladies, Haddon, 1516. Civ. & w., 1584.

*Mimms, South.* Thos. Frowyk, arm., 1448.

——*Northolt.* Arm., sm., 1452. Arm. & w., 1560. Vicar, 1610.

*Norwood.* Matth. Hunsley, 1618. Francis Awsiter, 1624.

*Pinner.* Anne Bedingfeld, in swaddling-clothes, 1580.

—— *Ruisclip.* John Hawtrey, civ. & w., 1593. Civ., c. 1600.

*Stanwell.* Rich. de Thorp, priest, demi, 1408.

*Teddington.* John Goodyere, civ. & w., sm., 1506.

*Tottenham.* John Burrough, civ. & w., 1616. Margt. Irby, qd. pl., 1640.

*\*Westminster Abbey.* Bp. John de Waltham, can., 1395. Archbp. Robt. de Waldeby, can., 1397. Alianora de Bohun, can., 1399. Sir John Harpedon, 1437. Sir Thos. Vaughan, 1483. Abbot Estney, can., 1498. Sir Humf. Stanley, 1505. Dean Bill, 1561, and fragments, etc.

*Westminster, St Margt.* Cole, civ. & w., qd. pl., 1597.

*Willesden.* Civ. & w., 1492. Lady, 1505. Priest in cope, 1517. Arm. & 2 ws., 1585. Lady, 1609.

## MONMOUTHSHIRE

*Abergavenny.* Hughes, vicar, 1631. Margt. Robertes, qd. pl., 1632.

*Llangattock-nigh-Usk.* Zirophaeniza Powell, qd. pl., 1625.

*Matherne.* Philip Williams, civ. & w., 1590.

*Usk.* A Welsh inscr., c. 1400.

## NORFOLK

*Acle.* Swanne, civ., sm., 1533. Thos. Stones, " minister," demi, 1627.

*Aldborough.* Herward, arm., c. 1480. Lady, 1485. Civ., c. 1485.

*Antingham.* Rich. Calthorp, arm., 1562. Arms & inscr., 1596.

*Attlebridge.* Chalice for Geo. Cuynggam, priest, c. 1525.

*Aylsham.* Priest in almuce, c. 1490. Civ. & w., c. 1490. 2 shrouds, 1499. Civ. & w., c. 1500. Shroud, 1507.

*Baconsthorpe.* Arms, Heydon, 1550. Lady, kng., heraldic, 1561. Arms, etc., Heydon, 1642.

*Barnham Broom.* Bryghteve, civ., 1467. Dorant, civ. & w., 1514.

*Barningham Northwood.* Hen. Pagrave, arm. & w., 1516.

*Barningham Winter.* John Wynter, arm., c. 1410.

*Barsham, West.* Arms & inscr., Gournay, 1641.

*Bawburgh.* Civ. & w., 1500. Priest in shroud, 1505. Chalice for priest, 1531. Priest in shroud, curious, 1660.
*Beechamwell.* Priest, *c.* 1385. Grymston, priest, demi, 1430.
*Beeston Regis.* John Deynes, civ. & w., 1527. Fragments, etc.
*Beeston St Lawrence.* Arms & inscr., Preston, 1630.
*Belaugh.* Chalice for John Feelde, priest, 1508.
*Binham.* Civ. & w., demi, *c.* 1530.
*Bintry.* Chalice for Thos. Hoont, priest, 1510.
*Blakeney.* Arms & inscr., Calthorpe, 1503.
*Blickling.* Bust of civ., *c.* 1360. Arm., 1401. Civ. & w., 1454. Lady, 1458. Child, 1479. Lady, 1485. Ditto, 1512, and many inscrs.
*Blofield.* Arms & inscr., Paston, 1630, 1641.
*Brampton.* Robt. Brampton & w., shrouds, 1468. Arm. & 2 ws., 1535. Civ. & w., 1622.
*Brisley.* John Athowe, priest, w. chalice, 1531.
*Broome.* Arms & frag., *c.* 1450.
*Buckenham, Old.* Chalice, *c.* 1520. A crane with scroll, *c.* 1500.
*Burgh St Margt.* John Burton, rector, kng., 1608.
*Burlingham, South.* Chalice for Wm. Curtes, 1540.
*\*Burnham Thorpe.* Sir Wm. Calthorpe, arm., canopied, 1420.
*Burnham Westgate.* Wife of John Huntely, 1523.
*Buxton.* Chalice for Robt. Northen, priest, 1508.
*Bylaugh.* Sir John Curson, arm. & w., 1471.
*Cley.* Civ., *c.* 1450, *c.* 1460. Merchant & w. in shrouds, 1512. Priest in acad., w. chalice, *c.* 1520.
*Clippesby.* Thos. Pallyng, civ. & w., 1503. John Clippesby, arm. & w., 1594.
*Colney.* Chalice for Hen. Alikok, priest, 1502.
*Creake, North.* Man in civil or monastic dress, w. church, canopied, *c.* 1500.
*Creake, South.* Pr. in cope, *c.* 1400. Ditto, with staff, & civ., 1509.
*Cressingham, Gt.* Arm. & w., 1497. John Eyre, lawyer, civ., 1507. Priest in almuce, 1518. Lady, 1588.
*Cromer.* Margt. Counforth, 1518.
*Dereham, East.* Priest, demi, 1479. Lady, 1486. Arms, etc., 1503.
*Ditchingham.* Philip Bosard, civ. & w., 1490. Civ. and son, 1505.
*Dunham, Gt.* Arms & inscr., Bastard, 1624.
*Dunston.* Civilian and 2 wives in shrouds, 1649.
*Ellingham, Gt.* A lady, *c.* 1500.
*\*Elsing.* Sir Hugh Hastings, canopied, w. saints & weepers, 1347.
*Erpingham.* Sir John de Erpingham, *c.* 1415.
*Fakenham.* Priest in cope, *c.* 1428. Civ. & 2 ws., 1470. 4 inscribed hearts, *c.* 1500. Lady, *c.* 1510.
*\*Felbrigg.* Civ. & w. and arm. & w., *c.* 1380. Sir Symon Felbrygge, K.G., 1416. Lady, *c.* 1480. Arm., *c.* 1608. Lady, 1608.
*Felmingham.* Palimp. inscrs., *c.* 1530 and 1591. Arms & inscr., 1628.
*Feltwell St Mary.* Francis Hetht, arm., 1479. Lady, 1520.
*Fincham.* A lady in shroud, *c.* 1520.
*Forncett St Peter.* Arms & inscr., Baxter, 1535.
*Fransham, Gt.* Geoff. Fransham, arm., 1414. Lady in shroud, *c.* 1500.
*Frenze.* Arm., 1475, 1510. Lady, 1519, 1521, 1551. Shroud, *c.* 1520.
*Frettenham.* Alys Thorndon, *c.* 1420. Lady, *c.* 1460.
*Garboldisham.* Merchant's mark & inscr., Carlton, 1579.
*Gissing.* Arms & inscr., Kemp, 1596. Shield, *c.* 1600.
*Gressenhall.* Arms & inscr., Estmond, 1604, 1609.

*Guestwick.* Civilian, *c.* 1500, 1505. Chalice for priest & father, 1504.
*Halvergate.* Bust of lady, palimp. of a monk, 1540.
*Hardwick.* Arms & inscr., Bakon, *c.* 1500.
*Harling, West.* Ralf Fuloflove, priest, 1479. Wm. Berdewell, arm. & w., *c.* 1490. Ditto, 1508.
*Haveringland.* Arms & inscr., Davye, 1561.
*Heacham.* Man in armour, *c.* 1485.
*Hedenham.* Chalice for Rich. Grene, pr., 1502. Arms, etc., Beddingfeld, 1594.
*Heigham.* Marg. inscr., Bateman, *c.* 1330. Thos. Holl, civ., 1630.
*Helhoughton.* Heart, with hand and scrolls, Stapilton, *c.* 1450.
*Hellesdon.* Rich. de Heylesdone, civ. & w., demi, *c.* 1370. Rich. Thaseburgh, priest, 1389.
*Heydon.* Arms, etc., 1517, 1580, 1618, 1630, and many inscriptions.
*Hillington.* Arms & inscr., Gaudy, 1642.
*Hindolvestone.* Edm. Hunt, civ. & w., 1568.
*Holkham.* Arms & inscr., Osborne, 1618.
*Holme Hale.* French inscr. for Sir Esmon de Illeye & w., 1349.
*Holme-next-the-Sea.* Herry Notingham, civ. & w., *c.* 1405.
*Honing.* Nich. Parker, arm., 1496.
*Horstead.* Arms, etc., Ward, 1645, and many inscriptions.
*Hunstanton.* Edm. Grene, civ. & w., *c.* 1490. Sir Roger le Strange, arm., canopied, 1506. Arms, etc., 1485, 1654.
*Ingham.* Fragments of two fine canopied brasses, Stapilton, 1438 & 1466.
*Ingoldisthorpe.* Thos. Rogerson, eccles., wife & dau., 1608.
*Kenninghall.* Group of daughters, *c.* 1500.
*Ketteringham.* Lady, *c.* 1470. Thos. Heveningham, arm. & w., heraldic, kng., 1499. Child in shroud, *c.* 1530.
*Kimberley.* John Wodehows, arm. & w., *c.* 1530.
*Kirby Bedon.* Heart & scrolls, *c.* 1450. Dussyng & w., in shrouds, 1505.
*Langley.* Robt. Berney, civilian, 1628.
*Loddon.* Heart, hands, etc., 1462. 2 shrouds, 1546. Arm. in tab., 1561. Civ. & w., 1516.
*Ludham.* Inscr., Honyngg, *c.* 1350, and many others.
*Lynn, St Margt.* Adam de Walsokne & w., German, 1349. Robt. Braunche & 2 ws., ditto, 1364, both very large qd. pl.
*Lynn, West.* Adam Owtlawe, priest, 1503.
*Martham.* Inscribed heart for Robt. Alen, priest, copy only, 1487.
*Mattishall.* Civ., *c.* 1480. Ditto, *c.* 1510. Civ. & w., *c.* 1540, and many inscrs.
*Melton, Little.* Arms & inscr., Angwish, 1604.
*Merton.* Wm. de Grey, arm. in tab. & 2 ws., 1520. Arm., 1562. Arms, etc., 1474, 1548, 1566 and 1644.
*Methwold.* Sir Adam de Clifton, arm., canopied, 1367.
*Metton.* Robt. Doughty, civ. & w., demi, 1493.
*Mileham.* Xpofer Crowe, civ. & w., 1526.
*Morston.* Rich. Makynges, rector, 1596.
*Morton-on-the-Hill.* Kath. Awdley, 1611.
*Mundham.* Arms & inscr., Harborne, 1617.
*Narburgh.* Civ. & w., 1496. Arm., 1545. Judge & w., her., kng., 1545. Arm. & w., kng., 1561. Arm., 1581. Palimp. inscr., 1556.
*Necton.* Lady, 1372. Vowess, 1383. Civ., 1528. Civ & w., 1532.
*Newton Flotman.* 3 men in armour, Blondevile, kng., 1571.
*Northwold.* Arms & inscr., Scott, 1616.

*Norwich—*
  *St Andrew.* Canopy, etc., 1467. Civ. & w., *c.* 1500. Mark, etc.,
    1527. Arms, etc., for John Underwood, Bp. of Chalcedon, 1541.
  *St Clement.* Margt. Pettwode, 1514.
  *St Etheldred.* Priest, 1487, and inscrs. from St Peter Southgate.
  *St George Colegate.* Wm. Norwiche, civ. & w., on a bracket, 1472.
    Mark & inscr., Warryn, 1514.
  *St George Tombland.* A civilian, *c.* 1450.
  *St Giles.* Civ. & w., 1432. Ditto, 1436. Chalice for priest, 1499.
  *St John Maddermarket.* Civ. & w., 1412, *c.* 1472, 1476, 1525. Ditto
    on brackets, 1524, 1558. Lady, 1506. Palimp. inscr., 1540, and
    many others.
  *St John de Sepulchre.* Civ. & w., *c.* 1530. Arm. & w., 1597.
  *St Laurence.* Civ., 1436, *c.* 1460, *c.* 1500. A prior, on bracket, 1437.
    Skeleton, 1452. Priest, 1485, and many inscrs.
  *St Margaret.* Anne Rede, 1577.
  *St Martin at Palace.* Arms, etc., 1588, and several inscrs.
  *St Mary Coslany.* Head of civ., *c.* 1460. Arms & inscr., Claxton,
    1605.
  *St Michael at Plea.* Skeleton, etc., 1588. Arms & inscr., Ferrer, 1616.
  *St Michael Coslany.* Man & w. in shrouds, 1515, and several inscrs.
  *St Peter Mancroft.* Arm., adapted palimp., *c.* 1470, and sev. inscrs.
  *St Peter Permountergate.* Skull & cross bones, inscr., Barny, 1620.
  *St Simon & St Jude.* Arms, Pettus, 1614.
  *St Stephen.* A prioress, *c.* 1410. Civ., 1460. Civ. & w., *c.* 1513.
    2 civs., 1513. Priest in cope, 1545.
  *St Swithin.* Civ. & w., 1495, and many inscriptions.
*Ormesby, Great.* Lady, demi, w. heart, *c.* 1440. Scrolls, etc., 1446.
  Sir Robt. Clere, arm., 1529.
*Outwell.* Rich. Qwadryng, arm., 1511.
*Oxnead.* Arms & inscr., Lambert, 1608. Ditto, Paston, 1608.
*Paston.* Erasmus Paston, civ. & w., shields palimp., *c.* 1580.
*Pentney.* Arms & inscr., Wyndham, 1620.
*Plumstead, Little.* Civ. & w., 1480. Sir Edw. Warner, arm., 1565.
*Potter Heigham.* Arms & inscr., Baispoole, 1613.
*Rainham, East.* Civ., *c.* 1500. Priest in acad., w. scarf, 1522. Labels,
  palimp., *c.* 1540.
*Raveningham.* Margt. Wyllughby, 1483. Arms & inscr., Castle, 1614.
*Reedham.* Elizth. Berney, 1475. Arms, etc., Berney, *c.* 1540.
*Reepham.* Sir Wm. de Kerdeston, arm. & w., can., mutil., 1391.
*Ringstead, Great.* Rich. Kegell, priest, 1485.
*\*Rougham.* Judge & w., *c.* 1470. Arm. & w., *c.* 1510. 2 chrysoms,
  1510. Civ. & 2 ws., 1586.
*Sall.* Civ., *c.* 1420. Civ. & w., 1440. Ditto, on bracket, 1441. 2
  ladies, 1453. Shroud, 1454. Palimp. inscr., *c.* 1480.
*Salthouse.* Chalice for Robt. Fevyr, priest, 1519.
*Sandringham.* Arms & inscr., Cobbis, 1546.
*Scottow.* Chalice for Nich. Wethyrley, priest, *c.* 1520.
*Sculthorpe.* Henry Unton, arm., kng., 1470. Civ. & w., 1521. Mark &
  inscr., Stebyrd, *c.* 1480.
*Sharington.* Arm., *c.* 1445. Priest, 1486. Lady, *c.* 1520. Arm. & w.,
  kng., 1593.
*\*Shernbourne.* Sir Thos. Shernborne & w., 1458.
*Sherringham.* John Hook, civ. & w., 1513.
*Shimpling.* Palimpsest inscription, 1692.

*Shotesham St Mary.* Edw. Whyte, arm. & w., 1528.
*Snettisham.* Lady, *c.* 1560. Civ. & w., 1610. Arms & inscr., Gurlin, 1644.
*Snoring, Gt.* Sir Ralph Shelton, mutil., & w., heraldic, 1424.
*Southacre.* Sir John Harsick, arm. & w., her., 1384. Thos. Leman, pr. in acad., kng., 1584. Frag. palimp., *c.* 1400.
*Sparham.* Wm. Mustarder, priest, *c.* 1490.
*Sprowston.* John Corbet, mutil., & w., kng., 1559.
*Stalham.* A civilian & wife, *c.* 1460.
*Stokesby.* Arm. & w., 1488. Pr. in acad., 1506. Lady, 1570, 1614.
*Stradsett.* Thos. Lathe, arm., 1418.
*Surlingham.* Alnwik, priest in acad., 1460. Chalice for priest, 1513.
*Sustead.* Arms & inscr., Damme, *c.* 1500.
*Swaffham.* Man in armour, *c.* 1480.
*Swainsthorpe.* Arms & inscr., Havers, 1628.
*Swanton Abbott.* Stephen Multon, priest, 1477.
*Tasburgh.* Arms & inscr., Baxter, 1586. Ditto, Burman, 1642.
*Themelthorpe.* Wm. Pescod, civ., 1505.
*Thornham.* Label, *c.* 1460. Initial on shield & inscr., 1464.
*Thwaite.* John Puttock, civ. & w., 1469. Arms, 1508.
*Tottington.* Margt. Unger, kng., 1598.
*Trowse.* Wife of Roger Dalyson, 1585.
*Trunch.* Heart & scrolls, *c.* 1530. Palimp. inscr., 1473.
*Tuddenham, E.* A civilian & 2 wives, *c.* 1500.
*\*Upwell.* Priest in cope, canopied, *c.* 1430. Henry Martyn, pr. in cope, with crossed stole, 1435. Lady, 1631.
*Wacton.* Arms & inscr., Sedly, 1623.
*Walpole St Peter.* Arms & inscr., Butler, 1630. Ditto, Frencham, 1652.
*Walsham, N.* Chalice for priest, 1519. Ditto, *c.* 1520. Arms, etc., Grocers', 1625.
*Walsingham, Little.* Civ. & w., 1485, 1509, *c.* 1540. Chalice and hands, *c.* 1520, and many inscrs.
*Warham All Saints.* Wm. Rokewod, arm., 1474.
*Weston.* Elizth. Rokewoode, 1533.
*Whissonsett.* Wm. Bozon, arm., *c.* 1485. Thos. Gybon, arm., 1484.
*Wiggenhall St Mary.* Heart & scrolls, Kervile, *c.* 1450.
*Wighton.* Arms & inscr., Bedingfeild, 1629.
*Witchingham, Gt.* Arms & inscr., Meares, 1626.
*Witton.* Dame Juliana Anyell, vowess, *c.* 1500.
*Wiveton.* Priest w. chal., 1512. Skeleton in shr., *c.* 1540. Arms, etc., 1558. Civ. & w., 1597.
*Wood Dalling.* Priest, 1465. Civ., 1504, and 1504. Chalice, 1510. 2 civs., 1518.
*Woodrising.* Arms & inscr., Sowthwell, 1586. Arms & Garter, Crane, 1636.
*Woodton.* Cristiana Bacon, kng., 1532.
*Worstead.* Priest, demi, 1404. Civ., *c.* 1500, 1520, and several inscrs.
*Yelverton.* Margt. Aldriche, 1525, and several inscrs.


# NORTHAMPTONSHIRE

*Addington, Gt.* John Bloxham, priest w. chalice, 1519.
*Aldwinkle.* Wm. Aldewyncle, civ., 1463. Arms & inscr., Pickering, 1659.
*Ashby Canons.* John Dryden, civ., 1584.

*Ashby, Castle.* Wm. Ermyn, priest in cope, w. saints, 1401.
*Ashby St Leger.* Civ. & w., canopied, 1416. Arm. & w., heraldic, can., 1494. Arm. in tab., kng., *c.* 1500. Priest in acad., 1510.
*Ashton.* Robt. Mariott, civ. & w., *c.* 1580.
*Aston-le-Walls.* Alban Butler, civ. & 2 ws., 1609.
*Barnwell St Andrew.* Christopher Freeman, civ. & w., qd. pl., 1610.
*Barton, Earl's.* John Muscote, prothonotary, & w., 1512.
*Barton Segrave.* Jane Floyde, qd. pl., 1616.
*Blakesly.* Matth. Swetenham, arm., 1416.
*Blatherwicke.* Sir Humphrey Stafford, arm. & w., 1548.
*Blisworth.* Roger Wake, arm. & w., 1503.
*Boddington.* Wm. Procter, rector, 1627.
*Brampton, Church.* Jone Furnace, skeleton, qd. pl., 1585.
*Brampton-by-Dingley.* Arm. & w., can., *c.* 1420. Simon Norwiche, arm. with B.V.M., 1468.
*Brington, Gt.* Priest, demi, on a bracket, *c.* 1340.
*Burton Latimer.* Lady in shroud, *c.* 1500. Margt. Bacon, 1626.
*Chacomb.* Arms, mark, monogram, etc., Myghell Fox, *c.* 1543.
*Charwelton.* Andrewe, civ. & w., can., 1490. Ditto, *c.* 1490. Arm. & w., *c.* 1541.
*Chipping Warden.* Wm. Smart, priest, 1468. Civ. & w., 1584.
*Cotterstock.* Robt. Wyntryngham, priest in cope, on bracket, can., 1420.
*Cranford.* Fossebrok, arm. & w., 1418. Ditto, civ. & 2 ws., 1602.
*Cransley.* Edw. Dalyson, arm. & w., 1515.
*Dene.* Sir Edm. Brudenell, arm. & 2 ws., qd. pl., 1584. Civ. & w., 1586. Arm. & w., *c.* 1600.
*Doddington.* French inscr. to Wm. de Pateshull, 1359.
*Dodford.* Cressy, arm. & w., 1414. Wylde, ditto, 1422. Lady, 1637.
*Easton Neston.* Rich. Fermer, arm. & w., 1552.
*Fawsley.* Knyghtley, arm. in tab. & w., 1516. Arm. & w., *c.* 1495.
*Floore.* Arm. & w., 1498. Ditto, 1510. Small cross & inscr., 1537.
*Geddington.* Henry Jarmon, civ. & w., *c.* 1480. Mark & inscr., Maydwell, 1628.
*Greens Norton.* Sir Thos. Grene, arm. & w., 1462. Lady, *c.* 1490.
*Grendon.* 2 men in armour & w., *c.* 1480.
*Harrowden, Gt.* Wm. Harwedon, arm. & w., 1433.
*Hemington.* Thos. Mountagu, civ. & w., 1517.
*Heyford, Lower.* Arms & inscr., Mauntel, *c.* 1400. Arm. & w., 1487.
*Higham Ferrers.* Priest, can., 1337. Cross, etc., Chichele, 1400. Civ. & w., can., 1425. Lady, *c.* 1435. Pr. w. chal., 1498. Civ. & w., 1504. Heart, *c.* 1510. Civ., 1518. Pr. in cope, 1523. Civ., *c.* 1540. Ditto, *c.* 1540.
*Horton.* Roger Salisbury, arm. & 2 ws., 1491.
*Kelmarsh.* Morrys Osberne, civ. & w., 1534.
*Kettering.* Edm. Sawyer, arm. & w., qd. pl., 1631.
*Lowick.* Hen. Grene, arm. in tabard & w., 1467.
*Marholm.* Sir Wm. Fytzwillyams, arm. & w., heraldic, 1534.
*Naseby.* John Olyver, civ. & w., 1446. Arms & inscr., Shukbrugh, 1576.
*Newbottle.* Peter Dormer, civ. & 2 ws., 1555.
*Newnham.* Letitia Catesby, 1467.
*Newton-by-Geddington.* John Mulsho, civ. & w., kng. to cross, 1400. Lady, qd. pl., 1604.
*Newton Bromshold.* Wm. Hewet, priest, sm., 1426. Rog. Hewet, pr., 1487.

*Northampton, St Sepulchre.* Geo. Coles, civ. & 2 ws., 1640.
*Norton.* Wm. Knyght, civ. & w., 1504.
*Orlingbury.* Wm. Lane, civ. & w., sm., 1502.
*Potterspury.* Agnes Ogle, sm., 1616.
*Preston Deanery.* Sir Clement Edmonds, arm. & w., sm., 1622.
*Raunds.* John Tawyer, civ. & w., 1470. Wm. Gage, civ., 1632.
*Rothwell.* Wm. de Rothewelle, priest in cope, 1361. Civ. & w., 1514.
*Spratton.* Robt. Parnell, civ. & w., 1474.
*Staverton.* Thos. Wylmer, civ. & w., 1580.
*Stoke Bruerne.* Rich. Lightfoot, rector, qd. pl., 1625.
*Sudborough.* Wm. West, civ. & w. and others, 1415.
*Tansor.* John Colt, priest, 1440.
*Wappenham.* Arm., mutil., c. 1460. Judge & w., mutil., 1481. L., 1499. Arm. & w., c. 1500. Ditto, c. 1500.
*Warkworth.* Arm., 1412, 1420 and 1454. Lady, 1420. Ditto, 1430.
*Welford.* Francis Saunders, arm. & 3 ws., qd. pl., 1585.
*Woodford-by-Thrapston.* Symon Malory, arm., c. 1580.
*Woodford-cum-Membris.* Nich. Stafford, priest, c. 1425.


## NORTHUMBERLAND

*Newcastle-upon-Tyne, All Saints.* Roger Thornton, merchant, & w., foreign, large, qd. pl., 1429.
*Newcastle-upon-Tyne, St Andrew.* Frag. of man in armour, 1404.


## NOTTINGHAMSHIRE

*Annesley.* Wm. Breton, civ., 1595.
*Clifton.* Clyfton, arm., 1478. Ditto, 1491. Arm. & w., 1587.
*Darlton.* Man in armour & w., c. 1510.
*Hickling.* Rad. Babyngton, priest w. chalice, 1521.
*Markham, E.* Millicent Meryng, 1419.
*Newark.* Alan Fleming, civ., foreign, large qd. pl., 1361. Arms, etc., 1532. Civ., c. 1540, 1557, and many inscrs.
*Ossington.* Reynolde Peckham, arm. & w., palimp., 1551.
*Radcliffe.* Anne Ballard, qd. pl., 1626.
*Stanford-on-Soar.* Priest w. chalice, c. 1400.
*Strelley.* Sir Robt. Strelly, arm. & w., 1487.
*Wheatley, N.* Palimp. inscr., Sheffeld, 1445.
*Wollaton.* Sir Rich. Willoughby, arm. & w., 1471.


## OXFORDSHIRE

*Adderbury.* Man in arm. & w., c. 1460. Jane Smyth, 1508.
*Aston Rowant.* Civilian & w., sm., 1441. Lady, mutil., c. 1470. Elynor Eggerley, 1508.
*Bampton.* Priest in almuce, demi, c. 1420. Pr. in cope, sm., 1500. Frances Hord, 1633.
*Barford, Great.* Wm. Foxe, civ. & w., sm., 1495.
*Brightwell Baldwin.* Eng. inscr. to John the Smith, c. 1370. Judge & w., sm., kng., and again, large, canopied, 1439.
*Brightwell Priors.* Rich. Crook, civ., 1549.

*Brightwell Salome.* Mores John, priest, sm., 1492.
*Broughton.* Philippa Byschoppesdon, large, 1414.
*Burford.* Civ. & w., kng. to bracket, 1437. Civ. & w., qd. pl., 1614.
*Cassington.* Cross fleury, 1414. Man in shroud, qd. pl., 1590.
*Chalgrove.* French inscr., *c.* 1360. Arm., 1441. Arm. & w., 1446.
*Charlton-on-Otmoor.* Thos. Key, priest in cope, 1476.
*Chastleton.* Kath. Throkmorton, sm., 1592. Edm. Ansley, civ. & w.,
　sm., 1613.
*Checkendon.* John Rede, civ., canopied, 1404. Soul & angels, *c.* 1430.
　Palimp. inscr., Rede, 1435.
*Chesterton.* Wm. Mawnde, civ. & w., 1612.
*\*Chinnor.* Flor. cross & head of pr., *c.* 1320. Pr. in acad., demi, 1361.
　Arm. & 2 ws., *c.* 1385. Arm. & w., demi, 1386. Pr. w. chal.,
　demi, 1388, and 6 others, mutil., *c.* 1390-1514.
*Chipping Norton.* Civ. & w., 1450, 1451, 1484. Civ., *c.* 1460. Lady, *c.*
　1500, 1507 and 1530.
*Cottisford.* Man in armour & w., *c.* 1500.
*Crowell,* John Payne, priest, demi, 1469.
*Cuxham.* John Gregory, civ. & 2 wives, sm., 1506.
*Deddington.* A civilian, demi, *c.* 1370.
*\*Dorchester.* Arm., mutil., 1411. Abbot Bewfforeste, *c.* 1510. Lady, *c.*
　1490. Civ. & w., 1513.
*Ewelme.* Thos. Chaucer, arm. & w., 1436. Pr., demi, 1458, 1467, *c.* 1470,
　Pr. in acad., 1517. Arm. & w., 1518. Civ. & w., 1599, and several
　inscrs. and arms.
*Garsington.* Thos. Radley, arm. & w., sm., 1484.
*Glympton.* Thos. Tesdale, civ., 1610.
*Goring.* Lady, canopied, 1401. Civ. & w., children palimp., *c.* 1600.
*Hampton Poyle.* John Poyle, arm. & w., 1424.
*Handborough.* Alex. Belsyre, in shroud, qd. pl., 1567.
*Harpsden.* Lady, *c.* 1460. Arm. & w., *c.* 1480. Walter Elmes, priest,
　1511. Sara Webb, 1620.
*Haseley, Gt.* Pr. in almuce, 1494. Shroud, 1497. Lady, 1581.
*Heythorpe.* John Aschefeld, arm. & w., 1521.
*Holton.* Wm. Brome, arm., 1461. Wm. Brome, child, 1599.
*Ipsden.* Thos. Englysche, arm. & w., sm., palimp., 1525.
*Islip.* Robt. Banks, Hen. Norrys & w., qd. pl., 1637.
*Kingham.* Catherine James, 1588.
*Lewknor.* John Alderburne, priest, demi, *c.* 1380.
*Lillingstone Lovell.* Heart & hands, 1446. Civ. & w., kng., sm., *c.*
　1460. Civ. & w., 1513.
*Mapledurham.* Sir Robt. Bardolf, arm., canopied, 1395.
*Nettlebed.* Arms & inscr., Taverner, 1637.
*Newnham Murren.* Letitia Barnarde, kng., 1593.
*Noke.* Wm. Manwayringe, Hen. Bradshawe, judge, & w., qd. pl., 1598.
*Northleigh.* Man in armour, *c.* 1415.
*Nuffield.* Beneit Engliss, civ., demi, *c.* 1360.
*Oddington.* Ralph Hamsterley, pr., skeleton, *c.* 1500.
*Oxford—*
　*St Aldate.* 2 civs., kng., qd. pl., 1607. Civ., qd. pl., 1612. Civ. in
　　hood, qd. pl., 1613.
　*St Cross, Holywell.* Lady in childbed, qd. pl., 1622. Lady, kng.,
　　qd. pl., 1625.
　*St Mary Magd.* Physician, in gown & hood, kng., 1580. Palimp.
　　inscr., 1574.

*Oxford—*

St Mary-the-Virgin. Pr. in almuce, 1507. Civ., qd. pl., 1581. Lady, 1584.

St Michael. Flexney, civ. & w., 1578. Pendarves, commoner, 1617.

St Peter-in-the-East. Civ. & w., sm., 1487. Civ. & w., qd. pl., 1572, 1599. Civ. & 2 ws., 1574.

St Peter-le-Bailey. Civ., 1419. Lady, c. 1420. Civ. & w., kng., c. 1640.

All Souls' Coll. Pr. in cope, kng., sm., 1461. Pr. in acad., 1490. 2 acad., demi, 1510.

Christ Church Cath. Civ., sm., 1452, c. 1460. Pr. in almuce, 1557. Students in acad., 1578, 1584, 1587, 1588, 1602 and 1613.

Corpus Christi Coll. John Claimond, President, in shroud, c. 1530.

Magdalen Coll. 9 academics, some demi, 1478-1523. Pr. in cope, 1480 & c. 1480. Pr. in almuce, 1515. Canon of Windsor, palimp., 1558.

*Merton Coll. Pr., demi, in head of cross, c. 1310. Pr. in tunic, in cross, c. 1360. 2 acad. on bracket, can., c. 1420. Acad., demi, 1445. Pr. in cope, can., 1471. Pr. in acad., w. chal., demi, c. 1520.

*New Coll. Archbp., 1417. Bishop, 1526. 5 pr. in cope and 8 in acad., 1403-1521. Pr. in shroud, 1472. Pr. in euch., demi, 1507. Notary, c. 1510. Physician, c. 1510, 1592, 1601 and 1619.

Queen's Coll. Acad., 1477. Pr. in cope, c. 1518. Bishop, qd. pl., sm., 1616. Eccles., ditto, 1616.

St John's Coll. Acad., 1571, 1578. Ditto, kng., 1573.

Rollright, Gt. Jas. Batersby, pr. w. chalice, 1522.

Rotherfield Greys. Sir Robt. de Grey, arm., canopied, 1387.

Shiplake. John Symonds, civ. & w., c. 1540.

Shipton-under-Wychwood. Elizth. Horne, in shroud, qd. pl., 1548.

Shirburn. Rich. Chamburleyn, arm. & w., 1493.

Somerton. Wm. Fermoure, arm. & w., 1552.

Souldern. Thos. Warner, priest, 1508. A child, c. 1620.

Stadhampton. John Wylmot, civ. & w., 1498. Ditto, 1508.

Stanton Harcourt. 2 civilians, sm., 1460. Lady, 1516. Priest, 1519.

Stoke Lyne. Edw. Love, civ. & w., 1535.

Stoke, North. Roger Parkers, Canon of Windsor, demi, c. 1370.

Stoke Talmage. John Adene, civ. & w., 1504. John Pettie, arm. & w., 1589.

Stokenchurch. Robt. Morle, arm., 1410. Ditto, 1412.

Swinbrook. John Croston, arm. & 3 ws., c. 1470. Anthony Fetyplace, arm. in tab., 1510.

Tew, Gt. Arm. & w., can., 1410. Fragments, c. 1500. Civ. & w., 1513.

Thame. 2 arm. & ws. on bracket, c. 1420. Arm., c. 1460. Civ. & w., c. 1500, 1502, 1503, 1508. Arm. in tab., kng., 1513. Civ., 1543 and 1597

Waterpery. Lady, sm., c. 1370. Curson, arm. & w., palimp., 1527.

Watlington. Civ. & w., 1485. Ditto, in shrouds, 1501. Civ., 1588.

Whitchurch. Thos. Walysch, arm. & w., c. 1420. Roger Gery, pr. w. chal., c. 1456. Peter Winder, curate, 1610.

Witney. Wenman, civ. & 2 ws., 1500. Ayshcome, civ., 1606.

Woodstock. Bailly, civ., 1441. Keyt, in gown & hood, kng., qd. pl., 1631.

M

## RUTLAND

*Braunston.* Kenelme Cheseldyn, civ. & w., 1590.
\**Casterton, Little.* Sir Thos. Burton, arm. & w., c. 1410.
*Liddington.* Lady, 1486. Edw. Watson, arm. & w., 1530.

## SHROPSHIRE

\**Acton Burnell.* Lord Nich. Burnell, arm., canopied, 1382.
*Acton Scott.* Thos. Mytton, civ. & w., kng., 1571.
*Adderley.* Prelate in pontif.⁋ mutil., c. 1390 Sir Robt. Nedeham, arm.
     & w., 1560.
*Burford.* Elizth. de Cornewaylle, c. 1370.
*Drayton.* Rowland Corbet, boy, kng., qd. pl., c. 1580.
*Edgmond.* Francis Younge, in shroud, & w., 1533.
*Glazeley.* Thos. Wylde, civ. & w., 1599.
*Harley.* A man in armour & wife, c. 1475.
*Ightfield.* Margery Calveley, can., mutil., c. 1495. Civ., 1497.
*Middle.* Arthur Chambre, civ. & w., 1564.
*Tong.* Sir Wm. Vernon, arm. & w., 1467. Priest in alm., 1510. Pr.
     in tippet, w. chalice, 1517.
*Upton Cressett.* Rich. Cressett, civ. & w., kng., qd. pl., 1640.
*Wenlock, Much.* Rich. Ridley, civ. & w., 1592.
*Withington.* John Onley, arm. & w., kng., 1512. Priest in cope, 1530.

## SOMERSETSHIRE

*Axbridge.* Roger Harper, civ. & w., kng., 1493.
*Backwell.* Rice Davies, civ. & w., qd. pl., 1638.
*Banwell.* Civ. & w., sm., c. 1480, 1554. Priest in cope, 1503.
*Bath Abbey.* Sir Geo. Ivy, civ. & w., 1639.
*Beckington.* Seyntmour, arm. & w., 1485. Compton, civ. & w., 1510.
*Burnett.* John Cutle, civ. & w., qd. pl., 1575.
*Cheddar.* Sir Thos. Cheddar, arm., 1442. Isabel Cheddar, c. 1460.
*Chedzoy.* A man in armour, large, c. 1490.
*Churchill.* Raphe Jenyns, arm. & w., 1572.
*Cossington.* John Brent, arm. & wife, 1524.
*Crewkerne.* Thos. Golde, arm., kng., sm., 1525.
*Croscombe.* Wm. Bisse, civ. & wife, 1625.
*Dunster.* John Wyther, civ & wife, c. 1520.
*Fivehead.* A lady, c. 1565.
*Hemington.* John Bawfelde, civ., sm., 1528.
*Hinton St George.* Adam Martin, civ. & wife, c. 1580.
*Hutton.* John Payne, arm & w., 1496. Thos. Payne, arm. & w., 1528.
\**Ilminster.* Sir Wm. Wadham, arm. & w., canopied, c. 1440. Nich.
     Wadham, arm. & w., 1618.
*Ilton.* Nich. Wadham, in shroud, 1508.
*Langridge.* Elizth. Wallche, 1441.
*Luccombe.* Wm. Harrison, civ., 1615.
*Lydiard, Bishop's.* Nich. Grobham, civ. & w., 1594.
*Minehead.* Lady, canopied, mutilated, 1440.

*Petherton, South.* Arm. & w., canopied, *c.* 1430. Lady, 1442.
*Portbury.* Sara Kemish, sm., 1621.
*St Decumans.* Wyndham, civ. & w., 1571. Ditto, arm. & w., 1596.
*Shepton Mallett.* Wm. Strode, arm. & w., qd. pl., 1649.
*Stogumber.* Margery Windham, 1585.
*Swainswick.* Edm. Forde, civ., 1439.
*Tintinhull.* John Heth, priest in cope, 1464.
*Weare.* John Bedbere, civ., *c.* 1500.
*Wedmore.* Geo. Hodges, civ., qd. pl., *c.* 1630.
*Wells Cathedral.* Priest in cope, demi, *c.* 1465. Willis, civ., qd. pl.,
    1618. Mitre for Bp. Lake, 1626.
*Wells, St Cuthbert.* Francis Hayes, civ.; sm., 1623.
*Yeovil.* A monk, demi, on lectern, *c.* 1460. Civ. & w., 1519.


## STAFFORDSHIRE

*Abbots Bromley.* John Draycote, civ., 1463.
*\*Audley.* Sir Thos. de Audley, arm., large, 1385. Wm. Abnet, 1628.
*Biddulph.* Wm. Bowyer, civ. & w., qd. pl., 1603.
*Blore.* Wm. Basset, civ. & wife., 1498.
*\*Clifton Campville.* A lady, demi, on a bracket, can., palimp., *c.* 1360.
*Elford.* John Hille, ecclesiastic, 1621.
*Hanbury.* Priest in cope, *c.* 1480.
*Horton.* John Wedgwood, civ. & w., qd. pl., 1589.
*Kinver.* Sir Edw. Grey, arm. & 2 wives, 1528.
*Leek, St Edw.* John Ashenhurst & 4 wives, qd. pl., 1597.
*Madeley.* John Egerton, civ. & w., 1528. Hawkins, boy, 1586.
*Norbury.* Hawys Botiller, can., *c.* 1350. Arms, etc., Skrymsher, 1667.
*\*Okeover.* Zouch & 2 ws., palimp., 1447, altered to Oker & w., 1538.
*Rugeley.* John Weston, civ., 1566.
*Standon.* Cross brass, *c.* 1450.
*Stone.* Thos. Crompton, arm. & w., qd. pl., *c.* 1615.
*Trentham.* Sir Rich. Leveson, arm. & w., 1591.


## SUFFOLK

*\*Acton.* Sir Robt. de Bures, arm., 1302. Lady, can., 1435. Arm., 1528.
    Civ. & w., 1589. Civ., *c.* 1590.
*Aldeburgh.* Civ., 1519. Lady, *c.* 1520, *c.* 1570. Civ. & w., 1601, 1606,
    1612, 1635.
*Ampton.* Civ. & w., kng., *c.* 1480. Lady, *c.* 1480. Ditto, palimp., *c.*
    1490. Children, *c.* 1490. Arms & inscr., Coket, *c.* 1500.
*Ashbocking.* Edm. Bockinge, arm. & 2 ws., 1585.
*Assington.* Man in armour & wife, *c.* 1500.
*Badley.* Arms & inscr., Poley, 1613
*Barham.* Robt. Southwell, civ. & w., 1514.
*Barningham.* Wm. Goche, priest in acad., 1499.
*Barrow.* Sir Clement Heigham, arm. & 2 ws., kng., 1570.
*Barsham.* A man in armour, *c.* 1415.
*Belstead.* A man in armour & 2 ws., *c.* 1520.
*Benhall.* Edw. Duke, civ. & w., 1598. Ambr. Duke, arm. & w., 1611.
*Bergholt, E.* Robt. Alfounder, civ., 1639.
    M*

*Bildeston.* Alice Wade, 1599.
*Blundeston.* Arms & inscr., Sydnor, 1613.
*Boxford.* David Birde, child in cot, 1606. Arms & inscr., Doggett, 1610.
*Bradley, Little.* Civ. & w., *c.* 1520, 1584, 1605. Arm., 1530. Arm. & w., qd. pl., 1612.
*Braiseworth.* Alex. Newton, arm., 1569.
*Bredfield.* Leonard Farrington, civ. & w., 1611.
*Bruisyard.* Two wives of Michael Hare, 1611.
*Brundish.* Priest, *c.* 1360. Arm., 1559. Arm. & w., 1560. Lady, *c.* 1570. Youth, kng., *c.* 1570.
*Bungay.* Arms & inscr., Throckmorton, 1599.
*Burgate.* Sir Wm. de Burgate & w., canopied, 1409.
*Bury St Edmunds, St Mary.* Civ. & w., kng., *c.* 1480. Pr. in almuce, *c.* 1510. Many arms and inscrs.
*Campsey Ash.* Alex. Inglisshe, priest w. chalice, 1504.
*Carlton.* A civilian, *c.* 1480.
*Cavendish.* Arms, Cavendish, *c.* 1530.
*Chattisham.* Mary Revers, 1592.
*Cookley.* Wm. Browne, civ. & w. (children palimp.), 1595.
*Cove, N.* Arms, etc., Sengylton, 1498, and several inscrs.
*Cowlinge.* Robt. Higham, civ. & w., 1599.
*Cratfield.* Arms & inscr., Warner, 1654.
*Darsham.* Ann Bedingfeild, 1641.
*Debenham.* Arm. & w., demi, *c.* 1425. Arms, etc., Gawdy, 1650.
*Denham.* Anth. Bedingfeld, civ., palimp., 1574.
*Denstone.* Henry Everard, arm. & w., heraldic, 1524. Lady, *c.* 1530.
*Depden.* 2 arm. & ws., kng., Waldegrave & Jermyn, 1572.
*Easton.* Arm, *c.* 1425. John Wingfeld, arm., 1584. Lady, 1601.
*Edwardstone.* Benj. Brand, civ. & w., *c.* 1620. Arms, etc., Brand, 1642.
*Ellough.* Arms, *c.* 1480. Lady, *c.* 1520, 1607. Arms, etc., 1612.
*Elmham, S.* Civilian & wife, *c.* 1520.
*Euston.* Civ. & w., *c.* 1480. Ditto, *c.* 1520. Lady, *c.* 1520. Arm. & w., *c.* 1530.
*Eyke.* Judge Staverton & w., *c.* 1430. Hen. Mason, eccles., 1619.
*Flixton St Mary.* Arms & inscr., Tasburgh, 1583.
*Fornham All Saints.* Thos. Barwick, physician, 1599. Sev. inscriptions.
*Fressingfield.* Wm. Brewes, arm. & wife, 1489.
*Gazeley.* Chalice, *c.* 1530. Arms, Heigham, *c.* 1500, Blennerhasset, *c.* 1560.
*Gisleham.* Arms & inscr., Bland, 1593.
*Glemham, Little.* Arms & inscr., Glemham, 1571.
*\*Gorleston.* Man in armour, of Bacon family, *c.* 1320.
*Hadleigh.* Lady, 1593. Civ., kng., 1637. Civ. & w., qd. pl., 1637. Palimp. inscr., *c.* 1560.
*Halesworth.* Civ., demi, 1476. Lady & palimp. inscr., *c.* 1580.
*Hawkedon.* Civilian and wife, *c.* 1510.
*Hawstead.* Boy, *c.* 1500. Girl, *c.* 1530. Lady, *c.* 1530. Sir Wm. Drury, arm. & 2 ws., 1557.
*Holbrook.* A man in armour, *c.* 1480.
*Honington.* Geo. Duke, civ., 1594.
*Hoxne.* Arms & inscr., Thruston, 1606. Ditto, 1613.
*Huntingfield.* Arms & inscr., Paston, 1595.
*Ipswich—*
    *St Clement.* John Tye, civ. & 2 ws., 1583. Wm. Cocke, civ. & w., 1607.

*Ipswich—*
   *St Lawrence.* Arms & inscr., Moor, *c.* 1580.
   *\*St Mary Quay.* Thos. Pownder & w., qd. pl., Flemish, 1525. Henry
      Toolye, civ. & w., kng., 1565. Lady, *c.* 1580.
   *St Mary Tower.* Notary, *c.* 1475. Civ. & 2 ws., *c.* 1500. Civ., notary
      & w., 1506. Civ. & 2 ws., on bracket, *c.* 1525. Arms, etc., 1697.
   *St Nicholas.* Civ. & w., 1475, *c.* 1500, *c.* 1600. Arms, etc., 1604.
   *St Peter.* John Knapp, civ. & w., 1604.
*Ixworth.* Rich. Codington, civ. & w., kng., 1567.
*Kenton.* John Garneys, arm & w., kng., heraldic, 1524.
*Kettleburgh.* Arthur Pennyng, civ. & 2 ws., 1593.
*Knoddishall.* John Jenney, arm. & w., 1460.
*Lakenheath.* Civilian & wife, *c.* 1530.
*Lavenham.* Civ. & w., shrouds, etc., 1486. Civ. & w., kng., qd. pl., *c.*
   1570. Chrysom, 1631.
*\*Letheringham.* Sir John de Wyngefeld, arm., heraldic, 1389.
*Lidgate.* Priest, once in head of cross, *c.* 1380.
*Livermere, Gt.* Arms, Clarke, *c.* 1520.
*Long Melford.* L., *c.* 1420. Civ., *c.* 1420. 2 ladies, heraldic, canopied, *c.*
   1480. Arm., 1557. Civ. & 2 ws., 1615. Civ. & 3 ws., 1624.
*Lowestoft.* 2 skeletons, *c.* 1500. Civ. & w., *c.* 1540, and sev. inscrs.
*Melton.* Pr. in acad., civ. & lady, canopied, *c.* 1430.
*Mendham.* Lady, 1615. Civ., 1616. Ditto, 1634. Arms & inscr., 1641.
*Mendlesham.* John Knyvet, arm., 1417.
*Metfield.* Arms & inscr., Jermy, 1504.
*Mickfield.* Peter Preston, civ. & w., qd. pl., 1617.
*Middleton.* Civ. & w., *c.* 1500. Anth. Pettow, civ., 1610.
*Mildenhall.* Sir Hen. Warner, arm., qd. pl., 1617. His son, ditto, 1618.
*Monewden.* Thos. Reve, acad., in gown, kng., 1595. Arms, etc., 1587.
*Nacton.* Arms & inscr., Fastolf, 1479.
*Nayland.* Lady, can., mutil., *c.* 1485. Civ. & w., *c.* 1500. Civ. & w.,
   1516.
*Nettlestead.* A man in armour, *c.* 1500.
*Occold.* Wm. Corbald, civ. & w., *c.* 1490.
*Orford.* Twelve civilian brasses, with ladies, *c.* 1480-1640.
*Pakefield.* John Bowf, civ. & w., 1417. Pr. in acad., 1451.
*Petistree.* Francis Bacon, civ. & 2 wives, 1580.
*Pettaugh.* A civilian and wife, *c.* 1530.
*\*Playford.* Sir Geo. Felbrigg, arm., heraldic, 1400.
*Polstead.* Priest, *c.* 1440. Civilian and wife, *c.* 1490.
*Preston.* Arms & inscr., Ryece, 1629. Ditto, 1638.
*Raydon.* Elizth. Reydon, 1479.
*Redgrave.* Anne Butts, 1609.
*Rendham.* Chalice, etc., to Thos. Kyng, vicar, 1523.
*Ringsfield.* Nich. Garnys, arm. & w., kng., qd. pl., *c.* 1600.
*Rishangles.* Arms & inscr., Grimeston, 1599. Ditto, 161/.
*\*Rougham.* Sir Roger Drury, arm. & wife, 1405.
*Rushbrook.* Arms & inscr., Badby, 1583.
*Saxham, Gt.* John Eldred, civ., 1632.
*Sibton.* Civ. & w., kng., 1574. Civ. & w., 1582. Ditto, qd. pl., 1626.
*Sotterley.* Arm., *c.* 1470, 1572 and *c.* 1630. Arm. & w., 1479. Lady,
   1578, *c.* 1630, & inscrs.
*Southolt.* Margt. Armiger, 1585.
*Spexhall.* Arms, Baynard, *c.* 1460. Silvester Brown, 1593.
*Stoke by Clare.* Lady, *c.* 1530. Civ., *c.* 1600. Alice Talkarne, 1605.

*Stoke by Nayland*. Lady, *c.* 1400.  Sir Wm. Tendring, arm., 1408.
  Lady, heraldic, *c.* 1535.  Arms, etc., 1590.  Lady, 1632.
*Stonham Aspall*.  John Metcalfe, eccles. in gown, 1606.
*Stowlangtoft*.  Arms, Wingfield, *c.* 1500.  Ditto, Ashfield, *c.* 1550.
*Stratford St Mary*.  Edw. Crane, civ. & w., 1558.
*Stowmarket*.  Ann Tyrell, child in shroud, 1638.
*Tannington*.  Ann Dade, 1612.  Arms & inscr., Dade, 1619.  Ditto, 1624.
*Thrandeston*.  Arms & inscr., Cuppledicke, 1619.
*Thurlow, Gt.*  Arm. & w., *c.* 1460.  Lady, *c.* 1460.  Arm. & w., *c.* 1530.
*Thurlow, Little*.  Man in armour & wife, *c.* 1520.
*Ufford*.  Civ. & 3 ws., 1483.  Skeleton, etc., qd. pl., 1598.  Arms, 1634.
*Waldingfield, Little*.  Civ. & w., 1506.  Arm. & w., 1526.  Lady, *c.* 1530.
  Civ., 1544.
*Walsham le Willows*.  Arms & inscr., Smalpece, 1602.
*Walton*.  Wm. Tabard, civ. & w., 1459.  Boy, kng., qd. pl., 1612.
*Wangford by Southwold*.  Arms & inscr., Rous, 1635.
*Wenham, Little*.  Thos. Brewse, arm. & w., canopied, 1514.
*Westhorpe*.  Arms & inscr., Elcocke, 1630.
*Wetherden*.  Arms & inscr., Daniel, 1584.
*Wickham Brook*.  Thos. Burrough, civ. & 2 ws., qd. pl., 1597.
*Wickham-Skeith*.  A lady, kneeling, *c.* 1530.
*Wilby*.  Civ., *c.* 1530.  Arms & inscr., Bayles, 1588, 1620, 1638, 1639.
*Withersfield*.  Arms & inscr., Bury, 1579.
*Wiston*.  Arms & inscr., Le Gris, 1630.
*Woodbridge*.  John Shorlond, child, 1601.
*Worlingham*.  Nich. Wrenne, civ. & w., 1511.  Arms & inscr., Duke,
  1615.
*Worlingworth*.  Children, *c.* 1530.  Arms, Barker, 1622.
*Wrentham*.  Ele Ufford, 1400.  Humphr. Brewster, arm., 1593.
*Yaxley*.  Andrew Felgate, civ., 1598.
*Yoxford*.  John Norwiche, arm. & w., 1428.  Lady, in shroud, 1485.
  Civ., 1613.  Lady, 1618, & inscrs.

## SURREY

*Addington*.  Thos. Hatteclyff, arm., 1540.  Leigh, civ. & w., 1544.
*Albury, Old Church*.  John Weston, arm., 1440.
~ *Barnes*.  Edith & Elizth. Wylde, small, 1508.
*Beddington*.  L., 1414.  Cross, 1425.  Civ. & w., *c.* 1430, 1432.  Arm.,
  1437.  L., 1507.  All under seats except 1432 and 1507.
*Betchworth*.  Wm. Wardysworth, priest w. chalice, 1533.
*Bletchingley*.  Lady, *c.* 1470.  Priest, 1510.  Civ. & w., 1541.
*Bookham, Gt.*  Lady, 1433, 1597.  Civ. & w., 1598.  Civ., 1668.
*Byfleet*.  Thos. Teylar, priest in almure, *c.* 1480.
*Camberwell, St Giles*.  Arm., *c.* 1470, re-used with palimp. inscr., 1538.
  Civ., 1497, 1507.  Arm. & w., kng., 1532.  Civ. & w., kng., 1577.
  Civ. & w., 1570, and inscrs.
*Carshalton*.  Nich. Gaynesford, arm. & w., *c.* 1490.  Pr. w. chalice,
  mutil., 1493.  Lady, 1524.
*Charlwood*.  Nich. Saunder, arm. & w., 1553.
*Cheam*.  Civ., mutil., *c.* 1370.  Civ., demi, *c.* 1375, 1459.  Civ. & w.,
  1458.  Arm., *c.* 1480.  Civ. & w., palimp., 1542.
*Chipstead*.  Lucy Roper, 1614
*Cobham*.  Adoration, *c.* 1500.  Arm., palimp. (pr. w. chal., *c.* 1510), *c.*
  1550.

*Compton.* Thos. Genyn, civ. & w., 1508.
*Cranleigh.* Resurrection, 1503. Priest, demi, 1507.
*Crowhurst.* John Gaynesford, arm., 1450. Ditto, 1460.
*Croydon.* Priest in cope, 1512. Wm. Heron, arm. & w., 1562.
*Ditton, Long.* Casteltunn, civ. & w., 1527. Hatton, civ. & w., 1616.
*Ditton, Thames.* Arm. & w., 1559. 2 civs. & w., 1580. Civ. & w., 1582, 1587, *c.* 1587 and 1590.
*Egham.* Anth. Bond, civ. & 2 wives, qd. pl., 1576.
*Ewell.* Lady, heraldic, kng., 1519. Lady, 1521. 2 ladies & civ., 1577.
*Farley.* John Brock, civ. & w., 1495
*Farnham.* Benedict Jay, civ. & w., qd. pl., *c.* 1580. Lady, qd. pl., 1597.
*Godalming.* Civ. & w., 1509. John Barker, arm., 1595.
*Guildford, Holy Trin.* Maurice Abbot, civ. & w., qd. pl., 1606.
*Guildford, St Mary.* Civilian and wife, *c.* 1520.
*Horley.* Lady, canopied, *c.* 1420. Civilian, *c.* 1520.
*Horsell.* John Sutton, civ., 1603. Thos. Sutton, civ., 1603. Thos. Edmonds, civ. & w., 1619.
*\*Horsley, E.* Civ., demi, *c.* 1400. Bishop Bowtho, kng., 1478. Civ. & w., 1498.
*Kingston-on-Thames.* Robt. Skern, civ. & w., 1437. John Hertcombe, civ. & w., 1488.
*Lambeth, St Mary.* Cath. Howard, heraldic, 1535. Thos. Clere, arm., 1545.
*Leatherhead.* A civilian, *c.* 1470.
*Leigh.* John Arderne, civ. & w., 1449. Susanna Arderne, *c.* 1450.
*\*Lingfield.* Lady Cobham, 1374, 1420. Sir Reg. de Cobh., 1403. Arm., 1417. Lady, demi, *c.* 1420. L., *c.* 1450. Priest, demi, 1445, 1458. Priest, 1469, 1503, the last under seats.
*Merstham.* Civ. & w., 1464. 2 ladies, 1473. Arm., 1498. Arm. & w., 1507. Children, 1587.
*Mickleham.* Wm. Wyddowsoun, civ. & w., 1513.
*Molesey, W.* Arms & inscr., Brende, 1598.
*Nutfield.* Wm. Graffton, civ. & w., *c.* 1465.
*Oakwood.* Edw. de la Hale, arm., 1431.
*Ockham.* Walt. Frilende, pr., demi, 1376. Arm. & w., 1483.
*Oxted.* Priest, mutil., 1428. Lady, 1480. Child, 1611, and 1613.
*Peper-Harow.* Joan Brokes, 1487. Cross, 1487. Elizth. Woodes, 1621.
*Putney.* John Welbeck, arm., 1478. Lady, *c.* 1585.
*Puttenham.* Edw. Cranford, priest, 1431.
*Richmond.* Robt. Cotton, civ. & w., 1591.
*Rotherhithe.* Peter Hills, mariner, & 2 ws., qd. pl., 1614, almost effaced.
*Sanderstead.* John Awodde, civ. & w., palimp., 1525.
*Send.* Laur. Slyffeld, civ. & w., sm., 1521.
*Shere.* Priest, 1412. Civ., 1512. Civ. & w., 1516. Lady, *c.* 1520. Sir John Towchet, arm., *c.* 1525.
*\*Stoke d'Abernon.* Sir John Daubernoun, sen., 1277. Ditto, jun., 1327. Lady, 1464. Chrysom, 1516. Civ. & w., qd. pl., 1592.
*Streatham.* Wm. Mowfurth, priest, 1513.
*Thorpe.* Bonde, civ. & w., 1578. Denham, civ. & w., qd. pl., 1583.
*Titsey.* Wm. Gresham, civ. & w., 1579.
*Tooting.* Wm. Fitzwilliam, civ. & w., qd. pl., 1597.
*Walton-on-Thames.* John Selwyn, park-keeper, & w., 1587.
*Wandsworth.* Serjeant-at-arms w. mace, 1420.
*Weybridge.* 3 skeletons, *c.* 1520. Civ. & 3 ws., 1586. Civ. & 2 ws., 1598.

*Witley.* Thos. Jonys, civ. & w., *c.* 1525.
*Woking.* Joan Purdan, 1523.  John Shadhet, civ. & w., 1527.
*Wonersh.* Elyot, civ. & w., 1467.  Ditto, 1503.


## SUSSEX

*Amberley.* John Wantele, arm. in tabard, 1424.
*Angmering.* Eden or Ellen Baker, 1598.
*Ardingly.* Wakeherst, civ. & w., can., *c.* 1500.  Culpepyr, arm. & w.,
    can., 1504.  Ditto, 1510.  Lady, 1633.  Children, 1634.
*Arundel.* Pr. in cope, demi, 1382.  Pr. in almuce, 1419.  Arm., mutil.,
    & w., can., 1430.  Pr., demi, *c.* 1450, 1474.  Pr., 1455.  Arm., 1465.
*Battle.* Arm., 1426.  Pr., *c.* 1430.  Arm., demi, 1435.  L., 1600.
    John Wythines, vice-chancellor of Oxford, 1615.
*Billinghurst.* Thos. Bartlett, civ. & w., 1499.
*Bodiam.* Arm., mutil., heraldic, *c.* 1360.  Pr. in shroud, 1513.
*Brede.* Robt. Oxenbregg, arm., mutil., & w., 1493.
*Brightling.* Civ. & w., *c.* 1480.  Thos. Pye, child, kng., 1592.
*Broadwater.* Priest in cope, can., 1432.  Inscribed cross, 1445.
*Burton.* Arm., *c.* 1525.  Lady in a man's tabard, 1558.
*Buxted.* Pr. in head of cross, 1408, and several fragments.
*Chichester Cath.* Heart, *c.* 1510.  Arms, Bp. Day, 1556.  Wm. Brad-
    bridge, civ. & w., qd. pl., 1592.
*Clapham.* John Shelley, arm. & w., her., 1526.  Arm. & w., 1550.  Ditto,
    qd. pl., 1592.
*Clayton.* Rich. Idon, priest w. chalice, 1523.
*Cowfold.* Prior Nelond, triple canopy, 1433.  Civ., *c.* 1500.
*Crawley.* Lady, *c.* 1520.
*Cuckfield.* Arms & inscr., 1509.  Arm., *c.* 1590.  Henry Bowyer, arm.
    & w., qd. pl., 1614.
*Etchingham.* Sir Wm. de Echingham, arm., mutil., 1388.  Arm., w. &
    son, canopied, 1444.  Two ladies, inscr. palimp., 1480.
*Ewhurst.* Wm. Crysford, civ., kng., *c.* 1520.
*Firle, W.* Arm & w., 1476.  Arms, etc., Gage, 1557.  3 Gage brasses, *c.*
    1600.  Lady in shroud, 1638.
*Fletching.* Sir Edw. Dallingridge, arm. & w., heraldic, canopied, *c.* 1380.
    Gloves & inscr. to Peter Denot, *c.* 1400.
*Framfield.* Edw. Gage, civ. & w., qd. pl., 1595.
*Friston.* Thos. Selwyn, civ. & w., sm., 1542.
*Goring.* Arm. & w., *c.* 1490.  Arms, etc., Cooke, *c.* 1510.  Ditto, 1707.
*Grinstead, E.* 2 men in armour, 1505.  Civ., sm. (misplaced), *c.* 1520.
*Grinstead, W.* Philippa Halsham, can., *c.* 1440.  Arm. & w., can., 1441.
*Hastings, All Saints.* Thos. Goodenouth, civ. & w., *c.* 1520.
*Hastings, St Clement.* Thos. Wekes, civ., 1563.  John Barley, civ.,
    1601.
*Hellingly.* A lady, *c.* 1440.
*Henfield.* Thos. Bysshopp, civ., 1559.  Ann Kenwellmersh, 1633.
*Horsham.* Thos. Clerke, priest in cope, 1411.  Lady, *c.* 1515.
*Hurstmonceux.* Sir Wm. Fienlez, arm., canopied, 1402.
*Iden.* Walter Seller, priest, 1427.
*Isfield.* John Shurley, arm., kng., 1527.  Shurley, arm. & w., 1558.
    Ditto, 1579.

£1.0.0. each    afternoon or morning

           2:00.p.m.         2 hrs. approx.

Rectory COBHAM Surrey 2502

Large Brass 7' x 2' 6"

Heelball  Monumental Brass Society  1/4 a stick

                                   T postage

    Mrs. H.F.O. Evans

      36 Rose Hill, Iffley, Oxford.

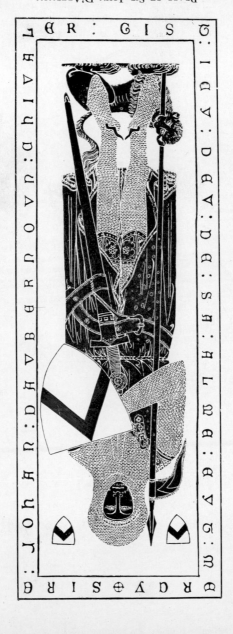

BRASS OF SIR JOHN D'ABERNON
THE ELDER, 1277

Copyright: the Rector of Stoke D'Abernon

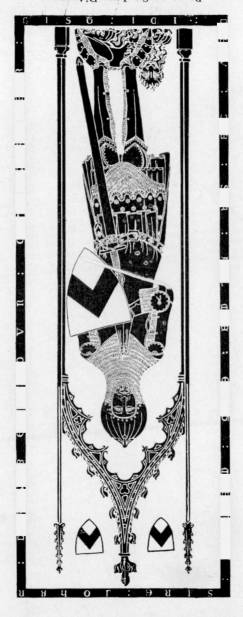

BRASS OF SIR JOHN D'ABERNON
THE YOUNGER, 1327

Copyright: the Rector of Stoke D'Abernon

*Lewes, St Mich.* Arm., mutil., *c.* 1430. Braydforde, priest, demi, 1457.
*Lewes, St Anne.* Arms & inscr., Twyne, 1613.
*Mundham, N.* Arms & inscr.—Nowell, 1583; Bowyer, 1594, 1610; *S. of Chich.*
 Birche, 1627.
*Northiam.* Robt. Beuford, priest, 1518. Nich. Tufton, civ., 1538.
*Ore, St Helen.* Civilian & wife, *c.* 1400.
*Poling.* Walter Davy, priest, demi, *c.* 1420. *(GB)*
*Pulborough.* Thos. Harlyng, pr. in cope, can., 1423. Civ. & w., 1452.
 Civ., 1478.
*Ringmer.* Arms & inscr., Mascall, 1631.
*Rodmell.* Palimpsest inscr. to John de la Chambre, 1673.
*Rusper.* John de Kynggesfolde, civ. & w., demi, *c.* 1370. Thos.
 Challoner, civ. & w., 1532.
*Rye.* Arms, *c.* 1600. Thos. Hamon, civ., 1607.
*Shoreham, New.* Civilian & wife, *c.* 1450. Arms & inscr., West, 1648.
*Slaugham.* John Covert, arm., can., 1503. Rich. Covert, arm. & 3 ws.,
 1547. Jane Fetyplace, 1586.
*Slinfold.* Rich. Bradbryge, civ. & w., 1533. Lady *c.* 1600. Arms, etc., *(A.29)*
 Cowper, 1678.
*Stopham.* Bartelot, civ. & w., *c.* 1460, 1601. Arm. & w., *c.* 1460, 1478,
 1614. Civ., kng., 1493. *(NEAR PULBOROUGH)*
*Storrington.* Henry Wilsha, ecclesiastic, 1591. *(NR. PULBOROUGH)*
*Thakeham.* Beatrix Apsley, 1515. Thos. Apsley, civ., 1517.
*Ticehurst.* Man in arm., *c.* 1370, and 2 ladies, *c.* 1510.
*Tillington.* Arms & inscr., Cox, 1697.
*\*Trotton.* Margt. de Camois, *c.* 1310. Thos., Lord Camoys, K.G., &
 w., can., 1419. *NEAR MIDHURST*
*Uckfield.* John Fuller, civ., qd. pl., 1610.
*Waldron.* Arms & inscr., Dyke, 1632.
*Warbleton.* Wm. Prestwyk, priest in cope, 1436.
*Warminghurst.* Edw. Shelley, civ. & w., 1554.
*Willingdon.* John Parker, arm. & w., 1558. Palimp. inscr., 1618.
*Winchelsea.* Civilian, mutilated, *c.* 1440.
*\*Wiston.* Sir John de Brewys, arm., 1426. *H.C*


# WARWICKSHIRE

*Astley.* A lady, mutilated, *c.* 1400.
*Aston.* Thos. Holte, in judicial robes, and wife, 1545.
*\*Baginton.* Sir Wm. Bagot, arm., heraldic, & wife, 1407.
*Barcheston.* Hugh Humfray, priest in acad., 1530.
*Barton.* Edm. Bury, civilian, 1608.
*Chadshunt.* Wm. Askell, civilian, 1613.
*Coleshill.* Priest w. chalice, 1500. Lady, 1506. Eccles. in gown, 1566.
 Arms & inscr., Beresford, 1651.
*Compton Verney.* Anne Odynsale, 1523. Rich. Verney, arm. & w., 1536.
 Arm., *c.* 1630.
*Coughton.* Sir Geo. Throkmorton, arm. & w., *c.* 1510. Arms & inscr.,
 1547 and 1580.
*Coventry, Holy Trin.* John Whithead, civ. & 2 ws., qd. pl., *c.* 1600.
*Coventry, St Mich.* Lady, 1594. Ditto, 1609. Arms & inscr., 1705.

*Exhall.* John Walsingham, arm. & wife, 1566.
*Hampton-in-Arden.* A civilian, *c.* 1500.
*Harbury.* Arms & inscr., Wright, 1685.
*Haseley.* Clement Throkmorton, arm. & w., palimp., 1573.
*Hillmorton.* A lady, *c.* 1410.
*Itchington, Long.* John Bosworth, civ. & 2 ws., qd. pl., 1674.
*Merevale.* Robt., Lord Ferrers, & w., 1412.
*Meriden.* Elizth. Rotton, 1633.
*Middleton.* Rich. Byngham, in judicial robes, & w., 1476. Arms & inscr., Fitzherbert, 1507.
*Preston Bagot.* Elizth. Randoll, 1635.
*Shuckburgh, Upper.* Shukburgh, lady, *c.* 1500. Arm. & w., 1549. Ditto, 1594.
*Solihull.* Wm. Hyll, civ. & 2 ws., 1549. Wm. Hawes, civ. & w., kng., qd. pl., 1610.
*Stratford-on-Avon.* Inscr. to Anne, wife of Wm. Shakespeare, 1623.
*Sutton Coldfield.* Barbara Eliot, 1606. Josias Bull, civ., 1621.
*Tanworth.* Margt. Archer, kng., qd. pl., 1614. Arms & inscr., Chambers, 1650.
*Tysoe.* Priest w. chalice, 1463. Lady, demi, 1598. Arms & inscr., 1611.
*Ufton.* Rich. Woddomes, eccles. & w., kng., qd. pl., 1587.
*\*Warwick, St Mary.* Thos. de Beauchamp, Earl of Warw., arm. & w., heraldic, 1406. Civ. & w., 1573.
*Warwick, St Nich.* Robt. Willardsey, priest, 1424.
*Wellesbourne Hastings.* Sir Thos. le Straunge, arm., sm., 1426.
*Weston-under-Weatherley.* Arms & inscr., Saunders, 1563.
*Whatcote.* Wm. Auldington, priest, 1511.
*Whichford.* Nich. Asheton, eccles. in gown, 1582.
*Whitnash.* Civilian & w., *c.* 1500. Priest w. chalice, 1531.
*Withybrook.* A civilian, *c.* 1500.
*\*Wixford.* Thos. de Cruwe, arm. & w., canopied, 1411. Child, qd. pl., 1597.
*Wootton-Wawen.* John Harewell, arm. & w., 1505.

## WESTMORELAND

*Kendal.* Alan Bellingham, civ., 1577.
*Morland.* Palimp. inscr. to John Blythe, pr., 1562.
*Musgrave, Gt.* Thos. Ouds, priest, 1500.

## WILTSHIRE

*Aldbourne.* Hen. Frekylton, priest, and chalice, 1508.
*Alton Priors.* Agnes Button, 1528. Wm. Button, from tomb, *c.* 1620.
*Barford St Martin.* Alis Walker, 1584.
*Bedwyn, Gt.* John Seymoure, civ., 1510.
*Berwick Basset.* Wm. Bayly, civ., demi, 1427.
*Bradford-on-Avon.* Thos. Horton, civ. & w., *c.* 1530. Lady, 1601.
*Broad Blunsden.* A lady, 1608.
*Bromham.* Lady, *c.* 1490. Baynton, arm., 1516. Arm. & 2 ws., 1578.
*Broughton Gifford.* Robt. Longe, tomb w. death, etc., 1620.
*Charlton.* Wm. Chaucey, arm. & w., 1524.

*Chisledon.* Francis Rutland, civ. & w., 1592.
*Cliffe-Pypard.* A man in armour, c. 1380.
*Collingbourne Ducis.* Edw. Saintmaur, child, 1631.
*Collingbourne Kingston.* Joan Darell, 1495.
*Dauntsey.* Sir John Danvers, arm. & w., 1514. Lady, qd. pl., *c.* 1535.
*Deane, W.* Geo. Evelyn, child, sm., 1641.
*Devizes, St John.* John Kent, civ. & wife, 1630.
*Draycot Cerne.* Sir Edw. Cerne, arm. & w., 1393.
*Durnford, Gt.* Edw. Younge, civ. & w., qd. pl., 1607.
*Fovant.* Geo. Rede, priest in acad., qd. pl., 1492.
*Lavington, W.* John Dauntesay, arm., palimp., 1559. Palimp. inscr.,
    1571.
*Laycock.* Robt. Baynard, arm. & wife, heraldic, 1501.
*\*Mere.* John Bettesthorne, arm., 1398. Arm., mutil., *c.* 1415.
*Minety.* Nich. Poulett, arm. & w., qd. pl., *c.* 1620.
*Newnton, Long.* John Erton, priest, 1503.
*Ogbourne St George.* Thos. Goddard, civ. & wife, 1517.
*Preshute.* John Barley, civ. & w., 1518.
*\*Salisbury Cath* Bishop Wyvil, demi, in castle, 1375. Bp. Geste, 1578.
*Salisbury, St Thos.* John Webbe, civ. & wife, 1570.
*Seend.* John Stokys, civ. & wife, sm., 1498.
*Stockton.* Elizth. Poticary, qd. pl., 1590. Potecary, civ. & w., 1596.
*Tisbury.* Civ. & wife, *c.* 1520. Laur. Hyde, civ. & w., qd. pl., 1590.
*Upton Lovell.* A priest, demi, *c.* 1460.
*Wandborough.* Thos. Polton, civ. & w., demi, 1418.
*Westbury.* Thos. Bennet, civ. & wife, 1605.
*Wilton.* John Coffer, civ. & wife, 1585.
*Woodford.* Gerrard Erington, civ., 1596.


## WORCESTERSHIRE

*Alvechurch.* Philip Chatwyn, arm., 1524.
*Birlingham.* Thos. Harewell, civ. & wife, qd. pl., 1617.
*Blockley.* Priest in academicals, kng., 1488. Priest, kng., *c.* 1500.
*Bredon.* Arms, mitre, etc., for John Prideaux, Bp. of Worcester, 1650.
*Broadway.* Anth. Daston, arm., 1572.
*Bushley.* Thos. Payne, civ. & wife, 1500.
*Chaddesley Corbet.* Thos. Forest, civ. & wife, *c.* 1500.
*Daylesford.* Wm. Gardiner, civ., 1632.
*\*Fladbury.* Arm. & w., 1445. Priest in cope, demi, 1458. Arm., 1488.
    Priest, sm., 1504.
*Hanley Castle.* Rich. Lechmere, civ. & wife, 1568.
*\*Kidderminster.* Sir John Phelip, Walt. Cookesey, arm. & w., canopied,
    1415.
*Longdon.* Wm. Brugge, arm. & wife, 1523.
*Mamble.* John Blount, arm. & wife, *c.* 1510.
*Stockton.* Wm. Parker, civilian, 1508.
*Stoke Prior.* Hen. Smith, civ., 1606. Robt. Smith, civ. & 2 ws., 1609.
*\*Strensham.* Russel, arm., *c.* 1390. Ditto, can., 1405. Ditto & w.,
    heraldic, 1562.
*Tredington.* Priest in cope, 1427. Priest in almuce, kng., 1482. Lady,
    1561.
*Yardley.* Wm. Astell, Simon Wheler, civs. & wife, qd. pl., 1598.

## YORKSHIRE

*Aldborough, near Boroughbridge.* Wm. de Aldeburgh, arm., heraldic, on a bracket, *c.* 1360.
*Allerton Mauleverer.* Mauleverere, arm., her., & wife, sm., qd. pl., 1400.
*Almondbury.* Arms & inscr., Netleton, 1621, and other inscrs.
*Anston.* Arms & inscr., Hutton, 1662.
*Aston.* Arms & inscr., Melton, 1510.
*Aughton.* Rich. Ask, arm. & wife, 1466.
*Bainton.* Roger Godeale, priest w. chalice, 1429.
*Bedale.* Arms & inscr., Wilson, 1681, Samwaies, 1693.
*Beeford.* Thos. Tonge, pr. in amice, alb & cope, w. book, 1472.
*Bentham.* Arms & inscr., Fetherstone, 1653.
*Birstall.* Elizth. Popeley, in shroud, qd. pl., 1632.
*Bolton-by-Bolland.* Hen. Pudsey, arm. & w., heraldic, kng., 1509.
*Bradfield.* John Morewood, civ. & wife, qd. pl., 1647.
*Brandsburton.* Priest, demi, on bracket, 1364. Sir John de St Quintin, arm. & wife, 1397.
*Burgh Wallis.* Thos. Gascoign, arm., 1556.
*Burton, Bishop.* Chalice, 1460. Lady, 1521. Estoft, arm. & w., 1579.
*Catterick.* Wm. Burgh, arm. & son, 1465. Wm. Burgh, arm. & w., 1492.
*Cottingham.* Nich. de Louth, pr. in cope, canopied, 1383. Civ. & w., 1504.
*Cowthorpe.* Brian Rouclyff, judicial, and fragments, 1494.
*Coxwold.* Arms & inscr., Manston, 1464.
*Crathorne.* Arms & inscr., Crathorn, *c.* 1420.
*Darfield.* Arms & inscr., Rodes, 1666.
*Darrington.* Arms & inscr., Farrer, 1684.
*Doncaster.* Arms, etc., Flower, 1662, Braylesford, 1683, Gibson, 1699.
*Easby.* Arms & inscr., Bowes, 1623.
*Escrick.* Arms & inscr., Robinson, 1636.
*Fishlake.* Arms & inscr., Perkins, 1663.
*Forcett.* Anne Underhill, recumbent, qd. pl., 1637.
*Halifax.* Arms & inscr., Barraclough, 1668, and other inscrs.
*Hampsthwaite.* A civilian, mutilated, *c.* 1380.
*Harpham.* Sir Thos. de St Quintin, arm. & w., canopied, 1418. Thos. St Quintin, arm., 1445.
*Hauxwell.* Wm. Thoresby, clv. & w., kng., qd. pl., 1611.
*Helmsley.* Arm. & wife, *c.* 1465, and inscrs.
*Hornby.* Thos. Mountford, arm. & w., 1489. Fragments, 1443.
*Howden.* Arm., canopied, *c.* 1480. Palimp. inscr., 1621.
*Hull, Holy Trin.* Rich. Byll, civ. & w., demi, 1451.
*Hull, St Mary Lowgate.* John Haryson, civ. & 2 ws., qd. pl., 1525.
*Ilkley.* Arms, etc., Heber, 1649 & 1658, Lawson, 1671, & other inscrs.
*Kirby Knowle.* Arms, etc., 9 brasses, 1676-1770.
*Kirby Malzeard.* Civ. & w., kng., sm., 1604. Arms, etc., Dawson, 1640, 1735.
*Kirby Moorside.* Lady Brooke, kng., 1604.
*Kirkby Wharfe.* Wm. Gisborne, pr. in cope, *c.* 1480. Arms, etc., Ledes, 1564.
*Kirkheaton.* Adam Beaumont, arm. & wife, 1655.
*Kirkleatham.* Robt. Coulthirst, civ., 1631.
*Laughton-en-le-Morthen.* John Mallevorer, arm., *c.* 1620.

*Leake.* John Watson, civ. & wife, *c.* 1530.
*Ledsham.* Arms & inscr., Foljambe, 1658.
*Leeds, St Peter.* Sir John Langton, arm. & w., 1459. Arm., 1467. Chalice for Thos. Clarell, priest, 1469. Civ., 1709.
*Londesborough.* Margt. Threlkeld, 1493.
*Lowthorpe.* Man in armour, sm., *c.* 1450. Arms & inscr., 1665.
*Marr.* John Lewis, civ. & wife, 1589.
*Masham.* Arms & acrostic inscr., Kay, 1689.
*Middleham.* Arms & inscr., Colby, 1727.
*Moor Monkton.* Arms & inscr., Hesketh, 1665.
*Otley.* Francis Palmes, civ., recumbent, qd. pl., 1593.
*Owston.* Robt. de Haitfeld, civ. & w., 1409. Arms, etc., Adams, 1667.
*Rawmarsh.* John Darley, civ. & w., 1616.
*Ripley.* Chalice for Rich. Kendale, priest, 1429. Arms, etc., Ingilby, 1682.
*Ripon Cath.* Arms & inscr., Crosland, 1670, and other inscrs.
*Rotherham.* Robt. Swifte, civ. & w., qd. pl., 1561.
*Rothwell.* Arms & inscr., Collings, 1682.
*Routh.* Sir John Routh, arm. & w., canopied, *c.* 1410.
*Roxby Chapel.* Thos. Boynton, arm., 1523.
*Ryther.* Arms & inscr., Robinson, 1619 & 1626.
*Seamer.* Arms & inscr., Lisle, 1694, and inscrs.
✓ *Sessay.* Archdeacon Magnus, in cope, palimp. 1550.
*Sheffield, St Peter.* Arms & inscr., Talbot, 1538, Lister, 1663.
⚬ *Sheriff Hutton.* Mary Hall, 1657. Arms & inscr., Wytham, *c.* 1480.
*Skipton-in-Craven.* A Holy Trin., *c.* 1560. Arm. in tab., kng., 1570. Arms, *c.* 1600.
*Sprotborough.* Wm. Fitz William, arm. & w., 1474.
*Tanfield, West.* Thos. Sutton, priest in cope, *c.* 1480.
⚬ *Thirsk.* Robt. Thresk, priest, demi, 1419.
*Thornhill.* Arms & inscr., Waterhouse, 1614.
*Thornton-le-Street.* Arms & inscr., Laton, 1664, Talbot, 1680.
*Thornton Watlass.* Geo. Ferrars, rector, in shroud, 1669.
*Thwing.* Arms & inscr., Stafford, 1671.
*Todwick.* Thos. Garland, civ., kng., qd. pl., 1609.
✓ *\*Topcliffe.* Thos. de Topclyff, civ. & w., foreign, qd. pl., palimp., 1391.
*Waddington.* Arms & inscr., Parker, 1673.
*Wadworth.* Arms & inscr., Pierrepont, 1653.
*Wath.* Rich. Norton, judicial, & w., 1420. Arm., *c.* 1490. Arms, etc., Ward, 1520.
*Wellwick.* Wm. Wryght, civ. & w., 1621.
*\*Wensley.* Simon de Wensley, priest, foreign, large, *c.* 1360.
*Wentworth.* Mich. Darcy, arm. & w., qd. pl., 1588.
❡ *Wilberfosse.* Robt. Hoton, arm. & wife., sm., 1447.
*Winestead.* Arm. & wife, mutil., *c.* 1540.
*Wycliffe.* Arms, etc., Wyclif, *c.* 1380. Wickliff, kng., qd. pl., 1606.

*York—*

*\*Minster.* Archbp. Grenefeld, 1315. Elizth. Eynns, demi, 1585. Jas. Cotrel, civ., demi, 1595.
*All Saints, North Street.* Thos. Atkinson, civ., demi, 1642. Symbols, etc., 1482. Arms, etc., 1609.
*St Crux Parish Room.* Robt. Askwith, civ., demi, 1597. Arms, etc., 1537, 1681.

*York—*
  *St Martin, Coney Street.*  Christopher Harington, civ., demi, 1614.
    Arms, etc., Colthurst, 1588.
  *St Michael, Spurriergate.*  Chalice for priest, 1466, and inscrs.
*York City.*  Many inscrs.  Total—40 brasses in 18 churches.


## IRELAND

*Dublin, St Patrick's Cath.*  Dean Sutton, in almuce, qd. pl., 1528.
  Dean Fynche, ditto, 1537.  Sir Edw. Fiton & w., qd. pl., 1579.


## SCOTLAND

*Aberdeen, St Nich.*  Dr Duncan Liddel, large, foreign, qd. pl., 1613.
*Edinburgh, St Giles.*  Arms & inscr., Jas. Stewart, Earl of Murray,
  Regent of Scotland, 1569.
*Glasgow Cath.*  Man in arm., Mynto fam., qd. pl., 1605.


## WALES

  *Anglesey.*
*Beaumaris.*  Rich. Bulkley, civ. & w., *c.* 1530.

  *Carnarvonshire.*
*Clynnog.*  Wm. Glynne, child, sm., 1633.
*Dolwyddelan.*  Meredith ap Ivan ap Robert, arm., kng., 1535.
*Llanbeblig.*  Rich. Foxwist, in a bed, qd. pl., 1500.

  *Denbighshire.*
*Llanrwst.*  6 lozenge-shaped plates, w. busts, Wynne fam., 1620-1671.
*Ruthin.*  Edw. Goodman, civ., 1560.  Edw. Goodman, civ. & w., 1583.
*Whitchurch.*  Rich. Middleton, civ. & w., 1575.

  *Glamorganshire.*
*Llandough.*  Wenllan Walsche, lady, 1427.
*Swansea.*  Sir Hugh Johnys & wife, w. Resurrection, *c.* 1500.

  *Montgomeryshire.*
*Bettws, Newtown.*  John ap Meredyth de Powys, priest w. chalice, 1531.

  *Pembrokeshire.*
*Haverfordwest.*  John Davids, civ. & wife, qd. pl., 1654.

# APPENDIX TO THE COUNTY LISTS
## CORRECTIONS RESULTING FROM THE WAR OF 1939-1945.

### ESSEX

*Horkesley, Little.*   Brasses are now in Colchester Castle Museum.

### GLOUCESTERSHIRE

*Bristol, St Peter.*   Brass destroyed.
*Bristol, Temple.*   Brasses destroyed.

### KENT

*Canterbury, St George.*   Brass now in Cathedral Chapter Office.
*Canterbury, St Mary Northgate.*   Brass removed to St Gregory.
*Canterbury, St Mary Bredin.*   Brass now in Cathedral Library.
*Dover, St James.*   Brass destroyed.

### MIDDLESEX

*London, Dutch Reformed Church, Austin Friars.*   Brass destroyed.

### NORFOLK

*Heigham.*   Brasses now in St Peter Hungate Museum, Norwich.
*Norwich, St Simon and St Jude.*   Brasses now in St Peter Hungate Museum.

### SUFFOLK

*Ipswich, St Mary Quay.*   Thos. Pownder now in Christ Church Mansion Museum.   Others still *in situ*.

### YORKSHIRE

*York, St Crux Parish Room.*   Brasses now in Castle Museum.

# INDEX

*(Exclusive of Bibliography and County Lists)*